3/26

ST MATTHEW AND ST MARK

THE EDWARD CADBURY LECTURES 1953-54

ST MATTHEW
AND
ST MARK

BY

AUSTIN FARRER .

DOCTOR OF DIVINITY AND FELLOW OF TRINITY COLLEGE
OXFORD

dacre press
westminster

FIRST PUBLISHED 1954

DACRE PRESS: A. AND C. BLACK LTD
4, 5 AND 6 SOHO SQUARE LONDON W.1

PRINTED IN GREAT BRITAIN BY ROBERT MACLEHOSE AND CO. LTD
THE UNIVERSITY PRESS, GLASGOW

PREFACE

Scholars of a generation and of half a generation ago reached the conclusion, more sound than surprising, that the Synoptic Gospels and especially St Mark's do not exhibit the sort of structure or sequence for which we are accustomed to look in a history or a biography. But they too easily despaired of finding any structure at all in them and wrote off their authors as little more than compilers. It begins now to occur to us to ask whether the Evangelists may not have used patterns more congenial to their time and place, adapted from the only literary tradition they respected and into which they were either born as Jews or grafted as Christians.

If the question is slow to obtain recognition, it is for the creditable reason that scholars are profitably occupied on the examination of oral forms and have so much the less attention to spare for literary influences. The pattern of the apostolic evangel, of the primitive catechism and of the typical sermon to the faithful are becoming clearer to our eyes and we rightly acknowledge the influence exercised by these things on the Gospels as well as on other New Testament writings. But the Gospels are no simple transcripts or compilations of oral matter, they are literary works and must be interpreted by their place in a literary history. Those who write books, read books and imitate what they read, not only in the matter of which they treat but in the manner in which they build it up. The Evangelists' sentences may often reflect the pulpit, but the organisation of their complex materials is a literary enterprise.

If the Evangelists followed any single obvious type of Jewish book we should know where to look for their literary models. Since they do not, we can scarcely hope to approach the Gospels ready equipped with an analysis of the existing forms which they must be expected to have imitated. It would be an endless undertaking to make a formal analysis of every Jewish writing inside the canon or outside it which might have influenced the form of the Gospels; and even if we achieved such a task our results would be useless to us. To be provided with a thousand and one tools only one of which is the tool for the job, and not to know which of them it is, would be worse than to have no tools at all. We are bound to begin with the job, and then look for the tools—to open up our analysis of the Gospel patterns on their own evidence, and let them suggest the scriptural types by the aid of which they are to be understood. What we have to expect is a constant two-way traffic between the two Testaments; the Gospels sending us to likely Old Testament models, and the more detailed examination of these casting fresh light on the Gospels.

If there is some difficulty about taking any simple and immediate step back from St Mark to a recognisable literary predecessor, there is none about taking a step in the opposite direction. We may not be able to say that St Mark begins where Daniel leaves off, but we can say that where St Mark leaves off St Matthew begins. He adapts St Mark's forms as well as his materials and a formal comparison between the two Evangelists cannot fail to yield results of high importance for the understanding of both.

The patterns we are led to ascribe to these Evangelists are built round a skeleton of numerical symbolism. The use which (in our supposition) they made of arithmetical form is unlikely to prove congenial to us, but how we feel about it is not the question. What did they do? Was such a numerical symbolism current coin in their world? It is not we, it is the Evangelists who (according to our argument) cast gospel facts into arithmetical patterns. We are not saying that Christ patterned his life in a ritual series of numbered acts, years or days; we are not even saying that the Evangelists thought he had. We are merely saying that they used a numerical symbolism of their own to pattern their exposition of what he did, meant, and was.

Surprising theories have, in our own time, been put forth by certain authors about Mediaeval English history. The attempt is made to persuade us that kings and archbishops actually arranged their lives and deaths to fit a preconceived calendar of magical numbers. We do not hold any theories of this kind about the life of Christ. We do not even say that the Evangelists held them. There is, indeed, a certain resemblance between the numerical form which we find in the Evangelists' narratives, and that which these authors employ in their histories. But the functions to which they put the form are very different. It is one thing to use an artificial arithmetic for drawing out the symbolical riches of a sacred narrative, another thing to employ it in the cool interpretation of human motive or the reconstruction of historical event. And those of us who find the historical theory unconvincing may still be willing to allow the sacred symbolism its proper rights. It is absurd to deplore that the Evangelists did not compose according to our historical rules. Our sole concern is to understand them, and the more we understand the less we deplore. The Evangelists' instruments were appropriate to their unique task.

The chapters which follow do not form a cumulative argument and the reader who looks to the end of the book for a conclusion will be disappointed. The first three chapters state the principal thesis, and the demonstration which they offer is virtually self-contained. They do, indeed, leave over some loose ends which are taken up later, but nothing on which the credit of the argument should depend.

The clearest evidence that a stone has fallen into a pond is offered by the sharp and immediate disturbance of the water surrounding the place where it fell; and yet it would be surprising if there lacked the further confirmation provided by the faint spreading of the rings over the remoter surface of the pool. So the clearest evidence of the sort of thinking we attribute to the Evangelists is to be found in the comparatively clear-cut pattern which our first three chapters bring to light; and yet it would be surprising if such thinking on the Evangelists' part remained within the boundaries of that pattern and did not spread into other regions of their work. It may be less evident in its further extensions, and yet it seems right that we should strain our eyes to follow it. A systematic endeavour of this sort occupies the next four Chapters (iv–vii). Among these the little Chapter vi is a sort of footnote to the argument of the rest. Since we have drawn certain of the numbers St Mark's Gospel contains into a pattern, it seems only reasonable to make a review of the remaining numbers in his text, and form an opinion of the Evangelist's attitude to number in general. And this is the task which Chapter vi undertakes.

The remaining four Chapters (viii–xi) deal with detached subjects of interest which have arisen in the course of the discussion. The suggestions which they offer are highly speculative, and I should be sorry to think that the credit of the previous seven would be made to depend on these four. As the argument of i–iii is independent of iv–vii, so the whole of i–vii is independent, I trust, of viii–xi. Yet discussions which are manifestly tentative and unfinished may serve for the advancement of enquiry.

The two Appendices contain retractations of a previous book called *A Study in St Mark*. It may seem portentous to treat what one has previously written with such seriousness, but on the other hand it may be less than honest to leave one's errors to propagate unchecked. The second appendix is miscellaneous and in no way essential to understanding the present work; the first rehandles a subject which I regard as of the very greatest importance and I have tried to write it in such a way as to be intelligible without reference to *A Study in St Mark*.

A last confession: try as I may, I cannot believe the Q hypothesis, but must suppose St Matthew's to be among those gospel accounts with which St Luke, as his preface claims, was acquainted. This book does not handle the question, but it contains remarks by the way which, without this warning, might mystify my readers.

My thanks are due to the University for honouring me with the lectureship out of which this book arose, and to two friends, Professor S. H. Hooke and Mr C. F. Evans, who persuaded me to rewrite most of what I had written at first.

Oxford, *March* 1954

CONTENTS

CHAPTER I

Chapter IV

The Marcan Pattern of Loaves

Mark viii 14–21 proposes an apparent riddle in the numbers of loaves and of thousands at the two miraculous feasts. The riddle must be answered by reference to the narratives of the feasts and to that of the Syrophoenician exorcism. A solution is suggested, pp. 57–70. As there are thirteenth persons healed and called, so there is a thirteenth loaf beside the five and the seven, pp. 70–73. Why there are only four thousands to eat the seven loaves, pp. 73–75. The distributions of bread stand on the background of the mention of David and the shewbread in Mark ii, pp. 75–80.

Chapter V

The Marcan Pattern of Apostles

The twelve apostles and the twelve loaves they distribute form a stream of continuous symbolism in St Mark and the twelve healings form a parallel stream. The apostolic series is progressive and dramatic in meaning, the healing series static and repetitive; yet it lends itself to the purposes of the other series to some extent, pp. 81–86. For example, (a) the placing of the miracle of resurrection: it fits the progress of the 'apostolic' symbolism, and its position both as eighth in all and as third in its group is significant, pp. 87–92. (The prefigurative significance of what he describes is drawn into the history itself by the Evangelist, pp. 92–94). (b) A triad of leading apostles is formally matched with two successive triads of healings and also with a triad of predictions concerning resurrection after three days, pp. 94–97. When the three days actually arrive they are initiated by a scene with the three apostles, and the four last days are similarly inaugurated by a scene with four apostles, pp. 98–105.

Chapter VI

Other Marcan Numbers

All the numbers to be found in St Mark apart from those already discussed are passed in review. It appears that St Mark follows certain conventions in the assignment of certain ranges of number to particular ranges of things, and that the matching of numbers with numbers is habitual with him, though not always equally meaningful, pp. 106–113. The author makes a few reflections on numerology, pp. 113–115.

150–152, or otherwise suggestive of the termination towards which the book is leading, pp. 152–153. St Matthew's final paragraph may be fairly viewed as the expansion of a single (lost) Marcan sentence into a short scene, in view of the general expansion of Mark xv 33 ff. in Matt. xxvii 45ff., pp. 153–159.

CHAPTER X

A consideration of Matthaean architecture in so far as it is non-Marcan may well start from the Sermon on the Mount, p. 160. The new 'Law from the Mountain' is shaped on the old: in Exodus ten commandments, in Matthew eight beatitudes, both followed by a fuller exposition, pp. 161–162. The order and structure of the beatitudes is examined, pp. 162–165, and related to the parts of the Sermon taken in chiastic order, pp. 165–169. The Lord's Prayer appears to influence both the beatitudes and the latter part of the Sermon (pp. 169–172) which is also influenced by Mark vi 30–viii 38, an influence confirmed by St Matthew's own version of this passage in xiv–xvi, pp. 174–175. Conclusions, pp. 175–176.

CHAPTER XI

The grand architecture of St Matthew has been thought to stand on five discourses; the five books of a new pentateuch. The sterility of this hypothesis leads the author to propose a new one; that St Matthew writes a hexateuch round six set pieces of which the genealogy is the first, pp. 177–185. Though such a scheme would be non-Marcan, St Matthew could have found the suggestion of it in St Mark, pp. 188–189. The admitted weaknesses of the new hypothesis (pp. 189–190) can be palliated by parallel instances, pp. 190–193. The hypothesis would serve to explain why St Matthew rearranged Mark i 1–vi 13 as he did, pp. 193–197.

APPENDIX A

The substance of three chapters in 'A Study in St Mark' is reconstructed so as to exhibit a corrected picture of the cyclic recurrences of theme in St Mark's Gospel.

CONTENTS

APPENDIX B

CHAPTER I

THE CHARACTER OF ST MARK'S GOSPEL

When the University of Birmingham did me the honour of asking me to deliver the lectures which form the substance of this book, it placed me in a dilemma. I wished, naturally, to take a subject which would accord most closely with the intention of the Cadbury foundation; but at the same time I wished to do my best, and to say the most important thing I had to say. The latter consideration, in fact, carried more weight with me. I have lectured on the interpretation of the Gospels because I had some ideas on the subject, and I thought that the ventilation of them might be of use to scriptural study. I say, the ventilation of them. For I will not be so absurd as to claim that my conclusions are certainly correct. What I do feel certain about is that I am worrying at real issues and running against genuine facts; and by stating what I have arrived at in this field, and provoking my hearers and readers to show me where I am wrong, I have more hope of contributing something to theological enquiry than by any other course I could take.

I call my work 'St Matthew and St Mark' because one must have a manageable title, but a true description would run more like this: 'The pattern of St Mark's Gospel, and of St Matthew's in so far as it throws light on St Mark's, with a few hints from St Luke's.' I make no attempt to cover the field which my title apparently marks out for me, or to give an equal and adequate treatment of my two chosen evangelists.

Our life is a continual repentance; and if we are so rash as to publish our opinions, that repentance will be in part a public one. I did publish a book called *A Study in St Mark*, and some of it, I hope, was right, but what is more present to me is the part I repent of. I hope it will not seem too egotistical if I make a remark now about the relation between what I published there and what I am going to say in this book.

There is an anecdote, at once touching and absurd, about an

I

academic figure of the last generation. Becoming aware (I do not know how) that an obituary notice about him was being prepared for the Press, he showed signs of strong irritation. It was not the implied intimation of mortality that distressed him. 'What is so infuriating,' he said, 'is to reflect how much better one could write it oneself.' No one who knew him could suppose that he desired unrestricted scope to sing his own praise; he was a man of scrupulous historical judgment, and he longed to tell the readers of *The Times* exactly what he had achieved and what had been his limitations. In the same spirit we might covet the opportunity to review our own books three years after writing them. Here, then, is my review of mine. At least it will be short.

The author of this book (I should say) began from a correct assumption—that St Mark was an able thinker who worked out a plan in composing his Gospel. We may also reckon it to the author's credit, that he made a number of separate observations on pieces of St Mark's design which deserve attention. But he failed to bring the pieces together into a convincing unity. His picture of the Evangelist shows us a writer keeping several different symbolisms going at once, like a juggler keeping six balls in the air together. We cannot help feeling that it is not the Evangelist who juggles but the interpreter who suffers from divided vision; he sees as six balls what is really only one ball in different positions and catching the light from different sides. When he begins to feel qualms about the psychological credibility of what he describes, the author takes refuge in mystery, invoking the intrinsic fertility and complexity of imaginative inspiration. We are willing to agree that this consideration has been in general too little applied by modern interpreters of the Gospels, but we are unwilling to accept it as an entire substitute for common sense. The author's fault is not that he has enquired too curiously into the inner workings of the Evangelist's mind, but that he has not enquired curiously enough; or that his curiosity has been sustained by too little patience. He who has come only so far as to see the complexity and variety of imaginative thought has not arrived at an understanding of the thinker. It is necessary to persevere until complexity settles and clarifies into unity.

That is how I should review *A Study in St Mark*, and what I have said will explain why I am pursuing the subject further here. Since I wrote that book, I believe that I have made two discoveries. First, I think I have found the grand mistake which vitiated my interpretation of St Mark. Second, I think I have found in St Matthew much light on the arrangement of St Mark. For where St Matthew rearranges, it is always with an understanding of what is being rearranged. The purpose of these chapters is to profit from those two discoveries—for let us hope that they are discoveries, not mares' nests.

So much in explanation of the fact that I am resuming a subject on which I published so lately and at such length. From my point of view, I am making my old work less faulty, but that is not how I will ask my readers to view my proceedings. I do not propose to plague them with references to my old muddles or my new repentances. I shall just try to say as much about St Mark as I can, with St Matthew to help me.

My question is: how did St Mark think his way through the matter he has recorded for us? And my first endeavour must be to get the question accepted. For many people's reaction to the raising of such a question will be to protest that St Mark did not think at all in any important sense, he just reported or transcribed. If the question about St Mark's thinking is to be admitted at all, it is concerned (such people will say) with the bias which colours his reports, or with the associations which lead him from one block of traditional anecdote to another. For he was a simple man, putting down what he knew; he was not a profound historical thinker like Tacitus, nor a profound symbolical thinker like St John, and it is an absurdity to set on foot an investigation into his thought.

Why is it so generally thought that St Mark is a simple writer? His Greek is unsophisticated, not to say vulgar, and if he were endeavouring something in the classical Hellenic manner, we should be justified in writing him down as a very simple person. But his literary tradition is Biblical, not Hellenic; his Bible is not the Hebrew original but the Septuagint version; he sees the splendour of biblical style through a screen of bad translation. It is true that Semitizing Greek can be developed into a fine language, as it was by St Matthew (to go no further afield). But St Matthew was a man of exceptional talent; there was no established standard for this sort of writing, no common proficiency which every Grecian Jew was taught at school, and which St Mark would be bound to attain unless he was an exceptionally simple person. The Revelation of St John provides an instructive parallel. It contains many hidden depths, but its Greek is often elementary.

Suppose we place the synoptic Gospels side by side, and (on the commonly held assumption that St Matthew and St Luke used St Mark) ask whether St Mark's contributions to the common tradition distinguish themselves by their intellectual simplicity. Where do we turn for simple material to present to simple minds? Is it not to the limpid and flowing parables, the copious exhortations of St Matthew and St Luke? St Matthew is St Mark's closest interpreter, and his characteristic attitude to St Mark is the desire to expound and expand. He finds his predecessor's thought too packed, too pregnant. Let us take an example. St Mark writes:

'As they were coming down from the mountain, Jesus charged his three disciples that they should tell no man what things they had seen until the Son of Man should have risen again from the dead. And they kept the saying in mind, discussing what was this "rising from the dead", and they put a question to Jesus thus: "The scribes say that Elias must come first". He said to them, "Elias comes first and works for general restoration, and what is the meaning of the scripture which says that the Son of Man suffers many things and is rejected? But I tell you both that Elias has come, and that they have done to him all that they wished, as it is written of him" ' (Mark ix 9–13).

In this paragraph St Mark may show himself a simple, in the sense of an unpractised or clumsy, writer. If we compose such paragraphs ourselves, our wiser friends advise us to rewrite them, bidding us to put in all the connecting links we have left out. They will accuse us, perhaps, of simplemindedness for imagining that we can communicate our ideas to others in the shorthand of our own thought. But they will not dream of telling us that what we have written is simple; what they do say is that it is simple of us to expect our readers to grasp anything so enigmatic. If our readers are to understand us, they will be obliged to make their own extended paraphrase of our compression, and that is what you or I find ourselves doing with the Marcan paragraph which I have just quoted. We might say something of this sort in paraphrase of it:

'Jesus forbade them to reveal what they had seen until the Son of Man should have risen again from the dead. "Risen again from the dead!" said the disciples to one another. "He cannot be put to death, to start with, for the scribes prove out of Malachi that Elias returns to earth to restore righteousness before Messiah comes. So when the Son of Man comes, he will be received with open arms, not killed." They put the difficulty to Jesus. He stated the question: "Elias comes on a mission of general restoration, according to Malachi, and how then can it be written in Isaiah that the Son of Man suffers many things and is rejected?" Then he gave his solution of the difficulty. "Elias has come already, and they have done to him all they wanted to do to him in the text about him"—that is, in the text which records Elias's complaint, *The children of Israel hunt after my life to take it away*.[1] "The mission of the returning Elias has been rejected, and so there is nothing to prevent the Son of Man's mission from being likewise rejected. Elias has been killed; he will be killed." '

Our indictment of St Mark's obscurity has been unjust in two ways. It ignores both the wider and the narrower context. The wider context embraces St Mark and his hearers; it consists in what we might call the commonplaces of Messianic prediction, and even in certain shorthand expressions for referring to them. He was writing for men who could take up easily references which we track down painfully; just as a poet whom I find enigmatic may be writing for a very remarkable body of men, soaked in Celtic antiquities and literary gossip; they can understand him; I cannot. I may, indeed, complain against the poet of a clique, that

[1] I Kings xix 10, 14.

5

he is writing as though the byways of literature which are the hobbies of his friends were the classics of our common culture. St Mark was open to no such complaint, for the scriptures held in the mind of those for whom he wrote an undisputed position which no classics since have ever attained. It is unfair, then, to suggest that St Mark's paragraph required as full a paraphrase to make it intelligible to his first readers as it requires to make it intelligible to us.

It is equally unfair to ignore the narrower context which previous, and especially recent paragraphs of his own book supply. When, for example, the disciples take the Son of Man's resurrection from the dead to mean his rejection, murder, and resurrection, they are simply interpreting Christ's new word about resurrection by the prophecy of rejection, death, and resurrection which he gave them a couple of pages back; and the attentive reader of St Mark should be able to recognise as much. Again, when St Mark makes the double supposition, that Elias's second appearance on earth runs much the same course as his first, and that his second appearance is in the person of John Baptist, he is picking up clues which his previous paragraphs have laid down. In particular, his recent story of John's martyrdom has been so told as to exhibit John in the part of Elias, Herod in that of Ahab, Herodias in that of Jezebel (vi 17-29). And so, when we are succinctly told that Elias has come, and that they have done to him what they wanted to in the scripture about him, it is not beyond reason that we should be expected to see that the new Jezebel has achieved what the old Jezebel could not, and compassed the death of the prophet of God.

It is not beyond reason that we should be asked to see these things, but it is beyond what St Matthew or St Luke is prepared to ask of his readers. St Luke cuts out the whole paragraph. St Matthew drops the two compressed appeals to the Old Testament and the whole issue of reconciling the preparatory mission of Elias with a suffering Messiah, and reveals in plain terms the equation between Elias and John Baptist. St Matthew's words are as follows:

'And as they were coming down from the mountain Jesus commanded them, saying: Tell the vision to no man until the Son of

Man be risen from the dead. And his disciples asked him, saying: Why then say the scribes that Elias must first come?' [That is, before Messiah and Resurrection.] 'And he answered and said, Elias indeed cometh and shall restore all things. But I say unto you that Elias is come already and they knew him not, but did unto him whatsoever they listed. Even so shall the Son of Man also suffer of them. Then understood the disciples that he spake unto them of John the Baptist.'

It would, of course, require a wide examination of St Mark's Gospel to show that the paragraph we have considered is at all typical of the whole,[1] but we will assume for the moment that it is, and ask what light it throws on St Mark's 'simplicity'. The paragraph suggested at first sight an author who is stylistically unpractised, but on further examination it shows us one who is systematically enigmatic; who writes paragraphs which fail to carry their meaning on their faces, but which can be unravelled by the aid of clues hidden in the preceding pages or contained in the common tradition. Having come so far, we may drop the stylistic question. Whether or not St Mark's Gospel can be accepted as a literary masterpiece once his systematically enigmatic purpose has been grasped, is a question which hardly concerns us.

We may, perhaps, obtain further light on the meaning of systematic enigma in St Mark if we take up another point of comparison between the other synoptists and him, and consider the parts he and they assign to action and to teaching respectively. It is a commonplace that St Matthew and St Luke assign more space to Christ's teaching than St Mark assigns it. It is often suggested that St Mark left the teaching mostly alone because it was already embodied in written form when he wrote, and that afterwards SS Matthew and Luke each combined into one book two writings, St Mark's gospel and the Teaching. Even if the suggestion is correct it leaves much still unexplained. Why did St Mark not wish to do what St Matthew and St Luke afterwards did, and write a good part of the Teaching into the Gospel? Moreover, we have

---

[1] Other enigmatic passages: iii 22-30, iv 21-32, viii 11-21, ix 49-50, xiii 14, xv 33-39.

said very little about St Mark's attitude to act and word respectively when we have simply measured the quantity of each that he chooses to admit. What is still more striking is the order in which the two elements are introduced. There is plenty of action from the start, but the teaching slips out sparingly at first and in slight hints from between the interstices of the events, and only gradually attains either scope or definition. The bulk of it steadily increases as far as xiii, after which the passion story begins and event necessarily predominates. Jesus spoke little while he suffered.

St Mark does not read like an author who relies on an existing book to instruct his readers in doctrine. He is himself careful to tell them sooner or later everything that a Christian must know for his soul's health. The Christ of St Mark's Gospel bids his disciples keep the Decalogue, under the supreme guidance of the two duties, love of God and of our neighbour (x 17-19, xii 28-34). He looses the laws of ritual impurity (vii 1-23), but forbids divorce (x 1-12). He enjoins political obedience (xii 13-17). He teaches us that God is the sole source of goodness and salvation, but calls those who desire to obey God to abandon themselves to the following of Christ. God is One, but the Son shares his throne (x 18-21, xii 29-37). Christ dies to live, and so must his disciples (viii 30-38). He is the example of the baptism (i 9-11), and the institutor of the Eucharist (xiv 22-25), by which his disciples are joined to him; he teaches them the sacrificial efficacy of his death (x 45) and the necessity of faithful prayer (ix 29, xi 22-25). He bids them to rely on the Holy Spirit (xiii 11), to shun worldly snares (iv 19, x 26-31), to fear hell and hope for a blessed resurrection (ix 43-50). He warns them of trial and promises them his second advent (xiii). He institutes the apostolic ministry (iii 13-19, vi 7-13), and exhorts his followers to unity and mutual humility (ix 31-42, x 35-45). St Mark's account of Christ's teaching is comprehensive and clear. Every essential of the creed and the catechism is covered. And if there is any writing on which he relies for supplementation, it is not any collection of Christ's words, which he nowhere implies, but the letter of the Old Testament, to which he constantly refers.

8

Since St Mark is going to bring out all this balanced scheme of Christian truth at last, why does he deal it so gradually and so sparingly? Why does the water of doctrine force its way so painfully through the banks of historical event, escaping as though by accident, wearing its own channel for itself as it runs, and scarcely running freely yet when the Gospel reaches its conclusion? St Mark, like St Matthew and St Luke, knows that from the first Jesus taught, or, as we should say, preached; that was, indeed, the substance of his activity; the healing was in a manner incidental and extorted from him by the crowds. St Matthew and St Luke, each in his characteristic way, hastens to give us a specimen of the teaching. With St Matthew it is the Sermon on the Mount, with St Luke a missionary sermon in the synagogue at Nazareth (iv 16–30). St Mark has nothing of the kind. He tells us that the teaching is given (i 21–22, 39, ii 2, 13); he does not tell us what it is, beyond the bare and general announcement 'The time is fulfilled and the Kingdom of Heaven is at hand. Repent and believe the good tidings' (i 15).

In the first three chapters Jesus acts, and his acts, it would seem, are significant in themselves. Such of his teaching as St Mark records in any detail is given in explanation of his acts to the prejudiced or the hostile, never on the divine teacher's own motion but always drawn from him by interference. The fourth chapter at length allows the word of Jesus to take the initiative; but even now it is thrown forth in parable which has all the concrete opacity of fact. Christ simply reminds the people how the corn grows anywhere in their fields and tells them to make what they can of it (iv 2–9). The parable of Jesus is nothing but God's living parable, the growth of the corn. Jesus does not begin to teach his own doctrine until his disciples' bewilderment draws it out. It flows more freely, certainly, on such an occasion than under the provocation of malice. Jesus gives something like a plain exposition of the Sower; and yet returns in his conclusion to the riddling style (iv 21–32). The next time he has to answer Pharisaic criticism (on clean and unclean) Jesus spontaneously extends his teaching to the crowds and answers his disciples further when they still do not

9

understand (vii 1–23). Half the Gospel is gone, and we are at Caesarea Philippi, before Jesus takes the initiative with his disciples. Even now it is to question, not to instruct; it is as though he needs a fact on which to comment, and when he has not one to hand, creates one in the shape of the answer his question evokes (viii 27–30). He proceeds to speak on the occasion so provided and ends, once more, by drawing in the crowd to hear the lesson of the discussion (viii 34–ix 1). The tenth chapter marks a fresh loosening in the flow of doctrine; Jesus gives direct answers to outside enquirers, who pose him with their questions; the Pharisees on divorce, the rich man on salvation, and, later, in the temple courts, the Pharisees and Herodians, the Sadducees, the Good Scribe (xii 13–34). Meanwhile the teaching given in answer to the disciples, or in comment on their behaviour, grows in volume, and reaches a climax in the apocalyptic prophecy of xiii.

What we have said needs to be guarded against misunderstanding. St Mark does not tell us that Christ's teaching was limited to the occasions on which the evangelist gives details of it, or that he taught more copiously later in his ministry than earlier. St Mark tells us, by way of bare statement, that Christ taught constantly and throughout his mission. But it seems that St Mark cannot bring himself to give any teaching but what is drawn from him by the movement of events. If he simply told us what Jesus said from time to time, he would not feel himself to be doing justice to the force of divine revelation. God's revelation is not what anyone says, even though the speaker be Jesus himself. It is a power, a fact, active in the world, and compelling recognition. The fact must be there before interpretation begins; and when interpretation comes, it can do nothing but interpret the fact. The fact is a riddle, until it has been read, and the first gleams of interpretation are themselves enigmatic until the later and fuller interpretations have supplemented them. And so St Mark's Gospel may be simple in style, but it is systematically enigmatic in its thought.

The Gospel is no collection of miscellaneous riddles, it is the riddle of Christ, the riddle which Christ is. To call Christ a riddle is no stroke of modern paradox; the thought is in St Paul and the very phrase almost is in the First Epistle to Timothy. 'Confessedly great', says this Epistle, 'is the Mystery of Religion, who' (not which, but who) 'was revealed in flesh, justified in spirit, seen of angels, preached to Gentiles, believed on earth, assumed in glory' (iii 16). The Mystery of Religion, according to the author to Timothy, is a person, Jesus Christ, not considered as a bare existence, but expressed in a pattern of divine action: a pattern of action set out in the text I have quoted: 'Revealed in flesh, justified in spirit,' etc. The Christian reader to whom the letter is addressed feels that the sequence of phrases is enigmatic in the sense that it cries out for exposition, and, he might say to himself, all the Christian teaching there has ever been or can be is no more than the drawing out of what those phrases implicitly contain. They are enigmatic by excess of meaning, not by the lack of it. They are not enigmatic as a sentence is enigmatic which we find in an author we are reading and are unable to relate at all to the general frame of his argument. 'The mystery of religion' which the facts about Christ constituted did not strike his disciples as an erratic block in the structure of God's purposes. They did not say 'How in the world are we to find any relation between this block of facts and what has otherwise been revealed about the action of God in human affairs?' What they said amounted to something more like this: 'Here is the group of facts in which whatever else we know of God's designs is focussed and brought to complete expression. Here is more than we shall ever be able to expound— who is sufficient for these things? Who can be the expositor of them, unless he is himself inspired by God?'

Such an attitude to the saving facts appears to find expression in the very form of St Mark's Gospel. The Mystery of Religion, or, to use a Marcan phrase, the mystery of the Kingdom of God, shoots into the world as a bud in which the growth that shall be is tightly packed and minutely folded together. Jesus himself taught, and that must mean that within the pages of the Gospel and in consequence of his teaching activity the bud of truth unfolded and displayed itself.

There is an apparent difficulty here. The simplest way to think of the Mystery of Religion is the way in which the author to Timothy does think of it. The mystery consists of Christ expressed in his completed work, Christ incarnate, crucified, risen, glorified. By these events God in Christ has written the text of the riddle; the exposition is the work of the Holy Ghost after Pentecost. But a scheme so clear-cut as this is inapplicable to the writing of a Gospel. For a Gospel is bound to carry the exposition back behind Pentecost, behind the Resurrection, behind the Cross itself, and lay it on the lips of Jesus in the days of his flesh. But if so, the very riddle to be expounded is not there, for it has still to be written, written in blood, and the blood has yet to flow.

One way out of the difficulty is to concentrate on Christ's predictive utterances. The text of the riddle was not yet written in blood but Christ predicted that it would be. In foretelling his death and resurrection he expounded the saving and revelatory power of what he prophesied. Yet a purely predictive Christ could never be the Christ of the Gospels. The 'Mystery of Religion' reveals himself in successive phases of action, but he is wholly present in each. Christ in the flesh is already the heart and lips of God, everything is somehow there, though so much is yet to come; for God is not divided or distributed, and where he is, he is. It is a present reality to which Christ testifies, and yet it is a reality of which the cross and resurrection are the indispensable revelation.

What then is the text of fact which the Galilean Christ is to expound? It is the present, seen as the prefiguration of what is to come. In one view the whole completed work of Christ is the folded bud of truth, which displays its leaves and flowers in the exposition which is the life of the Church. In another view Christ before his passion, Christ in Galilee is the folded bud, and the unfolding of what he contains is seen in his cross and resurrection. When he expounds to his disciples the present mystery of the Kingdom of God he is at the same time predicting how it will unfold itself: he who explains what the bud is foretells what the leaves and flowers will be.

The modern Christian may, in his own sense, accept such an account of the Gospel facts. The cross and resurrection, the world-wide mission and the Church were all prefigured in the presence of Jesus among men. The act of charity which healed the sick was identical in essence with the act of charity which consented to die for sinners. Christ's healing virtue was a manifestation of the power which emptied the Easter sepulchre. The society constituted round Jesus when he sat to table in Peter's house was in germ the Catholic Church. In all these examples, and many others, we might be willing to acknowledge a spiritual identity between present and future things and therefore a prefiguration of the future in the present. But we should be likely to reject any prefiguration expressed in the symbolism of physical detail. We should not admit that resurrection was any more prefigured in the raising of a bedridden person to his feet than in the cure of ulcerous sores. In this respect it really does seem plain that the Evangelists and their whole generation part company with us, and I hope it is not necessary to argue the point. In a work of apologetic theology, it would be appropriate to show that the symbolism of physical detail was not used by St Mark except to express and emphasise true spiritual identities. But this is not the place for such comforting reflections, but rather for insisting on the uncomfortable fact that the early Christian mind delighted in a detailed physical symbolism which disquiets our own.

From our modern point of view the enigma which is stated and progressively expounded in St Mark's Gospel is partly actual and partly artificial. It is actual in so far as it consists of the sheer facts concerning Christ present in the world; artificial in so far as those facts are presented as physically symbolic or prefigurative. Now there is a fine point of language here to which it is worthwhile to attend. Ought we to say that the admission of an artificial symbolism makes the enigma which St Mark's Gospel expounds partly artificial, or merely that it makes the exposition of the enigma a partly artificial exposition? If the artificiality is confined to the exposition, the factual statements which the Gospel contains are unaffected by it; St Mark merely places an artificially symbolical construction on the facts, in the comments he makes or records concerning the facts. But if the artificiality extends to the enigma, this means that the symbolism is written into the factual statements themselves; the story is so told as to bring out the symbolical qualities which the Evangelist sees in it and which he will later expound if occasion arises; or perhaps not expound, but merely call attention to by a significant parallel.

To take an example. It does not need to be argued that St Mark sees the martyrdom of St John Baptist as a foreshewing of Christ's passion. The modern believer would agree with the Evangelist both in a spiritual and in a political sense. Politically the death of John shewed the limits of toleration in first century Palestine, and the fate to which free preaching was likely to bring the preacher. And spiritually, the necessity for the prophet's word to be backed by the prophet's sacrifice pointed towards a Messiah who must die for the very reason that he incorporated in himself the fulness of the word of God. But however it comes about, the actual parallel between the Baptist's death and the Saviour's, as St Mark narrates the two, extends to details which go quite beyond such broad identities of principle as we have just suggested. Herod, like Pilate, is lukewarm and would spare the preacher if he could. But, like Pilate, he is subject to a pressure which in the end he fails to resist. In both stories the dénouement turns upon a feast-time boon. On an occasion arising out of the celebration of his birthday Herod offers his little daughter any boon she likes to ask. On occasion of the Passover Pilate offers the people the freedom of any prisoner for whom they like to intercede. The two offers look entirely different but the boons actually demanded turn out to be comparable. Moved by her mother, the girl asks, not for the expected trinket, but for the Baptist's death; moved by the priests the people decline to ask for Christ's life and demand Barabbas's instead. Pilate and Herod are both trapped by their princely promises; Jesus and his precursor are both executed (vi 14–28, xv 6–15).

The problem presented by such a parallel is difficult. If it stood alone we might call it fortuitous, but there are too many such parallels in the Gospel for chance to cover them. On the whole it is more likely that the passion of Christ has influenced the presentation of John's martyrdom than *vice versa*. The circumstances of Christ's death were open to public observation and were of intense interest to the Christian witnesses. John's tragedy was an intrigue within palace walls, a subject for conjectural rumour in the market place, and St Mark's story reads as though it were based on some such rumour. Perhaps there were more rumours than one and the Gospel retains the features most prefigurative of Christ's passion. Yet an influence in the reverse direction cannot be entirely ruled out. The episode of Barabbas is thrown into a form which is historically puzzling and it constitutes the very point in the passion of Christ where the parallel with John's martyrdom is most striking.

The difficulty which this parallel presents illustrates the question with which we are concerned. The enigma which is being unfolded at any point in the Gospel is the enigma presented by fact already existing at that point, for example, the fact of the Baptist's death from chapter vi onwards. If the account of John's death is purely historical, then while the interpretation of it as so detailed a prefiguration of Christ's death is in a modern view artificial, there is no artificiality in what is thus artificially interpreted. Whereas if the story of John's death is somehow pressed by the Evangelist into a prefigurative pattern, then there is something artificial not only about the interpretation of the factual enigma but about the factual enigma as presented for interpretation.

How far might the patterning of ordinary narrative with artificial themes go? To judge by the Jewish writings of the time most closely preceding the New Testament, it might go far; and these writings provide the only outside standard by which we can form an objective opinion of what to expect from the Evangelists. A very defective or dubiously relevant standard, perhaps, but the only standard we possess. In *A Study of St Mark* I called attention to the artificial or symbolical patterning to be found in books liable to have influenced the Evangelists, certain presumably pre-Christian pseudepigrapha and the canonical 'Daniel'.[1] To invoke the apocryphal writings is to explain what is obscure by what is

[1] Pp. 257–264, 348–357.

15

more obscure. If appeal is made to Daniel, it is made to a book with which all students of scripture are acquainted.

Daniel, like St Mark's Gospel, is a narrative evolving into a revelation of doctrine. The climax of doctrine in St Mark is, in fact, the Apocalypse of the Son of Man (xiii) of which the greatest among Daniel's revelatory passages (vii) is the acknowledged model. Daniel, like St Mark, begins with what appears to be straight story telling, based on traditional sources; but as the book proceeds it becomes clear that the stories prefigure the coming revelations both in a real and in an artificial way. They prefigure them really, because (for example) they describe the persecutions and vindications of individual Israelites under heathen tyranny, and the revelations, when they come, predict the final persecution and vindication of the whole Israel of God. But they also prefigure the coming revelations artificially, in so far as certain theological, and one is even tempted to say, allegorical themes which appear in the visions are already worked into the preceding narratives.

For example, in the great vision of vii the Saints of the Most High are typified by a figure in human form while the idolatrous powers are typified by wild beasts. For (the vision shows) the human form is the divine form. In the image of God the Lord made man, according to Genesis, and the vision shows the Almighty Himself as a man-like figure. Those who degenerate from the knowledge and worship of God degenerate from the divine form and brutify themselves—'They are altogether brutish, that set up their graven image.' But God made Adam king over the beasts, and the empire of those who preserve the divine image must ultimately prevail over idolatrous brutality. Such is the lesson of the vision. In a preceding historical episode Nebuchadnezzar, unrepentant in his idolatrous pride, suffers the penalty of brutification and eats grass like the ox. But when he is led to acknowledge that 'the heavens do rule' he regains his human nature. The exact appropriateness of the King's punishment eludes us at the time. It is only when we come to the vision of the beasts and the Son of Man that the relation between bestiality and the denial of divine sovereignty is made plain through the theology of Genesis i.

16

And the vision when it comes is linked to the episode of Nebuchad-nezzar's punishment by a precise reference. The first of the beasts in the vision is symbolical of Nebuchadnezzar's own rule, and it is said of this beast: 'It had wings like eagle's wings. I beheld till the wings thereof were plucked and it was lifted up from the earth and made to stand on two feet like a man and a man's heart was given to it.' (In the story, Nebuchadnezzar's hair grew like eagle's feathers in his brutified state; but afterwards he was restored to his former condition and rose on his two feet and recovered his human sense.)

The story of Nebuchadnezzar prefigures one aspect of the vision of the beasts and the Son of Man: I mean the relation between idolatry and brutification. Another aspect of it is prefigured in the story of Daniel in the den of lions, which immediately precedes the vision. Daniel is thrown to the lions, because of his religious fidelity; he is saved and restored to power as the King's chief vizier. In the vision the lions become the heathen empires under the form of various ravenous beasts, and Daniel becomes the Son of Man, the people of the saints, rescued from their persecutors and promoted to empire as the vicegerents of the King of Heaven. Daniel in the den had been a sign of the whole divine dispensation; but the fact was not evident at the time. It became apparent only when the subsequent vision expounded the riddle of the fact.

The visions and angelic instructions of Daniel vii–xii point for-wards even more than backwards—they interpret the enigmas of previous fact, but in so doing they point to a fulfilment yet to come which is what the factual enigmas signified. In the Gospel it is the same—the meaning of the facts is read in the promise of further facts. The Gospel being a Gospel actually contains the saving facts to which it points; not the apocalypse on the Mount of Olives but the passion and resurrection of Jesus are the last word. Whereas Daniel is prophecy only, and goes no further than apocalypse.

There is a profound unity of thought in Daniel, but it cannot be appreciated unless we pay attention to the artificial symbolism written into the early narratives by the author's art. Now the unity of St Mark's thought eludes us when we seek it on that straightforward historical level which is congenial to our own minds. We find that, after a strong beginning, marked by a swift forward movement and a sense of urgency, his story dissolves into a miscellaneous pile of healings and disputes and journeyings. It is at least worth seeing whether what restores to us the unity of Daniel's narrative[1] may not restore to us the unity of St Mark's, I mean the element of artificial symbolism. This, then, shall be our task: not merely to catalogue examples of such symbolism in St Mark's pages, but to see whether there is not a master symbolism unifying the narrative basis of the Gospel, and making visible the oneness of that factual enigma which is gradually unfolded as the Gospel proceeds.

[1] We have in fact mentioned certain particular connexions only. The general pattern of the Book of Daniel may be described as follows. The four heroes are introduced and undergo a mild temptation together (i). Daniel's three companions undergo a severe temptation (iii) and we are left expecting that Daniel himself will undergo one equally severe. He does so (vi). The first temptation is followed by a dream (ii), the second by a dream and a vision (iv, v), the third by a dream and three visions (vii; viii, ix, x–xii).

CHAPTER II

THE MARCAN PATTERN OF HEALING

Before turning to look for the piece of symbolism which supplies the basic unity in St Mark's story, it is well to recall where the lack of such unity is most felt. Not in the exordium, and not in the conclusion. The summary of John Baptist's mission, of Christ's baptism and temptation, and of his first public appearance (i 1–14) is closely written; there is nothing loose or miscellaneous there. The much longer story of the Jerusalem ministry and the passion (xi–xvi) is not, of course, so close, not being a summary. The transitions from episode to episode may sometimes baffle us, but the general effect is that of a continuous movement of events towards a single climax. It is in the Galilean and Peraean ministries (i 15–x 52) that the episodes so frequently have the feeling of being unplaced in any real context. We forget where we have got to in the development of events—if there is any development of events. Like a tired traveller on a flat road, we seem to pass the same haystack over and over again as we read one miracle of healing after another.

To one who has travelled in that region of Jewish writing which forms the background to the New Testament, it becomes almost a routine principle, if he is losing his way, to stop and count; count, that is, any items which are similar to one another and fall into a natural group. Now a feature as striking as any in the first ten chapters of St Mark is the repetition of individual acts of healing. We are told on several occasions that Christ healed multitudes of sick people, but a surprisingly large number of individual cases are selected for full narration. It appears natural, then, to try the experiment of counting these acts of healing; or, what comes to the same thing, of counting these persons healed, for in St Mark each healing story is concerned with a single patient only.

Jewish writers employed arithmetic for many purposes for which we should think it unsuitable and, among others, for providing an apparent continuity of historical development. A man of St Mark's age and education was not to conceive the task of a biographer as we should understand it. Faced with miscellaneous anecdotes such as provided the data for the middle part of the Gospel story, the Evangelist knew no art capable of placing them in a sequence which should reveal the systematic movement of events, the interplay of personality, the unfolding of human purpose. The author of Daniel, faced with the wider panorama of empire succeeding empire was, from the modern historian's point of view, equally powerless to organise his data. But neither author could be content with an appearance of haphazard. For Daniel the succession of empires was providential, a necessary series of steps leading to the Kingdom of God, and the acts of Christ's ministry are no less providentially ordered in the eyes of the Christian writer. They are the stages of the destined journey which leads to the cross and the Easter sepulchre.

A method used by Daniel for symbolising providential necessity is first to lay down a list having an intrinsic completeness about it, and then, by devices of literary magic, to transfer that completeness to another list of things which have no such natural completeness. One does not see why there should be four heathen empires oppressing Israel by turns from the fall of Jerusalem onwards, nor does one see why the fourth should be the last. But anyhow there are four points of the compass from which the four principal winds blow.[1] It is in the nature of things that there should be no more than four. In Daniel's vision the four winds break loose on the great sea (vii 2), and up come four monsters, one for each wind, representing four empires, Babylonian, Median, Persian and Greek. With the aid of an imaginative presentation the four empires can be assigned to the four points of the compass, for first Babylonia and Media took the South and North respectively of the old Assyrian domain, then Persia overthrew them both from the East, and Greece in turn overthrew Persia from the West. To the ancient mind there were six directions of space, four horizontal, right, left, forwards and backwards, geographically reckoned as

[1] Or, there are four worthy metals, gold, silver, bronze and iron, and when corresponding empires have reigned, the list is exhausted (Dan. ii).

south, north, east and west; and two vertical, above and below. Now it was from below that the four beasts arose; they were the product of Below and of the four horizontal directions, for they were begotten by the four winds on the great deep. 'Above' has still to play its part; it remains that a final empire should descend from above, and that the heavens should rule. And so, when we have seen the four beasts each have his day, we can look with confidence for the kingdom of the Son of Man, whose advent is not from the deep but from the clouds of heaven (vii 13).

It would be unjust to the writer of Daniel to suggest that he supposed this piece of geometrical history to have the force of argument. It is rather a piece of poetical persuasion; a way of making us feel the force of destiny, not a demonstration of it. What is true of Daniel in this respect we will suppose equally true of St Mark. Let his intention be to make the miscellaneous tradition of Christ's ministry exhibit the appearance of that inward divine necessity with which his faith credits it. He will arrange it round a fixed number of healings; and he will connect this number of healings with an identical number of some other things to which it intrinsically belongs that they should be just so many and neither more nor less.

What numbered set of things shall play the part of Daniel's four winds in St Mark's exposition? What but the twelve tribes? That Israel was a twelvefold people was an axiom unshaken by the accidents of history, and Christ himself had symbolised his claim to the whole people of God by appointing a body called the Twelve as his missionaries to them. St Matthew (with the support of St Luke) reports the words of Christ to his apostles, 'In the regeneration, when the Son of Man shall sit on the throne of his glory, ye also shall sit on twelve thrones judging the twelve tribes of Israel' (Matt. xix 28). It is the habit of St Matthew to write out St Mark's riddles in plain answers. No one who reads St Mark with attention can doubt that in this particular he meant just what St Matthew says. He presents the solemn institution of the Twelve in iii 13–19 complete with the list of their names, and he adds their sending forth on mission in vi 7–13.

It is reasonable to suppose that the Twelve, like the patriarchal sons of Israel, are both the destined heads of the tribes and also representative of the tribes. Christ sends the Twelve to the Tribes when he sends them on mission; but when he institutes them they stand for the Tribes. Their institution is a new covenant of God with the Twelve Tribes on a new Sinai, as the circumstances and details of St Mark's narrative sufficiently indicate. The call of the Twelve is both the firstfruit and the symbol of the call of Israel. But it is Christ's mission not only to call, but also to heal. The two sentences 'The whole have no need of the physician, but the sick' and 'I came not to call the righteous, but sinners' are equivalent (ii 17). Because those who are called are sinners, they must also be healed, for sin is sickness. Conversely, as the next preceding episode shows, sickness is the token or physical counterpart of sin, and healing is a sacrament of forgiveness. 'Whether is easier, to say to the sick of the palsy, Thy sins are forgiven, or to say, Arise and walk? But that ye may know that the Son of Man hath power on earth to forgive sins, arise then (this he said to the sick of the palsy) take up thy bed and go to thine house' (ii 9–11).

St Mark's symbolism will be perfect if he can show that as Christ called twelve, so he healed twelve. Evidently it is not possible that the persons should be the same. The twelve apostles were men in the vigour of their youth, they were not invalids. Christ did heal, not Simon indeed, but someone belonging to Simon, his wife's mother; but it would be absurd to suppose that there was a similar healing in every apostolic family. The twelve healed must simply be a different set of people, and their relation with the twelve called apostles must lie in numerical correspondence only. They must simply be a representative selection from the persons whom Christ was remembered to have healed in fact.

As the four winds according to Daniel's vision break loose all together on the great sea, so the twelve apostles are instituted as a body in St Mark's third chapter, and establish the canonical fixity of the number twelve. Whereas the twelve healings will have to take place one after another through the story of the ministry. When the last has been performed we shall know that the number is complete and the healing ministry fulfilled. When Christ heals blind Bartimeus, that will be the sign for him to send for the ass, ride into Jerusalem and face his passion (x 46–xi 7).

But are there, in fact, twelve Israelites healed in St Mark's Gospel? Yes, there are twelve Israelites, the demoniac in the synagogue (i 25), Simon's wife's mother (i 31), the leper (i 41), the paralytic (ii 11), the withered hand (iii 5), Legion (v 8), Jairus's daughter (v 23), the unclean woman (v 29), the deaf mute (vii 34), the blind Bethsaidan (viii 25), the epileptic boy (ix 25), blind Bartimeus (x 52); twelve Israelites,[1] and in addition one Gentile, the daughter of the Syrophoenician woman (viii 29).

There are not, then, twelve healings, but thirteen, and that may well appear to be a damning admission. If St Mark is really building upon a basis of twelve, surely he cannot depart from it. Christ's mission is to twelvefold Israel, expressed in the twelve Israelites he heals, and the Syrophoenician woman has no business to be there.

No, she has, in a sense, no business to be there, but then that is exactly what St Mark tells us. The Gentile woman has no business to find her place in Christ's healing mission, for his mission is to the Jews. When Jesus was in the territory of Tyre, he had no mind to be available to the heathen people; he entered into a house, says St Mark, and wished no one to know, but he could not remain hidden. A heathen woman of Syrophoenician race found her way in and fell at his feet to intercede for her daughter's cure. Jesus dis-

---

[1] The story of Legion has Gentile suggestions about it; Jesus goes over the 'sea' to a foreign (Decapolitan) shore, there are swine grazing, beasts for which Israelites should have no use, and the demons perhaps talk heathenishly: 'Most High God' is a title more often given to the God of Israel by strangers than by Jews. The man, on the other hand, once he has returned to himself, is treated as though he were an Israelite, as a messenger capable, without more ado, of telling his neighbours what 'the Lord' (his master, that is, his national God) has done for him. Certainly the episode prefigures the Mission, but the man is an Israelite, and the same must be supposed of the other Decapolitan (if he is a Decapolitan: the geography is ambiguous) in vii 31–37. The purpose of the somewhat surprising geography of the journey in vii 24–31 may rather be to associate Phoenicia with Decapolis, the Syrophoenician exorcism with the exorcism of Legion, so that we may note how the promise of Gentile healing in v 1–20 has been actually fulfilled in vii 24–30.

missed her. Let the children, he said, that is, the Israelites, have their fill first. It is not right to take the children's loaf and throw it to the dogs. But the woman would not take her dismissal. Might not the dogs, she said, hope for a crumb or two to drop from the table, even while the children dined? She got her crumb; For that word, said Christ, go and find the demon expelled from your daughter.

It could not be more plainly said that it is out of the ordinary for the dogs to feed until the children have feasted, or, to speak literally, for the Gentiles to have the physical and spiritual benefits of the Gospel while Christ is still preaching to the Israelites. And what St Mark expresses to us on the small scale in the symbolism of bread, dogs, and children, he expresses to us on the larger scale in the symbolism of numbers. The children, the children of Israel, have their archetype in the twelve sons of Jacob, and so it is natural that an evangelist free to select his material should exhibit Christ's healing mission to Israel in twelve narratives of single persons healed. And the intrusion of the Gentile dog begging for crumbs shows itself to be an intrusion by adding one too many to the number.

St Mark, then, makes the fixity of the twelvefold scheme a basis for the paradox of the Gospel. It belongs precisely to Jesus, himself a thirteenth beside his twelve companions, to go beyond twelvefold Israel and embrace the firstfruit of the Nations. It is no use our blaming the Evangelist for being a Christian.

The hypothesis, then, may stand for the present in spite of the thirteenth healing. But we can scarcely be satisfied with it as it stands. For we must surely feel that the mere number of twelve (plus one Gentile) might, after all, be fortuitous. How are we to be sure that St Mark counted his healings at all, or that he regarded them as constituting a group of any kind? Our confidence would surely be increased if we could see that St Mark followed any principle, or worked out any pattern, in the arrangement of the healing stories. For it is unlikely that he would build twelve-plus-one items into a pattern of any elaboration without becoming aware that there were twelve-plus-one of them. It is necessary, then, to discover whether the healings fall into any clearly marked pattern or not.

The investigation may begin from a fact about the last of the healings. It is a fact of simple repetition. A deaf stammerer and a blind man are healed in vii and viii respectively, a deaf mute and a blind beggar in ix and x. Two pairs, ears and eyes, ears and eyes; or rather, ears-and-tongue, eyes; ears-and-tongue, eyes.

It is not only that the same sequence of themes characterises successive pairs of narratives. The pairing seems conscious on the writer's part. The first two in particular of the four we are considering have a number of features in common. The deaf stammerer in vii is healed as though with difficulty, by the use of spittle, and with an attempt at secrecy, and all these three things are equally true of the blind man in viii. The pairing of the other two is less striking, but both contrast with the former pair in being crowd scenes, and both throw into relief the importunity which appeals to Christ for aid.

It hardly needs to be pointed out that ears and eyes make up a natural pair anyway, since they are the two most informative of our sense-organs, and the association of tongue with ears is no less natural. The tongue both utters what the ear will receive and repeats what the ear has received already. Common speech, and in particular Biblical speech, associates all three organs together, both in a literal and a spiritual application. Spiritually considered, men need eyes to see the works of God, ears to hear his word, and tongues to profess their faith. He that hath ears to hear, let him hear, is the Marcan conclusion to Christ's parables (iv 9, 23; ? vii 16); elsewhere Jesus is found moving his disciples to profess their faith in him (viii 29, 38), or making his own profession before the high priest (xiv 62). The immediate prelude to the healing of the blind man in viii is a rebuke administered by Christ to his disciples, and containing the words 'Have you eyes and see not, have you ears and hear not?' (viii 18). Indeed the whole of the area in which the four healings occur (vii–x) is largely occupied by the wrestling of the Master with his disciples' incomprehension. On the face of it, then, it appears that St Mark, matching the inward with the outward and the instruction of the mind with the cure of the body, has given emphasis to the theme of revelation by recording the restoration of ears and eyes at this point, and double emphasis by recording it twice over.

Within the area covered by the four miracles we have discussed, and indeed between the last two of them, there occurs a further spiritual saying about the value of the eyes. Though they are proverbially the most valuable of possessions, it would be better to pluck one of them out, than lose one's whole body. As we read this saying, perhaps we expect a parallel saying about the ears, but we do not find it there, and a moment's reflection will assure us that the parallel would not hold good. To pluck out one's eye is to lose half one's sight, to cut off one's ear is to spoil little but one's beauty. The Evangelist remains within his biblical tradition: the losses of eye, tooth, hand and foot were the traditional list of injuries calling for retaliation (Ex. xxi 24 etc.). We do not, then, find the cutting off of the ear mentioned in this context, but we find the cutting off of hand and foot. Hand, foot, or eye—that is the sequence. The hand and the foot are specialised organs like the eye or (as the wider Marcan context shows) the ear. To go, to do, to hear, to see, all have their particular instruments in the human body. Two powers of action, two powers of sense—it would be bad to lose the active powers, worse, surely, to lose the sensitive, but either would be well sacrificed for eternal life (ix 43–50).

In view of this text, it is natural to ask: And has St Mark nowhere exhibited the healing of foot and hand in a pair of successive narratives, as he has the healing of ear and eye? The answer is, Yes, he has. The paralysis of the paralytic in ii 1–12 may have been general, but what is emphasised is his inability to stand or walk before his cure, and his power to do these things afterwards. He came in on a bed carried by others, he goes out on his own feet and carries his own bed. It may be we are to understand that the gift of power to carry the bed includes the restoration of the arms that lift it. But St Mark does not tell us so, and how are we to know? Men paralysed from the waist down cannot carry their beds away, not matter how strong their arms may be. Everyone who reads the story of the paralytic is left with the general impression that what Christ has done is to 'make the lame to walk', and this would seem to be St Matthew's interpretation (Matt. xi 5, reflecting ix 5–7). If in reading the story we are inclined to think of it as a story of paralysed feet, we shall be still more inclined so to think of it on retrospect, when the next particular healing presents us with a companion-piece, the story of an atrophied hand (iii 1–6).

It may be complained that we are forcing the evidence here. If St Mark had wanted to say 'foot and hand', he would have said 'foot and hand', but whereas he says 'hand' right enough, he does not actually say 'foot' at all. His mind cannot, then, be shaping itself in the formal pairs we are trying to fix upon him. Such is the objection, and it is interesting, not because it is cogent, but because it calls attention to a very general problem of interpretation. How far did the Evangelist devise the pattern of his Gospel before he wrote it, and how far did it come to him as he went along? To take the particular point at issue—did he sit down to begin with the already formed resolve to write of foot and hand, ear and eye? When St Mark was writing about the paralytic, it is surely not necessary to suppose that he had yet conceived the idea of grouping the Lord's healings by a scheme of two active powers, let alone by a scheme of four powers, two active and two sensitive. Perhaps he comes to write of the paralytic in pursuit of quite another train of thought, and one that has nothing to do with feet, as such, at all. The paralytic appears to find a quite satisfactory place in a series of bedridden people raised to life and health (i 31, ii 12, v 42). It may not be until St Mark comes to choose which healing story he will place next, that he classifies the story of the paralytic as a story about palsied feet, and does so by the simple fact of coupling it with the story of an atrophied hand. So the pair of active powers may arise naturally as St Mark writes, and when he reaches vii–viii he may have the further idea of paralleling them with a pair of sensitive powers.

I said just now that St Mark 'couples' the paralytic with the withered hand. Perhaps 'couples' may seem unduly tendentious. Would it not be better to say just 'follows'—that the Evangelist follows the one story with the other? But the two stories really are coupled together by striking common features which the remaining healing-stories do not share. First, we have not merely 'use of feet' and 'use of hand', we have also 'paralysis' and 'withering', or 'atrophy', diseases which form a natural pair, the one attacking the action, and the other the very substance, of the limb affected. St Mark achieves a climax: it seems a greater miracle to put back the substance of a withered limb in an instant, than to give back to a whole limb its power of motion. Further, it is peculiar to these two healings that before Christ can perform them he has to refute an objection of the Pharisees to his doing so. In the case of the paralytic he is accused of blasphemy, in the case of the withered hand it is the sabbath-issue. In this regard also St Mark attains a climax. At the healing of the paralytic neither Christ's feelings nor his opponents' reactions are described. At the healing of the withered hand Christ 'looks on them with indignation, grieving at the hardness of their hearts', while as for them, they go out and plot his destruction.

It is not too much to claim, then, that in ii–iii we have a pair of healings wrought on feet and hand, just as in vii–x we have a repeated pair wrought on ears and eyes; and we have adduced evidence from ix to show that St Mark associated the pair of sensitive organs with the pair of active organs in his own mind.

There is one healing among those we have discussed which calls for special remark. The first of the two miracles which make up the last pair of all is the healing of a surprisingly complex disease (ix 14–27). Not only is the patient deaf and dumb, he is also possessed by a violent demon which hurls him about; indeed the deafness and dumbness are only two among the distressing symptoms of the demon's presence. The Gospel affords no parallel to so many-sided a malady. The nearest approach is the case of the deaf-and-tongue-tied man in the preceding pair (vii 31–37); here are two misfortunes joined in one, but they are really aspects of the same condition; the stone-deaf do not learn to talk properly.

A deaf and dumb demoniac is a different thing altogether; it sounds like the fusion of two types, the demoniac and the deaf-mute.

It sounds like the fusion of two types. Perhaps it *is* the fusion of two types. Where are we to look for those types in a pure state? The pure type for the deaf-mute of ix is to be found in the tongue-tied deaf man of vii, in parallel with whom we have seen the deaf-mute to stand; but where is the type of the demoniac to be found? We have not far to seek, for the tongue-tied deaf man follows directly upon a demoniac, with nothing intervening except a change of place (vii 24–30, 31–37). The facts can be stated as follows: in vii we have two stories. A parent intercedes for a demoniac child, with such persistent faith that the Lord's bare word heals the child without her ever being brought before him. The scene changes; they bring before Jesus a deaf tongue-tied man, whom he heals. In ix we have one story. A parent intercedes for a speechless demoniac child, with eager, but imperfect faith. At Jesus's bidding they bring the child before Jesus, and he is found to be deaf as well as dumb. Jesus heals him. Such are the common elements, making up two stories in the one case, and one in the other. Even certain elements which differ, differ in so pointed and antithetical a way as to suggest a contrasting pair. For example, in vii a mother begs on behalf of a daughter, in ix a father on behalf of a son. In vii the patient is described as having spirit unclean, πνεῦμα ἀκάθαρτον, and in ix as having spirit unspeaking, πνεῦμα ἄλαλον.

It seems, then, that the theme of the demoniac child stands in a curious relation to the last two pairs of healing miracles. Embodied in a distinct episode, it immediately precedes the first member of the former pair; but it is actually incorporated in the first member of the latter pair. Or let us say that the former pair has the exorcism as a sort of prelude prefixed to it, while the latter pair absorbs the prelude into itself.

Following the clues which we took up, we have been led to examine seven of St Mark's thirteen healing stories: six falling into three matching pairs, and a seventh which is a sort of prelude to the middle pair. There remain six more, three in front of the first pair and three in front of the second pair.

————, ————, ————, lame, maimed;

————, ————, ————, demoniac, deaf, blind;

demoniac-deaf, blind.

It begins to look as though the pairs were part of some overall pattern embracing all the thirteen healings. The first and second pairs match one another. Let us see whether the triads preceding these two pairs do not also match one another. The first triad is in chapter i: the demoniac in synagogue, Simon's mother-in-law, and the leper. The second triad is in chapter v: Legion, Jairus's daughter, and the woman with the issue. Do the two triads match in quality as well as in number? On the face of it, yes. The man in synagogue and the man with the Legion are both demoniacs; Simon's mother-in-law and Jairus's daughter[1] are both female relatives of named persons lying sick in bed; leprosy and issue are both levitical uncleannesses which defile by contact and are prescribed for in successive chapters of the Mosaic law (Leviticus xiii–xiv and xv).

The parallel between the two triads is already, surely, sufficiently striking, and even on the evidence so far disclosed we might hesitate to attribute it to chance. But the case has not yet

[1] In what order are we to take Jairus's daughter and the woman with the issue? By order of introduction into the narrative Jairus's daughter comes first, but by order of cure the woman with the issue comes first, for Jesus heals her on his way to Jairus's house. Either order, then, is theoretically open to us. It would, however, be unreasonable to take the order of cure rather than the order of introduction, in connexion with our present hypothesis. We are supposing that St Mark arranges the cures in v on the model of the cures in i. If so, the Evangelist will, in the second passage, pick up his themes in the order which the former passage has laid down. Having picked them up, he will go on to develop them as he sees fit, and in building up his story he is in fact led to interlace the narratives of Jairus's child and the impure woman in such a way that the order of their conclusions is reversed. In the course of developing his narrative St Mark changes not only the position but the quality of the cure. Jairus's daughter is introduced as sick in bed, like Peter's wife's mother. In the development of the story, and during the interval filled by the healing of the impure woman, she is found to have died, and so her healing becomes her resuscitation.

been heard; the parallel can be greatly strengthened by closer attention to detail. The two shouting demoniacs not only both shout, they shout the same thing: 'What have we to do with thee, Jesus of Nazareth?' says the one. 'Thou art come to destroy us. I know who thou art, the Holy One of God.' And the other: 'What have I to do with thee, Jesus, Son of God Most High? I adjure thee by God, torment me not.' The man in synagogue speaks as though for the whole people of the demons, 'What have *we* to do with thee? Thou art come to destroy *us*.' The man by the shore expressly declares that he is peopled by a regiment of demons: 'My name is Legion,' he says, 'for *we* are many.' There are no other individual demoniacs in the Gospel who speak or behave like these two; the only other victims of possession are the two children in vii and ix for whom their parents intercede, and who have nothing to say for themselves at all.

To proceed now to the comparison of Jairus's daughter with Simon's mother-in-law. Jesus enters Peter's house accompanied by Simon and Andrew and James and John; he enters Jairus's house with the same companions named, except that Andrew is now omitted. We are expressly told that he would have no other escort. Jesus takes Jairus's daughter by the hand and raises her up; he had done the same with Simon's mother-in-law. We may add a point which would not stand alone, but is perhaps worth mentioning in connexion with the rest. The mother-in-law, being raised from her bed, serves the company with food, for she is the mistress of the house. Jairus's daughter, being a twelve-year-old girl and recovered from mortal weakness, does not serve them with food, but is herself served with food at the direction of Jesus. No other healing miracle of Jesus beside these two has as its conclusion the serving of food.

The two healings of the unclean turn, naturally enough, on the act of touching, since the touch of the unclean defiles. Jesus touched the leper, the woman touched Jesus. Her presumption of his goodwill obtained his immediate favour; the leper's polite doubt of it (If thou wilt, thou canst cleanse me) earned a certain measure of his indignation. A further point is worth remarking.

We made our original comparison of the two incidents turn on their both being levitical defilements, prescribed for in contiguous chapters of the Mosaic law. We do not merely impute to St Mark an awareness of the Scriptural background to defiling sicknesses. He actually mentions it. The leper is dismissed to 'show himself to the priest and offer for his cleansing the oblations which Moses commanded' in Leviticus xiv, the chapter on which the discussion of sexual issues directly follows, where the case of the woman in Mark v is particularly described (Lev. xv 25 ff.).

So then, the two groups of healings in i and v match just as clearly as the pairs of organs or powers in ii–iii, vii–viii and ix–x. Since v matches i and vii–viii matches ii–iii we can put i and ii–iii together on one side and v and vii–viii together on the other and speak of a continuous parallel between the healings in i–iii and the healings in v–viii. We may then say that what St Mark has done is, considered in itself, something quite simple, though certainly surprising. He has arranged a series of five healing-miracles and gone over it again with a corresponding series. Then, as a sort of closing refrain, he has repeated the last two themes of the second series. A shouting demoniac, a female sick in bed, a case of Levitical defilement, palsied feet, withered hand; a shouting demoniac, a female sick in bed, a case of Levitical defilement, deaf ears, blind eyes; deaf ears, blind eyes. Five in the first line, five in the second line, and the last two repeated, twelve in all. Twelve, of course, for Christ's healing mission is to a twelvefold people, the twelve tribes of Israel; and if it is asked why twelve should be made up of two fives and two over, a very elementary fact will supply a sufficient answer. Our system of counting is decimal because we have two handfuls of five fingers each, that is why we take ten as our basic number. The Greek for 'twelve' is 'two (and) ten', *dodeca*. The ancients had no numerical notation that could be calculated with, the medieval Arabs were the first to think of that; the ancients counted with an abacus, or more simply on their hands; fingers were numbers to them. So, then, twelve is the proper number of healing stories for an evangelist to select and retail, since Christ's healing mission was to the twelve tribes; and two handfuls *plus* two over is as natural a way as any to make up the number twelve.

If the number twelve is to be divided, the division into two fives and a two may be as natural as any other, but why should any division at all be made? If the object of St Mark's numerical symbolism is simply to show Christ healing twelvefold Israel in the examples of twelve particular Israelites, the mere number twelve might seem to suffice for the purpose. But it is reasonable to credit him with other purposes besides. It is surely almost impossible to tell a story of twelve distinct healings without interesting oneself in the variety of diseases healed; and especially if it is Christ healing all Israel, his Evangelist will wish to show that he healed every disease. A list of twelve diseases all different, even supposing that they were all represented in current traditions of Christ's healing acts, might minister to medical curiosity rather than to religious edification. The distinctions which St Mark uses are such as were to be found in scripture, held a place in messianic prophecy, and were clothed with spiritual significance for his contemporaries.

His initial division of morbid conditions is fourfold—possession, illness (threatening death), defilement, incapacity;[1] the first four in each 'handful' illustrate this division in identical order. A further division subdivides incapacity, and this division is fourfold also—incapacity in foot, hand, ears-and-tongue, eyes. To make room for the subdivision, incapacity is spread over two healings in each handful, the fourth and the fifth. Thus the two handfuls allow scope for the whole system of cures. The pair of additional cures which make up the twelve merely repeat the last two of the last handful, incapacity of ears-and-tongue, incapacity of eyes. At first sight there may seem to be something clumsy about this addition, looked at from a merely formal point of view; as though St Mark had completed his scheme of variations in ten healings, and being

---

[1] Even these four are not the primary division. St Mark begins with impurity (by unclean spirits) and raising up (from fever), and then repeats with variation: impurity (by unclean sickness) and raising up (from paralysis). It is a fair conjecture that the initial division (purification, restoration of 'life') corresponds to the two baptisms (John's, with water; Christ's, with spirit) which have occupied St Mark's introductory paragraphs.

still short of the necessary twelve, simply repeated the last two from among the ten. But that would be an unjust criticism. The diseases in St Mark's primary division (possession, illness, defilement, incapacity) are all stated in the first handful and repeated in the second. The special subdivisions of incapacity are not thus repeated in the first ten; and two of them, deaf-muteness and blindness, are of the highest spiritual interest and surely deserve to receive the same sort of emphasis as the four diseases which make up St Mark's primary division. It should not surprise us, then, if St Mark makes up the twelve by repeating these two.

In the display of such a symbolism as St Mark lays before his readers repetition has, indeed, a value of its own. For if a list of various diseases is gone through once only, how is the reader to appreciate that it has any systematic character or any particular meaning? But if the list is gone over twice, and each time exhibits the same plan, there is a hope that the reader will begin to notice that there is a plan. So it is with music; without some recurrence of theme there is no tune to the ear.[1]

The repetition of the first handful of themes in the second handful serves a further purpose. It emphasises the intrusiveness, the numerical superfluity, of the Gentile healing. Not only is the Gentile healing a thirteenth, one above the sacred twelve, it also disturbs the otherwise perfect parallel between the second handful of healings and the first. For, as we saw above when we were examining the healings in detail, an anomalous prelude is inserted before the first healing of incapacity in the second handful; and this prelude is no other than the exorcism of the Gentile woman's daughter. If we count this healing in, the second handful is not a handful at all—not a five, but a six. But the whole point of the symbolism is that we should not count it in. For this is not the dealing of one of the twelve sacred loaves to the twelve children of Israel—'It is not meet to take the children's loaf and cast it to

[1] Repetition of types of cure is reinforced by the distinction between the secret and the manifest. Christ desires to keep the first two healings of the deaf and blind secret, the second two are manifest; the first impure disease is healed secretly, the second manifestly. For the whole topic, see *A Study in St Mark*, ch. x.

the dogs'. This is something else, a grant to the dogs of the crumbs which so abundantly fall from the children's table.

The symbolism is forcible and elaborate, and indeed there is more to the same effect, which we will examine later. Would the thing symbolised appear of sufficient importance to justify such symbolisation? St Mark was writing, it is commonly agreed, for a predominantly Gentile audience, who found themselves the inheritors of Israel. Their relation to the ancient people of God must have been to them of absorbing interest, and the writings of St Paul, to name no others, sufficiently show that it was so. The Gentiles wanted to be taught that Christ, ministering to the Jews, had made an exception even then in favour of a Gentile's faith; and that the transference of the Gospel to themselves was a mercy which they owed to Christ's agonising passion, inflicted on him by the Jewish nation. It is surely unreasonable to complain of any interpretation suggested for St Mark, that it makes him out to have over-emphasised points like these.

We made it the basis of our whole argument that the Evangelist who describes Christ's healing mission to the twelvefold people of Israel in twelve particular stories of healing also describes a preaching and healing mission to the same people administered by Christ through twelve apostles. Now in St Mark's handling of the apostolic list there is something similar to his handling of the healing list, an extra person, one over the twelve, one who does and who does not belong, Levi the son of Alphaeus.

While St Mark is building up his first handful of five healings, he is building up in strict parallel a first handful of five disciples. Four of them, Simon and Andrew, James and John, are called from their fishing, and accompanied by them Jesus heals four persons in quick succession. We noted above (p. 33) that the first four cures lay the foundation for that exposition of the varieties of disease which fills the twelve healing narratives, and it is interesting to observe that the calling of the twelvefold apostolate finds its first exemplification in the call of the four fishermen. We may go further—as the fishermen are paired (Simon and Andrew, James and John) so are the varieties of cure (purification from unclean spirits and raising from sick-bed, purification from unclean leprosy and raising from death-bed). The achievement of a fourfold work with a fourfold following is not, perhaps, of itself significant; but it prepares us for what is to come, the employment of a twelvefold following on a twelvefold task. The parallel between the four called and the four healed is enforced by the fact that one of those healed, Simon's mother-in-law, was the relative of one of those called, and that the four are expressly said to have been present at her healing (i 29).

Before Christ performs a fifth healing he calls a fifth disciple, Levi the son of Alphaeus (ii 13–14), and St Mark does everything possible to emphasise the parallel between the call of this one and the call of the previous four. The scene is the same—it is by the sea shore. The circumstances are the same—it is from the midst of his business that Levi is called. The summons is the same—'Follow me'—and the response is the same, he walks straight out and follows. Even the sequel is the same—Jesus is presently entertained in Levi's house as formerly in Simon's.

The convenience of counting with one's fingers is not merely that one can readily count by fives and tens, but that one can also count off five against five, the fingers of this hand against the fingers of that. So a reckoning in fives naturally suggests the comparison of one five with another five. After telling off five healings against five callings, as we have shown, St Mark begins again, and tells off five more healings against the first five. Is he to do the same with callings, and tell off five more, one for one, against the five already recorded? But surely that would be meaningless, for whereas a case of issue tells off against a case of leprosy, and one shouting demoniac against another, the apostles do not fall into similar significant pairs; Thaddaeus neither matches nor fails to match Bartholomew. No; St Mark does not tell off five disciples against five; what he does do, as soon as the withered hand completes the first pattern of five, is to record the corporate call and formal institution of the whole twelve together. And it is here that we meet with a surprise, a surprise comparable to the inclusion of the Gentile exorcism in the second handful of healings—the exclusion of Levi from the list of twelve apostles. Here are Simon, James, John, Andrew, but the next name is Philip, not Levi; we run on through the list, always expecting to find him, but he is not there. He was called to give up all and follow, but he is not one of the Twelve. There are the Twelve, and Levi,[1] just as there are the twelve healed, and the Syrophoenician's daughter.

Who, then, is Levi? He is not, indeed, like the Syrophoenician child, a Gentile; it was morally impossible for Jesus to include a Gentile among his travelling company during his ministry. But Levi was a publican, the representative of those apostate Jews who sold themselves to the service of the heathen conqueror, plundered their fellow-Israelites, and abandoned all serious attempt to keep the Law. Not a Gentile, but the next thing to a Gentile. And surely no one—certainly not the original readers of St Mark—could fail to see in Christ's receiving of publicans and law-breakers a prefiguring of the reception of Gentiles into the Church. Thus, 'the twelve apostles—and Levi' means the same thing as 'twelve persons healed—and the Syrophoenician's child'. Both of these surprising additions to the number of twelve point to a going outside official Israel.

St Mark's numerical pattern does not falsify any historical fact, or even the meaning of any fact. Jesus did receive publicans and call Levi, Jesus did make an exception in favour of a Gentile's outstanding faith, and these actions were the seeds from which the inclusion of Gentiles in the Church afterwards grew. Jesus did institute twelve apostles, and he did heal twelve sufferers—indeed, he healed many more besides, but it is surely open to St Mark to choose out twelve, or rather, thirteen, for particular commemoration.

[1] It is a singular fact that 'Levi' (the priestly tribe) 'and the Twelve' (lay tribes) is a form of reckoning in the Old Testament, e.g. in the Book of Numbers.

CHAPTER III

MATTHAEAN RECONSTRUCTION, i

The last chapter sketched out an analysis of St Mark. The object of this chapter is to obtain support for it from St Matthew and St Luke. As for the analysis of St Mark considered on its own evidence, the most that could yet be claimed for it is that it promises well. It remains open to many objections, of which the most general is, perhaps, that it is based on an arbitrary selection of material. If one is content to pick out forms and patterns from an irregular complex whole, such as the Gospel presents, could not one find a considerable variety of alternative figures, like faces seen in the fire? But if St Matthew and St Luke are patient of an interpretation which shows them to have arranged their matter on much the same principle as St Mark can so plausibly be shown to have used, the case is greatly strengthened. It requires a very wilful imagination, surely, to see the same face in three fires.

The Marcan thesis was that our second Evangelist records thirteen healing miracles, twelve for twelvefold Israel and one over for a Gentile. There were subsidiary points, but that was the main point. The support to be derived from St Matthew is, briefly, this. He gives a comprehensive view of Christ's healing work in viii-xii, and in that passage he records the healing of twelve Israelites and of a thirteenth who is a Gentile. Besides—and this is surely remarkable—he retains the Marcan reckoning of twelve as two handfuls and two over, and arranges the two handfuls in parallel with one another, just as St Mark does. As to St Luke, his Gospel contains exactly twice thirteen people healed, the two thirteenth persons being a Galilean heathen and a Samaritan heretic respectively. Why St Luke should double the Marcan number is a question certainly to be asked, but anyhow it is what he has done; no one can impugn the arithmetic.

Any attempt to emphasise the importance of schematic arrangement in St Mark's Gospel has hitherto run against an apparently unanswerable objection. It seemed in vain to contend that the

meaning of St Mark was intimately bound up with his arrangement, if his earliest expositor, St Matthew, did not think so, but
rearranged quite freely. Could we really suppose that we understood what St Mark was doing better than St Matthew did? The
argument appeared unanswerable so long as its factual basis was
granted. But now it seems that the factual basis of the argument
was false. To all appearance St Matthew was no less interested in
St Mark's order than he was in St Mark's matter.

An analogy may serve for illustration. A church has been pulled
down, and the stones are to be re-used. They may be re-used in
any of the following three ways. They may be carefully marked
as they are taken down, and re-erected in the same order on a new
site. Then we have virtually the same church; nothing is new but
the mortar and the fittings. Or, a second possibility, they may be
re-used quite regardless of their original purpose, to build (let us
say) a town hall. Or again they may be used to build a church, and
to the same essential design, say with aisles and transepts, but
larger, and with the addition of a narthex and side-chapels. The
old stones will not all of them go into the old places. The new
architect has, indeed, freely rearranged his predecessor's materials,
and yet he has had so high a respect for his predecessor's design,
that he has made it the basis of his own. His object has been not so
much to supersede it as to make it stronger and bolder.

It is this third sort of reconstruction that St Matthew undertook.
Undoubtedly he reconstructed. He did not even leave the stones
as they were, he squared and trimmed them to his liking. By
'stones' we mean 'paragraphs', so that what we are saying is that
St Matthew never copied a Marcan paragraph word for word.
What he did to the general lines of the architecture was, in fact, no
more drastic than what he did to the individual stones. Both are
reshaped, and both are recognisable. The same sort of reinterpretation as St Matthew applies to the paragraphs he applies also
to the main lines of the design. Now reinterpretation presupposes
comprehension. No one can reinterpret what he has not grasped.
If St Matthew reformed and reapplied the Marcan pattern, he had
grasped it; and if modern scholarship claims to have grasped it

too, it claims no more than to have seen a little of what St Matthew saw.

The difficulty of proving that St Mark made use of formal order lies in the necessity of admitting that if he used it, he very largely concealed it; he was 'systematically enigmatic'. No such difficulty arises in the case of St Matthew. Much formal, and even arithmetical, order appears on the surface of his work. He begins his whole book with a genealogy of Christ which he himself divides for his readers' instruction into three double sevens of generations, each double seven being made to correspond with a grand division in the history of God's people. The Sermon on the Mount is built round sets of things: eight beatitudes, six antitheses between the old law and its new interpretation, three works of merit. Within each set there is an almost rigid parallelism of form between the several items. All this is unmistakable, and the recognition of it has naturally inclined scholars to look about for further elements of schematisation which, though not so evident at first sight, may perhaps play an equally important part in the structure of St Matthew's book. Thus they have been led to observe that the narrative is punctuated at roughly equal intervals by five great discourses of Christ, each one of which is terminated by some close variant of the rubric: 'Now it came to pass when Jesus had completed all these words, that he . . .'

The division of St Matthew's book by the five great discourses is perhaps the most widely recognised structural characteristic of this Gospel as a whole. Now this division by discourses is clearly something entirely different from the Marcan arrangement of the narrative round twelve healings. It is, in fact, St Matthew's own; he may have found hints in St Mark suggestive of such an arrangement, but the arrangement itself is not in St Mark. It would be tempting to hazard the statement that as St Mark is written round twelve healings, so St Matthew is written round five discourses, and that this is just the difference between them.

At first sight it might seem that St Matthew's arrangement can leave no room at all for the Marcan healing pattern. But to leap to such a conclusion would be to overlook one of St Matthew's most notable peculiarities, arrangement by subjects. Christ's *halacha,* his interpretation of the Law as a way of conduct, is gathered together in the Sermon on the Mount, his predictive utterances are concentrated in the apocalyptic discourse of xxiv–xxv. Similarly the whole range and variety of Christ's healing work is gathered together in viii–ix, with a sort of appendix in xii.[1] It is here if anywhere that we must look for a Matthaean version of St Mark's twelvefold, or thirteenfold, scheme; but so telescoped or compressed that it can be fitted into a couple of interstices between St Matthew's great discourses.

Matt. viii–ix contains the story of ten Israelites healed in almost unbroken succession, with one Gentile healing inserted amongst them. If we bracket the Gentile healing and write out the Israelite healings in two lists of five, they correspond, the first in one column with the first in the other, the second with the second, and so on, just as the two Marcan 'handfuls' were found to do (the

St Mark

FIRST HANDFUL	SECOND HANDFUL
1. Demoniac in synagogue	1. Gerasene demoniac
2. Simon's mother-in-law	2. Jairus's daughter
3. Leprous man	3. Woman with issue
	(Syrophoenician's daughter)
4. Paralytic	4. Deaf stammerer
5. Withered hand	5. Blind Bethsaidan

TWO OVER
Deaf mute demoniac
Blind Bartimeus

St Matthew

FIRST HANDFUL	SECOND HANDFUL
1. Leprous man	1. Woman with issue
(Centurion's servant)	
2. Simon's mother-in-law	2. Jairus's daughter
3, 4. Two demoniacs	3, 4. Two blind men
5. Paralytic	5. Deaf-mute demoniac

TWO OVER
Withered hand
Deaf-mute blind demoniac

[1] But what of further healings in xv–xx? See pp. 120 ff. below.

five Israelites healed in Mark i–iii, and the five healed in v–viii). The 'two over' required to make up twelve, corresponding to the two in Mc. ix–x, are to be found in Matt. xii. The whole Matthaean pattern stands in an intimate relation to the Marcan pattern. It is simplest to summarise the two patterns in consecutive lists, and then to comment on the relation between them.

In commenting on the diagram, it will be convenient to take one after another the pairs which arise from the putting together of corresponding numbers from the two Matthaean 'handfuls'. And so we begin with the leprous man and the woman with the issue. This pair is a Marcan pair, the two levitical defilements. All that St Matthew has done is to move it back from third to first place. He follows on with another Marcan pair—Peter's mother-in-law and Jairus's daughter. Nothing could be more straightforward, but now we get a surprise. According to St Mark the two shouting demoniacs balance one another in the two handfuls; but St Matthew places them both in the first hand, a single story of two shouting demoniacs. Of St Mark's two stories, it is the second that provides the general model for St Matthew; his scene is on the Gadarene shore, not in the synagogue at Capernaum. Yet a careful examination will reveal verbal borrowing from St Mark's Capernaum story also. ('Thou art come to torment us,' say the two Matthaean demoniacs. 'Thou art come to destroy us,' says the Marcan demoniac in synagogue. 'I adjure thee, torment me not,' says the Marcan demoniac by the lakeside.)

St Matthew, then, pulls both the Marcan demoniacs over into the first handful, of which they make up the third and fourth items. What can he set over against them in the second hand? Another double, obviously; what but a double can match a double? He draws together the two blind men of Mark viii and x. The second of the two Marcan stories offers the better parallel to the vocal demoniacs, for blind Bartimeus is no less vocal than they. So St Matthew can obtain the balance he requires: the two demoniacs cry 'Away from us, Son of God' and the two blind men cry 'Mercy on us, Son of David'. But in the conclusion of the story St Matthew deserts the model of Bartimeus for that of the blind Bethsaidan in Mark viii. The scene is transferred to a private place, and secrecy is enjoined by Jesus on the recipients of the cure.

There remains the fifth pair only. St Matthew uses here another of St Mark's pairs—the paralytic and the deaf-mute. But the deaf-mute becomes a *demoniac* deaf-mute, like that other deaf-mute in Mark ix, and his cure is greeted with the comment: 'He casts out demons by the prince of demons'. This is the comment which according to Mark iii 28 and Matthew xii 31 was condemned by Jesus as blasphemy. And so the comparison between the two members of St Matthew's pair is enforced in a striking way. Christ, healing the paralytic, forgave his sins and was accused of blasphemy. Christ, exorcising the deaf-mute, is subjected to an accusation which is itself a blasphemy. Or, if you think the point too subtle, you will at least agree that paralytic and deaf-mute demoniac are both 'signs that are spoken against'. He blasphemes! He casts out demons by the prince of demons!

Let us pause here and make a cursory comparison between St Matthew's two handfuls and St Mark's two handfuls. We will ignore changes of order, and simply ask how many items are there in either Matthaean handful which are not to be found in the corresponding Marcan handful? The first Matthaean handful borrows a shouting demoniac from the second Marcan handful, and by way of compensation drops out the withered hand. The second handful, having surrendered a shouting demoniac to the first, borrows blind Bartimeus (as we have seen) from the Marcan 'two healings over'. To put it numerically: there is one item changed in each handful; the remaining four on each side stay the same.

Which, now, of the twelve Marcan healings have failed to find a place in either Matthaean handful? The withered hand, dropped from the first handful; and the second deaf-mute, also demoniac, one of the 'two over' in St Mark's arrangement. Does St Matthew forget the withered hand or the demoniac deaf-mute? He does not; they feature as his own 'two over' in chapter xii. And so the whole range of the Marcan healings is covered by St Matthew in viii–xii. He neither omits anything nor adds anything.

A retrospective observation may be permitted at this point. We sketched a pattern of healing-miracles in St Mark, and the clue to the pattern was the classifying of the miracles according to the quality of the disease healed: blindness, defiling sickness, or whatever it might be. Such a classification lay open to the accusation of arbitrariness. It might be that it could plausibly be made, but how were we to know that St Mark made it? The case is surely strengthened when it is shown that, supposing the same classification, we can see St Matthew to have made an intelligible re-arrangement of the Marcan scheme. Withdraw the classification, and the correspondence between the two Evangelists largely disappears.

That St Matthew classified healings by the nature of the disease healed is indeed obvious from his own words: 'Go tell John what ye do hear and see: the blind receive their sight and the lame walk, the lepers are cleansed, the deaf hear and the dead are raised up' (xi 4–5). Or again in xv 30–31: 'There come unto him great multitudes having with them the lame, blind, dumb, maimed, and many others . . . and he healed them, insomuch that the multitude wondered, when they saw the dumb speaking, the maimed whole, the lame walking, and the blind seeing.' These two lists together give us the whole classification we have used, except possession, which is in any case the most plainly distinct of all types of disease. Otherwise, here are the two physical incapacities (laming and maiming) and the two sensitive (deafness or dumbness, and blindness). Here is defiling sickness (leprosy and the like) and here is dangerous sickness, even to death itself. And so an interpretation of the Matthaean arrangement of the healing miracles which is based on such a classification cannot be called unreasonable.

To return now to the comparison between two handfuls of healings in Matt. viii 1–ix 8 and ix 18–34. We remember that St Mark used the otherwise perfect correspondence between his two handfuls to emphasise the intrusiveness of the Gentile healing, which disturbs it. St Matthew also introduces an extraneous and Gentile sixth into one of his handfuls; he places it in the first, whereas St Mark placed it in the second. The healing of the

Centurion's servant follows directly upon the healing of the leper; that is, it is the second of all the healing miracles in the Gospel.

It is not difficult to guess why St Matthew placed it in the position it occupies. He puts the leper first because the leper gives the best follow-on from the Sermon on the Mount which immediately precedes. The Sermon declares that Christ has not come to destroy the Law but to fulfil it. One jot or one tittle shall not fall till all is fulfilled. Examples of his moral teaching are given which all point in the same direction—Christ always asks more of men, not less, than Moses did. Now the healing of the leper is the only one of Christ's healing acts in which we are told that he showed himself solicitous about a point of literal Jewish law. 'Go thy way,' he says to the patient, 'show thyself to the priest and offer those things that Moses commanded, for a testimony unto them.' The leper is thus made typical of the Jew under the law and saved by Christ; and the typical case of the Gentile saved outside the law could have no more effective prelude. First the Jew, then the Gentile; first the leper, then the Centurion's servant; the Jewish leper must be scrupulous to make his levitical offerings, and yet, says Jesus in comment on the Centurion's faith, many shall come from the east and the west, and shall sit down with Abraham and Isaac and Jacob in the kingdom of heaven, but the sons of the kingdom shall be cast into outer darkness.[1]

Thus the leper receives the Centurion's servant as his immediate sequel, in place of the paralytic with four bearers, who follows the leper in Mark. Yet in phrasing the story of the Centurion's servant, St Matthew seems to have the paralytic in mind. For, to start with, the Centurion's servant is a paralytic; that is his disease. Then, further, the two stories have the same obvious point—the healing of a sufferer in consideration of his friends' faith. Seeing the faith of the bearers, Jesus spoke the words of reconciliation to the paralytic; finding in the Centurion such faith as he had not found in Israel, he healed his servant.

[1] The two episodes are held together by a common scriptural type. The most notable leper healed in biblical history is Naaman, and Naaman is a Gentile military officer (II Kings v, c.p. Luke iv 27).

The story of the Centurion fits its place perfectly indeed, and the matter is not yet exhausted. We have still to observe the place it occupies in the parallel between the two handfuls of healings. We said above, and it is true, that there is no healing in the second handful standing opposite to that of the Centurion's servant; but if a healing does not stand opposite to it, what does? The Centurion is halfway between the leper and Peter's mother-in-law. What, if anything, stands halfway between the corresponding pair of healings in the other handful? Nothing but a change of scene. After the scene of the healing of the impure woman, and before the scene inside the ruler of the synagogue's house where his daughter is actually resuscitated, we have the short scene of Christ's arrival at the entry: 'And when Jesus came into the ruler's house, and saw the flute-players and the crowd making a turmoil, he said: Give place, for the damsel is not dead, but sleepeth. And they laughed him to scorn.' We see that Jesus visits the house of a Jewish official[1] (the ruler) at the ruler's own request, so that (to quote an earlier verse) 'he may lay his hand on his child'; he goes, and is met with derision. The story of the Centurion shows us a Gentile official (the Centurion) declining Christ's offer to visit his house; his faith sees physical contact between healer and patient as something quite superfluous: his faith, pronounced by Christ greater than any he has found in Israel. The story of the Centurion is essentially the story of his declining Christ's offered visit. We are simply told by way of conclusion that his servant recovered at Christ's word. The healing never comes upon the scene of the dramatic narrative. In a sense, it is not there; and so if there is nothing to match it in the corresponding handful, it is the less surprising. The healing of the Gentiles does not belong on the scenes of Christ's earthly ministry.[2]

---

[1] St Matthew improves the parallel by dropping the name of Jairus. We are left with 'the centurion's servant—the ruler's child'.

[2] The story of the Centurion is commonly supposed to have been derived by St Matthew from Q. But surely the moral to be drawn from the extraordinary neatness with which the story nestles into its Matthaean context is that it was cast into written form for the first time by the man who placed it in that context, that is, by St Matthew himself. St Luke re-shapes the story somewhat, but

What general lesson is to be learnt from St Matthew's twelve (or, reckoning in the Centurion's servant, thirteen) healings? In spite of the many alterations he introduces, St Matthew holds fast to the Marcan pattern in its essentials; the two handfuls and two over, the extra item in one of the handfuls, the precise number of shouting demoniacs, of blind, of levitically impure persons, and so forth. What impresses us is his firm grasp upon the main lines of the Marcan pattern. If he had copied out the Marcan healings as they stand, we should never have known whether he appreciated the principle of their arrangement or not. But it would be little short of a miracle, if he made the alterations he has made, and still left the pattern intact, without ever having seen that there was a pattern there to be kept intact.

As for the rearrangements which St Matthew thought fit to make, no doubt he had his reasons for them, but we are under no obligation to investigate those reasons here. They do not affect the argument either way. We will, however, make a single observation on the subject, and we will begin from the general difference between St Matthew's plan and St Mark's.

In St Mark the twelve healings carry us to the very gates of Jerusalem. They must all be fulfilled; then, without delay, Jesus can enter the holy city and meet his passion. The climax to the twelve healings is the climax to the Gospel itself. There is no very evident climax of power in the healings as such, or of effect produced by them on the popular mind; nor is any such climax required. Our eyes are already on the coming passion by the time we reach Bartimeus.

even so it has no such vital or manifold connexions with the context in which he places it. The same is true of several other pieces of the so-called Q tradition: they appear to be made for their Matthaean place, and adjusted to their Lucan place. The fact is admitted by the friends of the Q hypothesis and actually twisted into an argument in support of it. St Luke, they say, could never have found his material in St Matthew, or he would not have dreamt of tearing it from the perfect setting it there has, to place it less happily in his own Gospel. It is wiser to say: St Luke, wishing to write his own book in his own way, rearranged the material he found in his authors. He did it skilfully, but no amount of skill could make an adapted context fit as tight as the context for which the material was composed.

47

In St Matthew it is very different. The whole scheme of twelve healing signs is completed before the middle of the Gospel is reached. The passion is far ahead; some sort of immediate climax is required. The twelve apostles have been sent; the twelve signs have been given. With what effect? The twelvefold people rejects them; as Moses' signs were rejected by Egypt, so are Christ's by Israel.

It is natural, therefore, that St Matthew should wish the end of his list of healings to be made up of miracles which provoked violent hostility. In St Mark's account, it is the first handful of miracles that works up the highest climax of immediate rejection.[1] When Christ healed the paralytic, they muttered about blasphemy; when on Sabbath and in synagogue he healed the withered hand, they went out and plotted his destruction (iii 6). Sixteen verses further on St Mark resumes the subject of the Pharisaic attitude to Christ's miracles. The scribes who came down from Jerusalem said, 'He hath Beelzebul, and by the prince of devils casteth he out devils' (iii 22). It was this accusation which called forth Christ's sayings about the source of his miraculous power, and about the significance of Pharisaic hostility to its exercise. The 'Beelzebul controversy', as it has been somewhat pedantically named, appears to provide the perfect climax to the whole topic of Christ's twelve-fold healing work. What, then, does St Matthew do? He provides the Beelzebul controversy with a particular occasion—it was not Christ's exorcisms in general which provoked the scribal accusation, but (says St Matthew) a particular exorcism. Let this exorcism be the twelfth and last of the healings, and let the withered hand be its predecessor. These two signs are above all others the 'signs spoken against', and they constitute the 'two over' which follow the second handful in St Matthew's arrangement. But, it may be asked, how can St Matthew introduce a new exorcism in connexion with the Beelzebul controversy without adding an extra to the Marcan list? Only by identifying it with an exorcism on the Marcan list. St Mark's last sign but one is the healing of a

---

[1] The end of the list brings us to ultimate rejection, i.e. the passion, but not immediately, nor are the healings themselves what is rejected there.

deaf-mute demoniac, and that healing is itself a cause of strife between a 'faithless generation' and Jesus. So the exorcism which provokes the Beelzebul controversy in St Matthew becomes the exorcism of a (deaf and[1]) dumb man. St Matthew adds 'and blind', thereby compensating for the disappearance of the Marcan blind beggar from the twelfth place in his own list.

There, then, we have the end of the Matthaean pattern of healing: the withered hand and the (deaf-[1]) dumb-blind demoniac are his 'two over'. They are divided from the 'two handfuls' by a considerable interruption, the apostolic mission (x) and the visit from John's disciples (xi). There is some danger, then, that St Matthew's readers should lose the thread of the twelve healings between the tenth and the eleventh. The Evangelist guards against such a loss of continuity by resuming the end of the second handful in the conclusion to the whole list. The last of the second handful is also a (deaf-[1]) mute demoniac, about whose cure Pharisaic malice says already, 'By the prince of devils he casts out devils'. The blasphemy passes without comment. That cannot surely be the end of the matter, thinks the reader of St Matthew. And indeed it is not. We read on, and in xii we find virtually the same exorcism, provoking the same comment. But this time the lightning falls; an extended and strengthened version of Christ's retort according to St Mark brings the whole matter to a fitting end (xii 25–45).

Whether or not the suggestions offered here illuminate the motive of St Matthew's rearrangements is irrelevant to the main point at issue. It is enough if it be granted that St Matthew does make the rearrangements, and that he preserves the pattern of the Marcan design in spite of them, and therefore surely not by accident.

St Matthew preserves not only the general outlines of the Marcan healing pattern, but also its relation to the twelvefold apostolate. The theme of the Twelve, like so many other Gospel themes, is gathered or concentrated by St Matthew in a place by

---

[1] κωφός may mean either deaf or dumb. St Matthew has both senses unambiguously elsewhere.

itself. In St Mark the Twelve are called and instituted in iii and on this occasion the list of their names is recorded; in vi they are sent out on mission and a brief account of the directions Christ gave them is added. St Matthew suppresses the separate account of their institution, transfers the list of apostolic names to the occasion of their sending on mission, and builds up a great missionary charge out of all the relevant sayings of Christ which his tradition contained. The resultant discourse takes its place as one of those five principal discourses which are commonly thought to lay down the main lines of St Matthew's architecture.

The position of the great mission charge is, for the purpose of the present enquiry, highly significant, for it stands in the midst of the pattern of twelvefold healing. For a merely diagrammatic purpose it will be convenient to use a doubtless unhistorical way of speaking and think of St Matthew with his five discourses arranged first, proceeding to fill the empty intervals between them. The first discourse is the Sermon on the Mount (v–vii), the second is the missionary charge to the Twelve (x), and the third is the Parables (xiii). Between the three discourses there are two intervals, flanking the mission of the Twelve on either side. How shall these two intervals be filled? How more appropriately than with that alternative expression of the theme of Christ's twelvefold ministry, the healing of twelve representative Israelites? The one interval (viii–ix) is completely filled with healings, for here the Evangelist sees fit to place both of the two handfuls, so that their mutual relation will be most plain; they stand so close together that they can be compared at a glance. The 'two healings over' are left to occupy the second interval (xi–xii) which, being only two, they by no means fill (xii 9–14, xii 22–24). But, being the end and climax of the healing series, they are the occasion of discourses rebuking Israel's rejection of the 'mighty works' (xii 25–45). What remains of the second interval is principally occupied by the episode of the message from John Baptist in prison. Christ's words to the crowd on that occasion also turn upon the rejection which has been the common lot of John's prophecies and of his own miracles (xi 1–24).

The first and simplest fact, then, about the relation between the twelvefold healing and the twelvefold mission is that the mission stands in the midst of the healing. A more detailed picture can be drawn from an examination of the list of apostolic names according to St Matthew (x 2–5). The occasion for the list, the sending forth of the Twelve, has its counterpart in Mark vi; though St Mark, for his part, gives the name-list in connexion with a previous episode (iii 13–19). St Mark says that Jesus sent them forth in pairs, an observation which naturally reminds us how Jesus had previously called four of them in pairs, Simon and his brother Andrew, James and his brother John. St Matthew does not tell us that the Twelve were sent out in pairs; he pairs their names in the list, and leaves it at that, placing first the couple of pairs that Jesus had called from their nets before he gave the Sermon on the Mount. The previous narration of their common call, and the present description of them in parallel form as pairs of brothers, have the effect of coupling these two pairs in our heads as we read the list; and so we are inclined to go on using the same unit of measurement, taking the next two pairs likewise together, and then the last two pairs. That gives us a list with three lines of two pairs each, an arrangement very close to St Matthew's own division of his other name-list, the genealogy (three lines, each containing two sevens: three lines, each containing two pairs).

Simon called Peter and Andrew his brother, James son of Zebedee and John his brother;
Philip and Bartholomew, Thomas and Matthew the publican;
James son of Alphaeus and Thaddaeus, Simon the Cananean and Judas Iscariot who betrayed him.

The first line of the apostolic list will then run from Peter to John, the second on from there as far as Matthew, the third on again to Judas Iscariot. And these simple facts remain unaffected by any serious variant in the MS. order—on any showing, John, Matthew, and Judas are the fourth, eighth and twelfth names in the Matthaean list.

With these facts in our minds, let us see the order in which the apostolic names make their appearance in this Gospel. The call of the two pairs of brothers from their nets in iv takes us through the first four names. The very similar call of Matthew from his tollbooth in ix takes us at a leap to the eighth name. Then the list of the whole apostolate in x takes us all the way to the twelfth name. It looks as though St Matthew's call were intended to mark a sort of middle between the call of the four and the mission of the twelve.

It is to be observed that our Evangelist has made two changes in his Marcan original, which ought to have something to do with each other. First, he has substituted the name of Matthew for the name of Levi in the story of the publican called from his tollbooth. Second, he has moved the name of Matthew on from seventh to eighth place in the apostolic list, by making Matthew and Thomas change places. What ought we to conclude from these two facts? Our Evangelist wishes to narrate the call of a publican who became an apostle, rather than of one who did not; St Mark's Levi was not an apostle, but Matthew was, and our Evangelist knows or believes him to have been formerly a publican. Further, wishing to represent Matthew's call as an intermediate point between the call of the Four in iv and the addition to them of the remaining Eight in x, he makes Matthew fourth among the additional Eight, or, what is the same thing, eighth among the whole Twelve.[1]

But if St Matthew's call is a bisecting point, what does it bisect? Obviously not the whole mass of material between the call of the Four and the calling together of the Twelve, for it is much nearer the end than the middle of the section thus delimited. What then does it bisect? It bisects the first ten healings, dividing them into the two handfuls. This, then, is how the healings are arranged in relation to the callings of the Apostles: after the call of the Four and the Sermon on the Mount, one handful; after the call of

[1] It is to be observed that St Matthew takes both the two previous call-stories, of the four and of the publican, into the apostolic list in an orderly manner, St Mark neither. His aim is exactly opposite—to point contrasts. Of the four called together, only three are chosen as 'pillars' and surnamed; of the five called in all, only four are chosen to be apostles.

Matthew, the other handful; after the calling together of the Twelve and the missionary sermon, the two over.

It remains that we should consider the testimony of St Luke. It is characteristic of his writings that the mission to Palestine is regarded as twofold; it is a mission to Jews and Samaritans (Acts i 8, viii 1). In the Gospel he, and he alone of the Synoptists, records a long journey of Christ in or about the Samaritan country (ix 51–xviii 30), as though anticipating the mission in Samaria begun by St Philip the Evangelist and continued by St Peter and St John (Acts viii 5–25). In the Acts Galilee is little mentioned, but in so far as it is, it appears to be viewed as attached to Jewry (ix 31, x 37; the latter of these two texts describes the Gospel as spread by Christ in the days of his flesh 'through all Jewry, beginning from Galilee'.) In the Gospel Christ's journey through the Samaritan region drives a wedge between his ministries in more characteristically Jewish regions, Galilee before and Judaea after. Nevertheless, so far as the arithmetic of the healing work is concerned, St Luke adds Galilee and Judaea together and balances them against Samaria. In Galilee and Judaea Jesus heals twelve Israelites and one Gentile, as St Mark had said; in the Samaritan region, between the first mention of Samaritan contacts (ix 51–56) and the last (xvii 11–19), Jesus heals another thirteen persons of whom one, the thankful leper, is said to be a Samaritan.

The splitting of the Judaean mission from the Galilean by the insertion of the Samaritan journey calls attention to a fact which in St Mark himself we scarcely notice—that St Mark records only one healing in Judaea, the opening of Bartimeus's eyes. In St Luke's picture the disproportion would be glaring—eleven in Galilee, only one in Judaea. In a case like this there is all the difference between two and one: that we should be able to say, 'There were *healings* in Judaea as well as in Galilee'. St Luke finds means to justify the indispensable plural. His predecessors had failed to record Christ's action in Gethsemane, when he mended the ear which his disciple's sword had severed (xxii 51). There were, then, two Judaean healings, and they formed a pair, according to principles which St Mark had already illustrated: Bartimeus's eyes, the ear of the high priest's servant. It is, moreover, congenial to the way of thought exhibited in Acts that the new healing-story should be sited at Jerusalem: the Gospel begins from Jerusalem (Lk. xxiv 47), it is testified to 'in Jerusalem and in all Judaea and in Samaria and to the end of the earth' (Acts i 8, cf. viii 1).

In developing his new missionary symbolism St Luke runs into a certain inconsistency. The older tradition had worked with the simple opposition 'Galilee–Judaea', and seen in the mixed population of the former some prefiguration of the Gentile mission-field. The 'Galilee of the Nations' had welcomed Messiah, Judaea and Jerusalem had crucified him. In Galilee Jesus had even healed an occasional Gentile in consideration of outstanding faith. Such was the older picture. St Luke puts Galilee and Judaea together on the one side, the field of a twelvefold mission to Jewry, with its own exceptional healed sufferer, the Centurion's servant, placed in the exact middle of the Galilean healings. On the other side he puts a mission in the Samaritan region, where an equal number of persons are healed, among whom a Samaritan stands out as the exceptional figure (xvii 16). And this is confusing. For if the two missions are to be characterised by the exceptional person they contain, then we have (a) a mission carrying the promise of the conversion of the Gentiles (b) a mission carrying the promise of the conversion of the Samaritans; and Jewry appears nowhere in the classification. If, on the other hand, the two missions are characterised by the persons to whom they are normally directed, then both missions are directed towards Jews, Jews domiciled in Jewry, and Jews domiciled in Samaria. If St Luke could say that Christ had preached (a) to Jews (b) to Samaritans, as St John does say (iii 22–iv 42), the picture would have been clear. But his interpretation of the historical tradition was that Jesus had merely prefigured the Samaritan mission of the Church by skirting Samaritan territory and making occasional contact with an individual Samaritan; even the geography of ix 51–xviii 30 is left vague. Is Jesus in Samaria all that while, or is he not?

We should hesitate in adopting an interpretation of St Luke which attributed to him such an inconsistency of presentation, were it not that we find him willing to run into similar inconsistencies elsewhere. They form in fact the characteristic *cruces* of Lucan exegesis. Was the miracle of Pentecost the first example of a high ecstatic utterance which disdained the trammels of articulate speech, or was it a clear message delivered to many nations in the mother tongue of each one? Were the Seven an impartial board of Charity-Commissioners set up to relieve the Apostles of a financial task and allay the mutual suspicions of Aramaic and Grecian Jews, or were they, as their names suggest, a purely Grecian body with whom the Aramaic Twelve might collaborate in matters affecting people of both tongues? What was the subject of debate at the so-called Council of Jerusalem—the circumcision of Gentile converts, or the conditions of table-fellowship between Gentile and Jewish Christians? We are not suggesting that the problems posed in such questions are insoluble, we are merely stating that St Luke's presentation of his history is so confused as to give rise to them.

A proposed interpretation which imputes confusion to its subject cannot pretend to certainty, and so let us in conclusion recall the simple facts. Between the first and last mentions of the Samaritan scene Jesus according to St Luke heals thirteen persons of whom one is said in so many words to have been a Samaritan. In the rest of the Gospel he heals thirteen persons of whom one was the servant of the Gentile Centurion. And those facts, however interpreted, suggest that St Luke paid attention to St Mark's having recorded the healing of thirteen persons, one of them a Gentile; and that he thought what his predecessor had done in this regard was significant.

St Luke's rehandling of the Marcan list may be summarised as follows. The Samaritan healings do not affect the question, being entirely non-Marcan; the first story is Matthaean (Luke xi 14= Matt. ix 32, xii 14) the other three purely Lucan. For the rest, St Luke concentrates St Mark's concluding theme of ear and eye in Judaea wholly (Bartimeus and the High Priest's servant). So the deaf and the blind (Mark vii 31, viii 43) disappear from their places in the second Galilean handful. The handful is compensated by two accessions, one at the beginning, the other at the end: the

Lucan story of the widow's son (vii 15) and the Marcan story of the epileptic boy (ix 42). These alterations so dislocate the second handful that it no longer corresponds item for item with the first. St Luke's plan is not to range the varieties of disease in parallel columns but to count their total number. Christ rids twenty-four Israelites of twelve evils: violent possession (iv 35, viii 32, ix 42), leprosy (v 13, xvii 14), untimely issue (viii 44), fever (iv 38), paralysis (v 25), atrophy (vi 6), curvature (xiii 13), dropsy (xiv 4), death (vii 15, viii 55), and affections of tongue (xi 14), eye (xviii 43), ear (xxii 51). Perhaps St Luke was a physician, after all.

The argument of the foregoing chapters can be treated as complete in itself. It claims to establish the strong probability of a twelve- or thirteenfold scheme of healing in St Mark and his imitators. The next three chapters will endeavour to develop the theme. If they are unsuccessful they will still not overthrow anything which these first chapters have validly established.

CHAPTER IV

THE MARCAN PATTERN OF LOAVES

At an early point in this book we called attention to the enigmatic passages which St Mark's gospel contains. We used an example for the purpose of showing that enigma in this Evangelist, though it may appear sporadic, is really systematic—the riddling passage reflects themes in the preceding context and can be understood by reference to them. We will now examine another example of the same kind. After the second miracle of loaves and fishes, Jesus and his disciples depart by boat towards the unknown district of Dalmanutha. There they are met by Pharisees requiring of Jesus a sign from heaven, which he sternly refuses, and returns again by boat. 'And' we read 'they forgot to take bread, and had not in the boat with them more than one loaf. And he charged them saying, Take heed, beware of the leaven of the Pharisees and the leaven of Herod. And they reasoned one with another, saying, We have no bread. And Jesus perceiving it saith unto them, Why reason ye because ye have no bread? Do ye not yet perceive nor understand? Have ye your heart hardened? Having eyes see ye not? And having ears, hear ye not? And do ye not remember? When I broke the five loaves among the five thousand, how many creels full of broken pieces took ye up? They say unto him, Twelve. And when the seven among the four thousand, how many baskets full of broken pieces took ye up? They say unto him, Seven. And he said unto them, Do ye not yet understand?' (viii 14-21).

This passage, on the face of it, is extremely difficult. The difficulties can be put under two heads. First, the unity of the scene escapes us. And second, we are at a loss to account for the emphasis and gravity of Christ's rebuke to his disciples.

Let us consider the problem of unity first. The apparent form of the paragraph is one familiar from the Bible as a whole and in particular from St Mark. A single image, or symbol, is played upon in one saying after another. Though the several sayings play upon the same symbol they apply it in different ways. Nevertheless there is an underlying unity of meaning in the sayings, and the hearers or readers are to show their penetration in grasping it. For example: 'If a house be divided against itself the house will not be able to stand, and if Satan hath risen against himself and is divided, he cannot stand but is at an end. But no one can enter into the house of the strong man and spoil his goods except he first bind the strong man, and then he will spoil his goods' (iii 25–27). Here are two sayings about houses; what is the relation between them? Satan has been mentioned under the name of Beelzebul, which means 'Master of the House', and Jesus has been accused of exorcising by his power. Jesus replies in two riddles: (a) If the Master of the House attacks himself the House is divided and the Mastery is at an end (b) The House of the strong cannot be plundered unless the Master of the House is first gagged and bound. We are to infer: (a) Satan does not attack himself, for if he did his power would collapse by dissention without the trouble of our fighting it, which is plainly not the case, and so it remains that (b) he is a powerful lord who would not allow his household, *i.e.* the unclean spirits, to be made havoc of by the exorcist, if the exorcist had not first put Satan himself under restraint.

To take a more difficult example—it would, says Christ, be better to forfeit the hand, foot or eye that causes you offence than to consign your whole person to the place where the worm does not die and the fire is not quenched, 'for everyone shall be salted with fire. Salt is good, but if the salt lose its saltness, wherewith will ye season it? Have salt in yourselves and keep peace one with another' (ix 49–50). The fires of the last day will salt, that is, disinfect or sweeten, *all* self-will, and not only in those whose case is incurable, who are everlastingly scorched and never cleansed, whose maggot never dies.[1] The sin which Christ has spoken of as

---

[1] All the comment necessary is in St Paul. 'Every man's work shall be manifest, for the day of judgement will show it; for it opens in fire, and the fire will test what every man's work is like. Whoever's work stands fast will receive reward, whoever's work is burnt will pay the penalty, but himself be saved, yet as pulled through the fire. Know you not that you are the temple of God and the Spirit of God dwells in you? Whoever *destroys* (or violates) the temple

sinking the soul in hell is the overthrow of others' faith through uncharitable self-assertion, the breakdown, that is, of fellowship, the failure of the 'bond of salt'. The salting (of the fellowship) will not go on unless the salt is salty; the disciples must have salt in themselves, that is, they must have the discipline which sacrifices hand, foot or eye and anticipates the salting action of the judgment fire. If they have that salt in themselves, the peace between them will keep sweet.

In the passage we are proposing to examine 'bread' plays the part of 'salt' in ix 49–50. 'Bread' is the common image variously applied. In this case the image is not chosen entirely at will by the speaker but suggested by the circumstances. The disciples have their minds on bread because they are short of it. Their divine Rabbi catches their attention with what looks like a warning against tainted sources of supply but turns out to be a figurative exhortation. 'Beware of the leaven of the Pharisees, and the leaven of Herod,' that is, beware of infection from their unregenerate ways, of compromise with the existing order, whether political or ecclesiastical. The disciples continuing to worry about their lack of bread, Jesus accuses them of hardness of heart for doing so, for having no use of their eyes, ears or memories; he recalls to them in exact detail the numbers of loaves and recipients at each miraculous feeding and makes them supply the number of creels on the one occasion and baskets on the other that they filled with fragments remaining. Then he says to them, Do ye not yet understand?

The Lord's protest can be understood in the letter, but the analogy of the previous saying suggests that it ought not to be. In the literal sense it reminds the disciples of the miraculous power which has fed nine thousand men with a dozen loaves. How much more easily could the same power make one loaf suffice a dozen

of God, God will destroy him. For the temple of God is sacrosanct, and you are that temple.' That is, the fire of ultimate perdition is for those who subvert the brotherhood (I Cor. iii 13–17). The judgement can be anticipated by self-discipline: 'If we judged ourselves we should not be judged. Being judged by the Lord we are disciplined, that we may not be damned with the world' (*Ibid.*, xi 31–32).

men? If, on the other hand, we go beyond the letter and run the sense on from the previous saying, what is the meaning? If, warned against the leaven of Pharisees and Herod, the disciples persist in saying 'We have no bread' the metaphorical sense must be: 'We cannot cut ourselves off from Pharisaic and Herodian leaven, for we have only one loaf and one loaf is really no bread at all.' On such an interpretation the sense is mysterious; for whereas 'leaven' has a clear and fixed sense, 'the pull of the unregenerate past', 'bread' or 'loaf' has no such clear sense. What is it that ought to be sufficient to support a life independent of Pharisaic and Herodian 'leaven'?

The 'spiritual' sense may be mysterious but it seems we must pursue it. For Christ's urgent appeal to his disciples not to close their eyes, ears and hearts to the truth suggests that some great mystery is at stake and not only whether or no they ought to expect to go hungry until they next see a baker's shop. The language which Christ uses is in strict parallel to his earlier citation from Isaiah of a divine oracle about the judicial blindness of Israel: 'That looking they may look and not see, and hearing may hear and not understand, lest they should turn and receive forgiveness' (iv 12). Christ is there expressing his grief and surprise that his disciples should share the incomprehension of 'those without';[1] and their incomprehension of what? Of the spiritual sense, of the mystery of the kingdom of heaven expressed in parable. And in what parable? The parable, in particular, of the cornfield, where the good ground bore 'thirty and sixty and a hundredfold'; there was a crop, though the bad patches of the field failed to bear. The analogy to the text before us is very close. The few loaves, the five and the seven, had multiplied so that they sufficed thousands and yielded whole basketfuls of remainders besides. Surely the bread of Christ and his company is independent of Pharisaic or Herodian 'leaven', and surely the multiplication of Christ's bread, like the multiplication of the corn, is to be understood in the spirit and not in the letter alone.

[1] In the language of viii 15, that they fail to purge themselves from 'the leaven of the scribes, and the leaven of the multitudes'.

The necessity of supposing a spiritual sense is confirmed by the sequel, the healing of the blind man. We have just learnt that for the disciples not to understand what Christ commends to their attention is for them to be deaf and blind. Christ had opened the ears of the deaf after the first miraculous banquet; now he opens the eyes of the blind, thereby completing the enacted symbolism of illumination. The blind eyes once opened, Christ without more delay challenges his disciples to use their tongues and confess their faith in what they have seen and heard. They confess, but their confession proves most imperfect; they confess Messiah but refuse the practical consequence of his breach with Pharisaic and Herodian 'leaven', the necessity that he should suffer many things and be rejected by the elders, high priests and scribes. It would seem that the mystery which the disciples failed to see in connexion with the loaves and thousands was essentially the same mystery which they still could not see in a clear light at Caesarea Philippi. If so, it ought to have some bearing on the rejection of Messiah by the Jews. Now the literal sense of the saying we are considering has nothing at all to do with the rejection of Messiah but merely with his power to guarantee a supply of bread. The spiritual sense is as yet undetermined by us, but such indications as we have so far observed may be said to point in the required direction. If the mysterious 'bread' of Christ's company is something which is to be uncontaminated by Pharisaic and Herodian leaven, its special characteristics may very well have something to do with the rejection of Messiah by Israel. For Israel is permeated with Pharisaic and Herodian leaven.

When in an earlier chapter we examined an example of Marcan enigma, we found the clues for its interpretation in the paragraphs preceding it. To follow that line of enquiry in the present instance is no mere speculation of ours, however reasonable; it is the course plainly recommended to us by the Evangelist. For the enigma here consists in nothing but the concise statement of what he has previously described in full. When the five loaves were broken to five thousands twelve creels were filled with fragments from the feast, and when the seven loaves were broken to the four thousands, seven baskets were so filled. If we want to understand the riddle, what can we do but turn back to the full narratives which it summarises? As we go about our task, we carry something with us which the riddle has given us—the assurance that what we are looking for has something to do with the numbers of loaves, thousands fed, and creelfuls or basketfuls remaining. The numbers of these things barely stated in the riddle may not be intelligible by themselves but only when they are filled out with the detail of their previous context. But in that context the numbers will be intelligible; the sense that we must look for is in some way centred in the numbers.

Such a suggestion ought surely to be welcomed by any expositor who is trying to understand the two miracles of loaves on their own account and quite apart from any attempt to read the riddle of the subsequent conversation in the boat between Christ and his disciples. For what is on the face of it so puzzling about these two stories is the relation of the second to the first. It appears to add nothing, it is just the same story over again with some of the picturesque detail omitted and the miracle itself diminished. There are fewer people, they are kept waiting longer before they are relieved, more loaves are used to feed them and fewer baskets of a smaller sort are needed for the fragments remaining. It used to be suggested (in the days when such things were more readily believed) that St Mark was the victim of his sources here, and having received two accounts of the same event from two persons or places, failed to observe that they were both speaking of the same event and put both stories down in all innocence. Such an accident is not inconceivable, but what does seem inconceivable (to judge by the rest of St Mark's writing) is that he should so have placed and phrased the two stories as that the second should give the impression of nothing but bathos when compared with the first. But now, in the light of the 'riddle' passage in viii 11–21, we may expect to find that St Mark's reason for writing the second story as the mere shadow of the first was to concentrate our attention on the sole significant novelty, the variation in the numbers; and in addition, that he intended the numbers to be not the numerical expression of a bathos but the symbolical expression of a mystery.

What, then, is the mystery contained in the numbers? We have already brought to the surface a simple numerical system in St Mark's book and it seems intrinsically probable that it will help us with the further pattern of loaves, thousands, and basketfuls. We have seen St Mark to take the acknowledged fact that Christ instituted and sent forth twelve apostles and to make it the framework of his gospel. Christ sent twelve men to twelvefold Israel, he also healed twelvefold Israel in twelve representative sufferers exhibiting between them the several powers and parts of man and their several disorders. Such was (we saw) St Mark's basic scheme, but he was not satisfied to leave it at that. For he was writing to Gentiles in a Gentile tongue and he was careful to record how among and in addition to the twelve Israelites Christ healed the firstfruit of the Gentile world, even though his personal mission was to Israel only. This additional or thirteenth sufferer was the daughter of the Syrophoenician mother, and the narrative about her stands midway between the two miracles of loaves (vii 24–30). There she stands, the Gentile exception among the twelve Israelites healed; there she stands in a middle place between the distributions of the twelve loaves, five before her and seven after her. Moreover, though the thing she asked for was healing, Christ chose to discuss it with her under the figure of a loaf: 'It is not proper to take the children's loaf and throw it to the dogs.' It would seem that in the symbolism of this gospel one person's healing is to be somehow equivalent to one person's portion of bread —for we must remember that the 'loaf' is not a pound loaf but a cake of bread for one person. If the Israelite people are conventionally represented as the Heavenly Father's family of twelve children, then twelve loaves are their portion, and it would be most unmeet to take any one of the children's loaves and cast it to the dogs. If, however, the children are satisfied and still leave crumbs, who will complain if the dogs receive them? Now we observe about the two stories of miraculous sustenance not only that twelve loaves are distributed in them, but also that crumbs in great number are taken up and carefully preserved for some future use. And surely out of these the 'dogs' are to be fed.

One loaf is one person's portion of bread. But to judge by the first miraculous feast (which is all we yet have to judge by when we meet the story of the Syrophoenician) one person's portion is multiplied by divine blessing a thousandfold. The stories of feeding make explicit what is also implicitly true of the healing narratives. The sufferer healed is a representative person standing for the multitudes whom Christ saves; the healing of the twelve persons is, through the mystery of the Passion, to become the healing of twelvefold Israel. And this truth receives equivalent expression when the first five of the twelve loaves are found sufficient not for five persons but for five thousand persons. The twelve 'Children' or 'Sons' of Israel are the conventional embodiments of twelve tribes, each tribe, perhaps, comprising many thousands. In the scenes of the gospel story the many thousands of Israel cannot be all present together, but only a manageable number of persons representing them. Each tribe may be represented by a single individual, as in the healing stories, or by a conventional number, as in the narratives of feeding; when, it appears, a thousand is to be the conventional number for a tribe. Each of the loaves belonging to a child of Israel suffices, by divine blessing, for a thousand.

Putting together the feeding of five thousand and the Syrophoenician episode, we might incline to propose the following straightforward interpretation. The twelve loaves are eternal life seen as the portion of twelvefold Israel. The thousands eating the loaves are the Israelite tribes receiving their portion; the fragments left over are the crumbs for the Gentile world. But this interpretation is faulty. It can only be obtained by reading St Mark's book backwards, and books are not written to be read backwards. It is only if we approach the feeding of the five thousand with the subsequent episode of the Syrophoeness already in our heads that we are inclined to the view that the crumbs remaining are simply the portion of the Gentile 'dogs'. If we take the narrative as it comes, we shall form no such impression. For nothing as yet suggests that the crumbs are for the dogs; on the contrary, they may seem to be marked out for the twelve children by the fact that they are taken up in twelve creels.

The feeding of the five thousand (vi 33–44) is the direct sequel to the mission of the twelve apostles (vi 7–13, 30–32), an event which impresses upon us both the unique commission of the apostolate and their determinate number. When the apostles return from the mission which scattered them two by two, and are now all together with Christ, resting in the wilderness, they are surprised by the crowds. Jesus bids his disciples feed the multitudes themselves, and that they should use their own provision for the purpose. It turns out that the twelve have not even a loaf apiece, but roughly half, say half a day's food, their supper, five loaves in all—two fishes besides; but the fishes do not enter into the arithmetic. Bread is the staple of the meal and a loaf is a portion. If there is some fish as well, by way of relish, so much the better; but fishes do not come in standard sizes, nor is it necessary that each person's relish should be a standard amount.

The twelve apostles, then, are found not to have twelve loaves among them but only five; and presently it turns out that there are five thousands to receive, a symmetrical result, a thousand to a loaf. The five thousands sat down in companies, by hundreds and by fifties, a further symmetry (just in case we might be doubting whether St Mark attended to such points or not). For five thousands are either one hundred fifties, or fifty hundreds. The twelve apostles having five loaves among them fed five thousand men, through Christ's blessing. Suppose that the twelve had had their full or proper complement of loaves, twelve, they might then, by the same reckoning, have fed twelve thousands of men, a complete symbolical Israel. Even as it is they take up twelve creelsful of remainders, as though they were laying up future provision for all Israel, and not for five 'tribes' only.

The suggestion with which we are left (for we have not yet heard of the Syrophoenician mother) is that divine bounty, by instituting twelve apostles and making twelve creels to abound with remainders from the feast, has made ultimate provision for all the twelve thousands of Israel, but that so far only five thousands have feasted. The feeding of the multitude is not apparently to be taken as symbolising their feeding once for all with everlasting bread, but the beginning of a heavenly diet for whose continuance provision is also made. And as twelve measures of remainders are taken up, we are to see that five of these measures represent future provision for the five thousands already introduced to the messianic table, while the seven other measures are for the remaining seven thousands not yet fed.

When, therefore, the unexpected story of the Syrophoenician mother intervenes and we learn that the dogs may have the children's crumbs, our reaction is not 'Of course; there are lots of crumbs from the children's table' but 'How will that be arranged? The crumbs are for the twelve tribes. Are some of the tribes to go short?'

The Syrophoenician episode and the feeding of five thousand, taken together, leave two unsolved questions. The feeding of the five thousand leaves us asking 'And when will the seven thousands be fed?' The Syrophoenician episode leaves us asking 'What portion of the crumbs is diverted to the use of the Gentiles?' The second miracle of loaves and fishes gives a combined answer to both these questions.

How are the seven surplus creels of crumbs from the feast of the five thousand given to further thousands of men? Obviously the form of the story cannot be that further thousands are fed from those actual creelsful taken up on the previous occasion. If multitudes are again in straits for food in desert places, the apostles cannot be supposed to have all this load of old broken bread handy, not to mention that, even if they did have it handy, it would no longer be fit to eat. In literal fact the remainders from the first feast must be supposed to have been distributed next day to anyone who could use them. The twelve creels remaining are not, but merely symbolise, a future provision for the five thousands already fed, and for seven thousands more. When further thousands are fed in the wilderness, there can be no more than a symbolical relation between the seven extra creelfuls previously gathered up, and what is now set before hungry men. What is, in fact, set before them is not seven creelfuls of crumbs but seven fresh loaves.

It belongs to each man to have his portion of bread and so it belongs to the twelve apostles to have twelve loaves. At the first feeding they found they had only five out of their whole ideal number, at the second feeding they are found to have the rest of it, seven: as though the first five of their 'proper' provision of twelve had been used for the five thousands and the rest remained for use on the second occasion; as though the loaves found in their hands the first time had been those brought for the common use by Peter, Andrew, James, John and Philip, and those they had the second time were the contribution of Bartholomew, Matthew, Thomas and the rest. We make the picture clearer to ourselves by thus pressing the details, we do not attribute such curiosity to the Evangelist. A loaf for a man, twelve loaves for twelve men, five and seven are twelve—these simple figures are enough for him— the offering of seven loaves to further thousands sufficiently shows the fulfilment of the promise implicit in the seven creelfuls 'too many' remaining from the first feast.

But now to take the second question propounded above. How is it shewn that crumbs from the children's table have been given to the Gentiles? The guests at the second feast are not Gentiles but further Israelite thousands, required for making the thousands up to twelve; and if there is to be any consistency of symbolism between the two feedings, the crumbs taken up after they have eaten must also be for their future provision and not for the Gentiles. The five have been dealt with, their present need and their future provision; when the remaining seven loaves are distributed to present hunger, it is proper that seven measures of remainders should be taken up for the future need of those who eat them.

Where, then, are the 'crumbs for the dogs' to be found? Not in what is taken up from the second feast, but in what is not taken up from it. The abundant remainders from the first feast appear to prefigure the provision of a creelful each not only for the five Israelite thousands present but for the Israelite thousands still to come. But when the seven loaves are in due course distributed, the remainders are taken up not in creelfuls but in basketfuls, a creel (*cophinus*) being a bigger vessel altogether than a basket (*spyris*). But surely the initial divine bounty cannot be withdrawn nor the fulfilment be less than the promise? No, the bounty cannot be withdrawn but it may be diverted. There was a time when the full creels of heavenly provision were for the thousands of Israel. But now that crumbs have been allotted to the Gentiles, only a basketful in every creelful is kept for the children, the rest falls to the dogs.

It might well appear that in the interpretation we have suggested too much is made to turn on the fact that different words are used for the vessels filled with remainders in the two narratives. It is no doubt true that if a Greek speaker pointed at two vessels standing side by side and called one a *cophinus* and the other a *spyris* he meant that they were of quite different shapes and sizes, but surely one might use either word indiscriminately for a wicker vessel casually mentioned in the course of a story, without ever asking oneself whether it was square and large or comparatively small and round. When St Luke tells us (Acts ix 25) that St Paul descended the wall of Damascus in a *spyris,* who is to suppose that he said to himself, 'Certainly it was a *spyris,* not a *cophinus*; they would have found a *cophinus* much too unwieldy?' So might not St Mark write *cophinus* in vi and *spyris* in viii and never note the difference? It is very possible he might; but what he would surely not have done is to repeat the two words side by side in successive sentences of the 'riddle' passage, unless he meant to stand by the difference between them. 'When I broke the five loaves to the five thousands, how many *cophini* of fragments did you take up?— They answered, Twelve.—And when I broke the seven loaves to the four thousands, how many *spyrides* of fragments did you take up?—They answered, Seven' (viii 19, 20). It appears, then, that St Mark was conscious of the difference throughout, and that one of the factors in the riddle, alongside of the ratios between the numbers, is the ratio between *cophinus*-capacity and *spyris*-capacity.

We have not yet done with the riddle of the loaves, but before we take up further points we may usefully consider here whether

what we have so far observed seems likely to meet the requirements we laid down. There were two: the mystery must justify
the deep seriousness with which Christ speaks of it; and it must
have something to do with the mystery of mysteries which Christ
revealed and St Peter rejected at Caesarea Philippi. The two
requirements reduce to one, for if the riddle of the loaves bears on
the mystery revealed at Caesarea, no more need be said to justify
the seriousness with which Christ speaks of it.

The riddle tells us that the faith of the 'dogs' is destined to be
rewarded with a great part of the crumbs. The Gentile healed by
Christ was but one in thirteen, or (since the healing stories are
artificially selected) one, it may be, in several hundred. But all
except a *spyris* in each *cophinus* of the bread Christ breaks to mankind is marked for the future nourishment of the Gentile world.
How will so surprising a division be brought about? By the very
same train of events as will consecrate to human use the bread of
salvation. If Christ blesses bread and breaks it in the wilderness, it
is by way of anticipating his action in the upper room. The actual
and intended parallel between Christ's miraculous and sacramental eucharists, as St Mark describes them, is generally admitted.
But Christ has no body and no blood to give away in bread and
wine apart from his passion, nor does he suffer any passion but
what the treason of his nation inflicts on him. There is sacramental
bread because Israel rejects Messiah, and because Israel rejects
Messiah the greater part of the present blessings of the Gospel goes
to the Gentiles.

The salvation of the world through Israel's rejection of Christ is
not a mystery among mysteries, it is, to the mind of St Paul and
of the first Greek Christians, the mystery of mysteries, God's
masterpiece (Rom. xi, Coloss. i 25–27, Ephes. iii 1–12). If the disciples understood this they would understand everything, until
they understand this they understand nothing; they may acknowledge Christ but they blaspheme his suffering destiny. 'Having
eyes, see they not, having ears, hear they not?' Christ's words fly
over his disciples' heads and find their target in St Mark's readers.
All that the disciples witnessed has been unrolled by the Evangelist

before his readers' eyes. They have read how John Baptist's death was made strangely and hideously present at a royal banquet, and how Jesus was hailed as a second Baptist by the Baptist's murderer. They have read on the next page how Jesus broke five loaves to five thousands, employing eucharistic actions which can have to the Christian mind one sense and one only. They have seen him grant crumbs to the Gentiles, and then go on dealing bread to Israelite thousands, but with a much diminished store of crumbs for their continued provision. If the disciples could not penetrate the mystery, surely St Mark's readers, illuminated by Easter and Pentecost, can penetrate it.

The situation which gives rise to the conversation in the boat, and, in the course of it, to Christ's propounding of the riddle, stands in formal parallel with the two situations which had led to the distributions of the loaves. When the disciples had five loaves, and when they had seven, they reckoned themselves to have no bread to any purpose, in face of hungry thousands; and now that there is one loaf only on board, they say that they have no bread. If the parallel holds so far, ought we not to take it further? The five loaves on the first occasion, and the seven on the second, appeared to us to make up a sum; on the two occasions taken together it was as though all the loaves belonging to an ideal provision for all the twelve apostles had been distributed. But if the seven loaves of the second occasion are properly to be added to the five loaves of the first, can we withhold ourselves from adding the one loaf of the third occasion to the five and to the seven? If so, what does it mean? The five and seven are for the twelve, the one is a thirteenth over.

Here is a third exemplification of what we have met twice already. Twelve Apostles are called—and Levi the publican. Twelve Israelites are healed—and the Syrophoenician's daughter. Twelve loaves are mentioned as blessed in provision for Christ's company—and this one loaf besides as at least able to be blessed for their provision. 'They' (the disciples, that is) had forgotten to bring loaves. They 'had with them' in the boat one loaf, which they, presumably, had not brought, but there it was. They said to one another, 'We have no loaves', whereas on the two previous occasions they had owned to having five and seven. It is as though the twelve loaves of the twelve apostles have been spent. There is, however, a thirteenth loaf here.

Let us follow out the train of thought and, placing the provision offered by the one loaf in parallel with the provision offered by the five loaves and the seven, consider what its symbolical significance may be. The five loaves and the seven are offered to the 'thousands' of Israel, the five before a grant of crumbs has been made to the Gentile dogs, the seven afterwards. Apart from the intervening grant to the Gentiles there would be no significant difference between the two feasts; no interest would attach to the fact that the 'thousands' of Israel were fed in two parties and not all together in one. As it is, the reservation of seven loaves for a second distribution allows the diminution in Israel's 'crumbs' to be felt: a *spyris* per loaf, instead of a *cophinus*. But hitherto the Gentiles have not put in an appearance *en masse* to receive their 'crumbs', nor, within the framework of the Gospel story, can they reasonably do so. Jesus made an exception in favour of the Syrophoenician's faith and so a thirteenth healing found a place beside the typical twelve, but there is no place for Gentile multitudes coming to be fed before Pentecost. Even in St John, where the prefigurative sense of the Gospel events is stretched to the limit, the Greeks who come to the feast and desire to see Jesus are anticipating the hour when the seed corn, which will provide their mysterious nourishment, will have fallen into the earth and died (John xii 20–24).

When, therefore, the twelve loaves of the twelve apostles have all been distributed to the Israel for whom their very number stands, and (in connexion with a mysterious thirteenth loaf) a further situation of need is anticipated but neither encountered nor described, what does this anticipated situation typify? What but the Gentile mission? The Lord's riddling answer in fact assures the disciples of two things: (a) they have—this is presupposed— one loaf (b) of the original bounty of twelve *cophini* of crumbs, all but seven *spyrides* of the last seven *cophini* remain unused. To appreciate the relation between these two facts we must allow ourselves to be guided by the conventions laid down in the two distributions of loaves. In the first distribution five loaves were used, in numerical proportion to the thousands present; but the promise of provision for all the Israel of God was shown in the taking up of twelve *cophini* of crumbs, not five. The promise is implemented presently in the distribution not of the actual seven extra *cophini* of crumbs (which would be historically impossible) but of the corresponding number of loaves, seven. Seven *spyrides* only being taken up, the original bounty is still not exhausted and we are left looking for an occasion when the contents of the seven *cophini* (minus the seven *spyrides*) will be taken up. By analogy, they will be taken up when bread is broken, but what bread? 'We have no loaves', say the Twelve, the twelve loaves of the twelve apostles are exhausted, and in any case 'it is not meet to take the children's loaf'—any one of the twelve, that is—'and throw it to the dogs'. No, but just as there is a thirteenth healing, so there is a thirteenth loaf. There is only one healing of a Gentile in the Gospel, but it is the promise of myriad Gentile baptisms in the Church; there is only one loaf for the 'dogs', but it will yield more broken pieces, more communicants' portions, than seven loaves given to Israel.

St Mark's numerical symbolism, if we interpret it rightly, balances two ways of thinking about the Gentiles. They are additional to twelvefold Israel, their loaf is a thirteenth. Yet they are part of the spiritual Israel of God, and the twelvefold bounty originally given, the twelve *cophini* of broken bread, includes a provision for them.

If the one loaf is to suffice the Nations, it must indeed be kept free from the leaven of Pharisaism and Herodianism; neither Jewish legalism nor Palestinian political compromise will provide the Gospel of a world-wide mission. A universal Church must preach and live and eat and drink Jesus Christ alone, who died at the hands of the Judaean government, both lay and priestly, Pharisees and Herodians lending themselves to the plot (Mc. xii 13–17).

It is difficult indeed to resist the impression that the thirteenth loaf—the one loaf—is specially expressive of Jesus Christ. It is a company of thirteen which puts out in the boat; the twelve have brought no loaves, their loaves are all used, but they have a loaf with them in the boat, just as they have Christ with them in the boat. Christ has appointed twelve apostles for the twelve tribes; but that there is a thirteenth with them, not, after all, Levi the publican, but Christ himself, is precisely what makes the new Israel Christian and breaks the closed number of old privilege. When, in fact, will the giving of holy bread to the nations begin to be possible? When Jesus, rejected by Israel, goes to his death, after having distributed his body to the Twelve.

The whole setting of the feedings is for St Mark's contemporaries undisguisedly eucharistic. What, then, in a eucharistic context are the suggestions of 'one loaf'? One loaf was broken at the last supper and the company was bound together by all eating of the one loaf. In the eucharists of the primitive church numbers might necessitate the breaking of more loaves than one. It was a material imperfection and for symbolical purposes ignored. 'The loaf we break' says St Paul 'is it not a communion of Christ's body? Because there is one loaf we many are one body, for we all partake of the one loaf' (I Cor. x 16–17). Eucharistic reality is revealed at the point where the bread is to be broken for the Gentiles, that is, when, rejected by Israel, the body of Christ is broken on the cross. Let not those who have one loaf say they have no bread. In the only relevant sense, they have all the bread there is.

We have observed certain relations between the pattern of twelve healings and the pattern of twelve loaves. In both there is a thirteenth, and the thirteenth healing, that of the Syrophoenician's child, is brought into close connexion with the thirteenth loaf, because it is talked about as being a loaf—it looks as though one of the children's loaves were taken and thrown to the dogs, but it is explained that no such violation of the promises to Israel is really contemplated. But there is another common feature of the healings and the loaves which leaps to the eye—division after the first five. Five disciples are called and five persons healed in chs. i–iii.

73

After that there is a new departure in apostolic calling, the whole twelve being instituted at once, and there is also a new series of healings, running over the same types of disease in order as the first five did. The theme of the loaves is likewise introduced with a double five—five loaves are dealt to five thousands; then there is the division marked by the Syrophoenician episode, and a further distribution follows.

The twelve loaves do not begin to make an appearance until the series of healings is two-thirds completed, and then it is as though the distributions of bread set about to catch up with the gifts of healing already bestowed. The first five loaves cover at a single stroke the only group of healings so far completed—for the first handful of cures are finished and we are still in the midst of the second handful when Christ feeds the five thousand. Then follow the extra (Gentile) healing and another Jewish healing, and then, before there are any further healings, the second feeding of thousands and the voyage with one loaf on board follow in quick succession. Let us say that in this last pair of episodes the theme of the loaves draws level with the series of healings. The first five loaves 'covered' the first handful of healings; how many healings have there been since then? Out of the remaining seven healings granted to Israel four have so far found beneficiaries, the Gerasene, the impure woman, Jairus's daughter and the deaf stammerer. In addition the one anticipatory Gentile healing has been performed. The theme of bread keeps exactly in step with that of healing; out of the seven Israelite thousands numerically provided for in the distribution of seven loaves and the gathering of seven basketfuls, only four thousand actual recipients are present; and in addition the one anticipatory Gentile loaf is provided against future need.

It is truly surprising that St Mark should carry the balance between his thousands fed and his Israelites healed so far as that the seven loaves should have four thousands only to receive them, not seven. And he would not, perhaps, have been so influenced by mere formality of numbers without the supporting persuasion of more material considerations. If the twelve are all called and all sent on mission, no suggestion results of Christ's work being completed, but only that it has been fairly set on foot. But if either the twelve typical Israelites are all healed or the twelve representative thousands are all fed, what is represented must appear to be the completion of the saving work. The twelve are indeed all healed in due course, but then there is no danger of our thinking that the Gospel is rounded off; for the last healing is at the very door of Jerusalem and it is by then plain that the train of events is moving which will carry Christ to his passion. The symbolism of the loaves is all condensed by St Mark into a comparatively short space towards the middle of his book (vi 33–viii 21) and at that point it would give the wrong impression so to handle the theme as to leave no part of the feeding of Israel unperformed.

The question suggests itself—If St Mark's purpose was indeed to keep the thousands fed in step with the sufferers healed, why should he not have given four loaves rather than seven to the four thousands and, perhaps, recorded a later gift of the remaining three loaves to the remaining three thousands? The answer, surely, is that such a handling of the theme (even if the traditions about Christ's miracles had allowed of it) would not have helped St Mark to say what he wanted to say. He is interested in a single division only—the bread dealt initially to part of Israel before the grant of crumbs to the Gentiles and the bread dealt to the rest of Israel after that grant. He wants to tell us that the rest of the loaves (seven) produce only a *spyris* of remainders apiece. It is a secondary point, saved up to be mentioned last, that only four of the seven thousands hitherto unfed were as yet present to receive them.

The basis of the whole interpretation we have offered is the assumption, that twelve loaves belong naturally to the twelve apostles; and we illustrate such an assumption from the twelve symbolical loaves of the old covenant, the shewbread set before the Lord 'on behalf of the sons of Israel', of the twelve patriarchs, that is to say, as represented in the tribes descended from them (Levit. xxiv 8). Our assumption is confirmed by St Mark's actually mentioning the shewbread. And we must not say, 'What of it? Are not biblical authors always mentioning shewbread?' For in fact St Mark's development of the topic is unique in the whole

New Testament. The Author to the Hebrews, as one might expect, places the shewbread in his inventory of the contents of the temple (ix 2) but pays it no attention. St Mark (ii 26) is alone in basing any Christian argument on the shewbread, or would be alone in doing so were it not that St Matthew and St Luke have thought fit to transcribe him. Jesus permitting his hungry disciples to pluck corn on Sabbath is seen as a second David, forcing the law of the temple and giving shewbread to his lay companions. It is not unreasonable to suspect that such a topic should recur to the Evangelist's mind when Messiah's company are faced with a crisis of hunger, and loaves must be found for thousands of people. It is true, indeed, that the story of the five thousand is written on the lines of a tradition about Elisha (II Kings iv 42–44) with Mosaic touches besides (Num. xi 13, 22); but it is not without its Davidic features. David, the shepherd-psalmist of Israel, acknowledges his dependence on a divine shepherd in the twenty-third Psalm, and the Psalm appears to be echoed in the combination of phrases: 'He had compassion on them as sheep not having a shepherd . . . he commanded that they should lie down . . . on the green grass.'

There is certainly time for the memory of the shewbread to have faded between the mention of it in ii 26 and the first mention of loaves given to thousands in vi 38. Yet memories do not fade in direct proportion to distance; they fade if there has been nothing intermediate to keep them bright. The mention of the shewbread in ii 26 plays in fact a highly significant part in a cycle of themes which recurs and in the recurrence of which the two feedings of thousands find their place. To give a full account of cyclic recurrence in St Mark's Gospel would belong to another occasion;[1] we will briefly state here the facts which concern us.

St Mark's narrative cycles are most simply to be described as the sequences of subjects which lead up to each healing of a particular person, or (where such healings follow one another without any interval) to each group of such healings. The mention of the shewbread is to be found in the sequence leading up to the cure of the

[1] See below, Appendix A.

withered hand (iii 1–6). A fresh sequence leads to the three great healings of v, another to the Syrophoenician exorcism and the Effatha in vii, and another to the first cure of blindness in viii. The Marcan cycle is of course modified at each repetition and we cannot lay down a fixed form for it throughout, but the headings 'calling, nourishment, healing' will give us a convenient division to start from.

Call of Levi, ii 13.	Episode of Cornfield, ii 23.	Withered hand, iii 1
Call of the XII, iii 13.	Parables of Cornfield, iv 1	Gerasene demoniac, etc., v
Mission of the XII, vi 7.	Feeding of 5,000, vi 34.	Syrophoenician, etc., vii 24.
	Feeding of 4,000, viii 1	Blind Man, viii 22.

We will now concentrate on the middle column and exhibit the correspondence of the successive items in more detail (See over).

The whole of this parallel is instructive but, for our present purpose, we need once again the middle column only. In the first cycle the themes of corn growing in the field and of loaves distributed to hungry men are introduced side by side, for the disciples' 'harvesting' of the corn by Christ's permission is compared to the reception of the loaves at David's hand by his hungry companions. In the second cycle the theme of the growing corn is developed, while the third cycle returns to the theme of the distribution of loaves. One might say at first sight that the second and third cycles develop two themes from the first independently and without reference to one another, but a closer observation shows that it is not so. The third synthetises its two predecessors. The first deals with the simple relief of hunger with physical bread and corn, the second deals with the spiritual sense of the growth of corn, the third combines the two—actual hunger is relieved with actual bread, and yet the bread carries a symbolical and sacramental sense besides. A second point of synthesis—the bread with which the third cycle is concerned must be looked for in the first, not the second, but the wonderful multiplication of the bread even to a thousandfold finds its type in the miracle of nature de-ii 18 Jesus' disciples criticised because they do not fast.

iii 20 Jesus criticised because he and his disciples give themselves no time to eat.

ii 23 Jesus in the cornfield compared with David who gave loaves of shewbread to his hungry companions.

iv 1 Parable of cornfield: the Sower's seed multiplies in good ground 30, 60, 100 fold.

iv 10 Alone in boat with Jesus his disciples ask about cornfield parable and are rebuked for sharing the incomprehension of those without concerning the 'mystery'. They have no sight in their eyes or hearing in their ears. Jesus recalls, with comments, the details of the parable, including the numbers of increase.
Continuing the voyage Jesus stills a storm.

vi 31 Jesus and his disciples have no leisure to eat and withdraw (with provisions) into a quiet place.

vi 33 Five loaves given by Jesus and his disciples to hungry people multiply 1,000 fold.

vi 45 Voyage of the disciples, and contrary wind. Jesus walks over the water to their assistance. They were amazed, not having understood concerning the loaves, for their heart was hardened.

viii 1 Seven loaves given by Jesus and his disciples to further crowds multiply in like proportion.

viii 14 Voyage of Jesus and his disciples with one loaf. Disciples rebuked for their incomprehension about the loaves, for having hardened hearts, unseeing eyes and deaf ears. Jesus recalls the details of the feedings, especially the numbers.

scribed in the second cycle: the corn multiplies even to a hundredfold, whereas the loaves obtained for his men by David do not multiply at all.

To understand the doctrinal relation between the cornfield parable and the mysterious banquets succeeding it we should have to go deep into the strangely two-sided symbolism of primitive eucharistic thought. We are what we eat; we eat the bread of God, the body of Jesus, but at the same time we are a bread of God sown by his word in the field of the world, gathered into his church and kneaded into one body. This is not the place to explore such mysteries. Let us return to the prosaic theme of numerical pattern.

When in vi St Mark takes up again the theme of loaves distributed to hunger, it is to tell us of five loaves distributed out of twelve in all. Now though St Mark does not say so, it is recorded in the text of I Samuel to which he refers (xxi 3), that David asked the priests for *five* loaves; and they supplied him out of the shewbread, which in any case numbered twelve. These are simply facts. It will hardly be supposed by anyone who has followed us so far, that they are chance coincidences. St Mark began with the picture of the Lord's. Anointed taking five loaves out of the holy twelve on a given occasion. It must seem to him, as indeed to any Jewish thinker, that the remaining seven are left for a future occasion.

There is nothing whatever mysterious or designing about the introduction of the comparison between Christ and David in the first cornfield episode. The saying of Christ which contains it is presumably traditional and illustrates the point at issue, the 'loosing' of sabbath in case of hunger. But the comparison once written down proves endlessly suggestive and St Mark returns to it again and again. It is only in the later applications of it that the number of the loaves David borrowed becomes of interest. In ii 23 it would be completely irrelevant to mention any figure. However many or however few holy loaves are eaten by laymen, the same violation of the literal law takes place.

When St Mark takes up the theme of the twelve loaves in vi-viii we have observed how he brings it into step with his other twelve, the healing miracles. Of the healing miracles one set of five has been already completed and a second is under way. So he gives us first a distribution of five loaves and then presently in a second distribution he deals with the still incomplete remainder. Five healings in the first 'handful', five loaves taken by David—a happy concord. It may be further remarked that the mention of David and his loaves occurs at the very point at which the first handful of five healings is completed by the healing of the withered hand. The story of the cornfield containing the saying about David is one part of the theme of the 'loosing of sabbath' in Mk. ii–iii, the healing of the withered hand is the other part of it, and the passage from the one part to the other is immediate. It is all the easier, then, for the evangelist, when he picks up the five healings in the five loaves of the five thousand, to pick up David and the shewbread at the same time.

The riddle of loaves is a riddle indeed. It is propounded as a riddle, and the context is full of elements for a solution. But what is the solution? We have been led to an answer which has not the neatness necessary for entire convincingness. Is St Mark's meaning as complicated as we have made it out to be, or have we walked blindly round the missing piece which unifies the puzzle? If we must be content with an open verdict, we are still not left with a wholly negative result. For this much is plain—the true answer has something to do with the extension of the children's bread to the Gentiles; and even so bare a conclusion as this may suffice to carry the weight of our succeeding arguments.

CHAPTER V

THE MARCAN PATTERN OF APOSTLES

In the last chapter we suggested not only that St Mark relates the form and meaning of the loaf-pattern to those of the healing pattern, but that in his handling of the loaf-pattern he shows himself aware also of the precise point which the healing series has reached in the part of his gospel which the loaf-pattern occupies. In Mark i–vii a complete set of five healings, a handful as we have called it, has been followed by four ordinary healings more, together with one exceptional healing, that of the Gentile's daughter; and accordingly in vi–viii first five thousands are fed with miraculous loaves, and then four thousands, while there is also provision made in a mysterious thirteenth loaf for the multitudes of the Gentiles. To suggest that a writer pays so much attention to the precise position in a formal series at which some piece of his subject-matter falls, is to raise the question whether he did not feel the serial position of that piece to be specially significant. Whether, indeed, to speak more boldly, he did not assign it that position, because he saw it to belong there? In any case, let us ask why St Mark placed the topic of the loaves round about the ninth Israelite healing—or, as we have called it, the fourth healing in the second handful.

The answer we may be tempted to give is that the fourth healing in the second handful is the healing which has the extra or Gentile healing prefixed to it, and it is obvious that the topic of the loaves, as St Mark has conceived it, centres round the award of crumbs to the 'dogs'. But the answer merely carries the question a step further back. Why did St Mark place the Gentile healing just at that point in the healing series? We might just as well begin at the other end, and fix the position of the Gentile healing by the position of the loaf-narratives, saying that the healing which gives crumbs to the dogs had to be so placed as to fall in the middle of the history of the loaves and thousands. To place the Syrophoenician exorcism and the loaves by reference to one another gets us nowhere. What we have to do is to place them both by reference to something else.

At least part of the answer must be that they are placed by reference to the institution and mission of the twelve apostles. In so far as the twelve loaves belong to the twelve apostles and are distributed in token of the mission of the twelve to twelvefold Israel, they clearly belong to the sequel of the commission and sending forth of the Twelve. In fact the story of the loaves begins at the very point at which the Twelve, after being sent forth on mission, make their first report back to their Sender.

At the risk of excessive formalisation we might even say that the theme of the twelve loaves is the continuation of the theme of the twelve apostles. We have said that St Mark writes his Gospel round three twelves; apostles, loaves and sufferers healed. But plainly the three twelves do not play an identical or equal part in the general pattern of his narrative. The sufferers who are healed constitute a series which stretches steadily on from the beginning of the Ministry to the entry into Jerusalem. Whereas the whole number of the Twelve have been both instituted and commissioned by the beginning of the sixth chapter, and as for the pattern of loaves and thousands, the whole thing is deployed within the space of two chapters and a half.

We might perhaps experiment with a form of description which reckoned two parallel streams of twelvefold symbolism running side by side, one stream consisting of the healing series simply, and the other containing both the apostles and the loaves. Certainly the beginning of the Gospel suggests that the Evangelist had such a two-stream symbolism in mind, for, as we saw at an earlier point, the first five healings he records count off against five disciples called. Jesus calls two pairs of brothers, Simon and Andrew, James and John, and heals two pairs of sufferers, the demoniac and Simon's mother-in-law, the leper and the paralytic. After that he calls Levi and he heals the withered hand.

So far the two streams of calling and healing have run side by side, but now the simplicity of the parallel is disturbed. It looked as though the Twelve were being built up man by man, but Levi, being the thirteenth man called and not one of the Twelve, precipitates a change in the development of the apostolic series. Now the whole body of the Twelve are both instituted and named at once, so that it becomes clear in a moment who are of the Twelve (for example, the two pairs of brothers) and who (for example, Levi) are not.

We might (if so trivial a comparison can be tolerated) think of a game of cards for two hands, twelve, or shall we say, thirteen, being held by each. They begin putting down card for card to the number of five turns each; then the hand which holds the apostle cards throws down all he holds at once face upwards upon those he has already played. The other hand, which holds the healings, wants to go on playing one card at a time, but there are no cards (it would seem) in the opposing hand for him to play them against. The apostles have all been used. If the game is to continue they must be picked up and used again.

St Mark goes on steadily placing the healings one after another, and as for the apostolic theme, his first method for sustaining that is to repeat the whole twelve. Called in iii and instituted that they might be sent on mission, they are in vi sent on mission. We may say that iii and vi between them contain the two halves of the empowering of the twelve for their apostolic task; now the whole theme has been stated and the way is open for a fresh development. What shall it be? The twelvefold task has found expression so far in the equipment of a twelvefold force to undertake it. The next phase should express the twelvefold contact they make with their twelvefold objective. It is of course true that in vi 7–13 the twelve are not commissioned only, they actually go forth and preach to the twelvefold people, but this side of the matter is not brought within the terms of the numerical symbolism. They simply go forth and teach whom they can make attend. The relation of their work to the whole scope of their twelvefold field goes unexpressed. It is expressed in the symbolism of the loaves and thousands.

It is surely possible to appreciate the reason for the difference in the evangelist's handling of his two basic twelves, the apostles and the sufferers. The story of the sufferers is simply the story of their cure, and when that in all its variety has been displayed, there is nothing left to be revealed but the saving passion, in which is gathered the whole substance of a healing power so variously applied. Christ heals Israel in the sufferers, he calls Israel in the apostles; but the story of the apostles is not simply the story of their call, for they are fellow-agents in the healing work. If we suppose a Gospel written in free phantasy without the control of factual tradition it might conceivably take the form projected by Spenser for his Faery Queene—twelve successive missions or quests entrusted to apostles called one by one for each occasion. Thus a correspondence with the healings of twelve individual sufferers could be kept up. Yet such a way of expressing twelve-fold mission, even supposing that the factual tradition would have borne it out, would not have appealed to our Evangelist, since it fails to give direct symbolical expression to the unity of the Israel of God. All the knights and those they had delivered were to meet in a high feast at Gloriana's court; a final tryst in Heaven is not the only unifying factor in the Church, even when taken in conjunc-tion with a single Master of Quests. The twelve are commissioned in a body; the unity of their ministry and of those to whom they minister is already displayed in earthly rehearsals of the high feast in heaven. St Mark, therefore, may begin by showing how Israel is both called and healed, in his balanced double series of five dis-ciples and five sufferers; but after that he must disturb the sim-plicity of the parallel. The theme of suffering healed remains pas-sive and individual, the theme of the mission becomes active and corporate: the twelve, called and instituted in a body, themselves go forth to preach and heal; through their hands and with their own twelve loaves the thousands of Israel are fed.

One way of putting the contrast between the Evangelist's hand-ling of the two themes is this—the apostolic theme is progressive, the healing theme is repetitive and static. One person after another is healed; it is a catalogue of cures; it displays the variety of the divine action, but it expresses no development of purpose, it em-bodies no forward march of events. Whereas the apostolic pattern is a diagrammatic history of our holy Religion. It shows us disciples individually called, instituted as an apostolate, sent out on their mission, and ministering to a sacramental church, first of Jews only, then of Jews and Gentiles as well.

Such a description of the contrast is substantially true: what we may call the serial principle of the healings is simple and repetitive, that of the apostolic pattern is historical and progressive. Yet the contrast admits of qualification on the side of the healing series. Even if it has no real forward movement of its own, it accommodates itself to that of its rival. Just when the apostolic pattern has reached the stage of adumbrating the admission of the Gentiles the healing pattern throws up the Syrophoenician exorcism, prefixing it as an extra to the ninth regular healing.

Nor is this the only example of the healing pattern accommodating itself to the requirements of the apostolic pattern. In the cure next before the Syrophoenician exorcism there is an equally striking instance. It may be true that all the healing miracles prefigure the saving death and resurrection of Christ, but it cannot be denied that the miracle in Jairus's house does so in an eminent degree, being itself a resurrection. Now the adumbrations of Christ's resurrection and of the admission of the Gentiles to the privileges of Israel lie within the ministry of Christ, for they are the resuscitation of the Jewish girl and the exorcism of the Gentile girl respectively. But the things which they adumbrate lie beyond the ministry, when, first, Christ rose from the dead and then Peter, taught to account nothing common or unclean, entered the house of Cornelius.

The order of the adumbrations is the same as the order of things adumbrated—first the resurrection, then the reception of the Gentiles. That, indeed, is not by itself surprising, for after all there are only two orders in which two narrated events can stand relatively to one another, and the actual order of the two miracles is a fifty per cent statistical probability. But it begins to look more interesting when we observe how the apostolic pattern is fitted to this simple sequence of two items in the healing series. The facts can be most clearly set forth in a table.

(a) Institution of the Twelve (iii 13–19)
(b) Miracle of Resurrection (v 35–43)
(c) Sending of the Twelve on mission (vi 7–13)
(d) Five loaves given—all crumbs for Israel (vi 35–44)
(e) Miracle gives 'crumbs to the dogs' (vii 24–30)
(f) Effatha miracle (vii 31–37)
(g) Seven loaves given—great part of crumbs withheld from Israel (viii 1–10)
(h) One loaf, added to the five and seven, entirely suffices (viii 14–21)

The prefigurations are within the Ministry of Christ, the things prefigured run out beyond. Jesus instituted the Twelve (a), died and rose from the dead (b), sent the Twelve out on a mission (c) to feed Israel with the bread of life (d), shewed mercy to the Gentiles (e) while continuing to heal the Jews (f), and so brought it about that the most part of the heavenly manna provided in the original and single bounty went to the Nations, and yet the predestinate from among the old twelve tribes had no lack (g, h).

The eighth healing sign is Resurrection, and the Evangelist takes special pains to make it eighth. When we were previously tracing the pattern formed by the varieties of suffering cured, we saw how a second 'handful' of five sufferers was built up in parallel to a first handful, and how Jairus's daughter, as the female relative of a named person lying sick in bed and raised up by the hand, corresponded with Simon's mother-in-law. Each sufferer is second in her respective 'handful', and so Jairus's daughter is not eighth but seventh in the whole series. But her case is held over while the impure woman is both introduced and healed.

Two consequences follow from the interruption. First, a narrative filling is introduced which helps the reader to appreciate the passage of time, a device repeated by St Mark in the next chapter, where the artfully introduced parenthesis about the end of John Baptist fills the otherwise empty period between the setting out of the Twelve on mission and their return to Christ. So the episode of the impure woman provides a lapse of dramatic time, a scene before the drop-curtain while the stage-set is being changed. And in this lapse of time Jairus's daughter dies, and her healing is changed from a cure of the bedridden to a raising of the dead. That is the first change produced by the intrusion of the impure woman; and the second accompanies it—the healing of the girl is transferred from seventh to eighth place in the whole series and from second to third in the 'handful' to which it belongs.

The sign of resurrection, then, is both a third and an eighth, like the day of resurrection. That Jesus rose on the third day (after his passion) is, of course, a fact much emphasised by St Mark in the latter half of his Gospel. Jesus also rose on the first day (of the week), that is, on the day next following the week which contained Good Friday. If we want to exhibit Easter day as at once third (from Good Friday) and first (in the week) we shall require a fortnight in which to place it, and it will appear as eighth[1] in the fortnight:

$$i, ii, iii$$
$$1, 2, 3, 4, 5, 6, 7, 8, 9, 10 \ldots \ldots \ldots 14$$
$$1, 2, 3 \ldots \ldots \ldots 7$$

'The *day* of resurrection may be a third and an eighth, but St Mark' (it may be objected) 'is not placing the day of resurrection in relation to other days, he is placing the act of resurrection in relation to other qualities or forms of healing act. The two things have nothing whatever to do with one another.' To answer the objection fully would take us far afield; we must be content to give shorthand replies. In general, the Biblical mind does not distinguish as we do between the empty form of time (Friday, Saturday, Sunday) and the historical filling of time (passion, entombment, resurrection). Neither do we, indeed, when we forget to be pedants: 'What a day I've had.'—'He ruined my whole week-end.'—'We had a most moving Good Friday at St. X's'— 'An Easter Sunday never meant so much to me before.' 'Easter' is,

---

[1] Justin Martyr (Trypho 138), presumably interpreting I Peter iii 20 (cf. II Peter ii 5), says without justification offered that Christ rose on the eighth day, and goes on to expound the eighth as the beginning of a new age ('week' of the world), after that which had mystically died on the cross; as the old world had perished in Noah's flood, and Noah, himself an eighth (person saved) had established a new world. The Gnostics made their own characteristic elaborations of the 'ogdoad'.

in fact, ambiguous in our vocabulary; it is either the Sunday standing in a certain relation to the full moon and to the Equinox, or it is the resurrection of Jesus as present in the Church's sacraments; and we pass readily from the one sense to the other. The same sort of ambiguity should not surprise us when we meet it in our Evangelist.

More in particular, the extended application of the form of the week is a familiar Jewish phenomenon. It was revealed to Daniel (ix) that when Jeremiah had predicted a captivity of seventy years, he had really demanded patient expectation for seventy times seven, for seventy weeks of years, seventy weeks of which the days are not days, but years, and in which the history of Israel's oppressions up to the middle of the second century is periodised. These seventy somethings which Jeremiah had foretold were no mere aggregates of hours, they were blocks of event: things tend to take a week of years in which to happen, if they do not take several such weeks. It is all the more remarkable that the end of the whole reckoning of seventy 'weeks' should be a week cut in half—there is only half a week of years (a time, times, and half a time) left for the last phase of oppression, the terrible tribulation such as has not been since the world was. Daniel gives the greatest possible emphasis to the point—an archangel comes to swear to him by the living God that the period will be no longer. Things may tend to take a week of years, but this thing, the tribulation, has been cut short by the mercy of God and will take but half a week. As St Mark recounts in Christ's version of the last act of Daniel's prophecy: 'Those days shall be tribulation, such as was not from the beginning of the creation which God created until now, and never shall be. And except the Lord had cut the days short, no flesh had been saved; but for his elect's sake whom he elected, he has cut short the days' (xiii 19–20).

'Weeks of years' are an artificial form; even more artificial are 'weeks of generations', for here the items counted are not even chronologically equal. The very important short apocalypse in I Enoch 93 f., called the Apocalypse of Weeks, is constructed on such a form. Building on the biblical genealogies from Adam down, it divides history into weeks (of seven generations each),[1] and exhibits a pattern of recurrence in the characteristic events of these weeks, which supplies us with a philosophy of history and a pointer to the kingdom of God. St Matthew, commonly admitted to be the most Enochian of major New Testament writers, constructs a genealogy of Christ on the same model, pairing the six 'weeks' of generations which lead from Abraham to the 'sabbatical' age of the Church, so that they appear as three 'fortnights'. St Luke's genealogy is also written in sevens—eleven 'weeks' (77 names) bring us from Adam's Creator to the threshold of the blessed twelfth 'week'.

But perhaps even more illuminating for our present purposes is the oldest and simplest example of all. God made the world in six days and rested a seventh, and even before there was sun, moon or star to measure the periods of time, his successive creative acts constituted three days of creation-week. According to St John, the Son does the works of his Father, restoring what the Father had made through him; and so it is appropriate to set forth the ministry of Christ in six mighty works and a holy feast (John i–xii, xiii ff.). The Johannine Apocalypse is made up of sevens, one 'week' after another of divine acts, the seventh act being in almost every case a sabbath, a scene of heavenly worship.

The mass of evidence to which we have alluded is somewhat disproportionate to the very simple point we have to illustrate. St Mark, writing a series of Christ's miracles, feels the force of the traditional 'week of divine works' and the appropriateness of so placing Resurrection that it should begin a fresh seven and stand third in a group of three.

That the raising of Jairus's daughter is the eighth particular healing is evident by dead-reckoning and no more need be said about it. What the Evangelist must take special pains to make plain is that the three miracles of which it is the last constitute a group apart. And there is no question but that he shows this. First, these three miracles, Legion, the impure woman, and Jairus's daughter,

---

[1] The counting is strict as far as Solomon; after that the periods called 'weeks' are quite artificial.

are cut off from the five preceding them by that division into fives or handfuls of which we have said enough already. Second, they are bound together among themselves by the simple fact that they follow directly upon one another without any interval, whereas a wide interval separates them on either hand from the next healings before and after. Third, their 'threeness' is emphasised by the parallel introduction of another three—the three principal apostles, Peter, James and John.

Peter, James and John would not seem to us to have anything whatever to do with Legion, Jairus's daughter, and the impure woman were it not for the general parallel between Israel expressed in twelve princes and Israel expressed in twelve sufferers, a parallel initially commended to our attention in the four apostles called and the four persons healed of chs. i–ii. The apostolic prelude to the three first healings of the second handful is not three more apostles called, but the whole Twelve instituted (iii 13–19). But in the institution of the Twelve a special place is given to the three leaders, in virtue of the fact that they alone received special surnames from Christ. The grammatical structure of the story is certainly curious, and its effect is to make the surnaming of the three almost as much the subject of description as the institution of the twelve.

'He made twelve to be with him and to be sent preaching by him and to have the power of casting out demons;

He [made the twelve, and] gave Simon the surname Peter; James also the Son of Zebedee and John his brother, them he gave the surname Boanè-R'ges, that is, Sons of Thunder;

Andrew also and Philip and Bartholomew and Matthew and Thomas and James the Son of Alphaeus and Thaddaeus and Simon the Cananaean and Judas Iscariot who betrayed him.'

There follows in due course the group of three healing miracles (v). It has, if such minutiae are really worth observing, a certain structural similarity to the list of surnamed apostles. Peter comes first alone, having a surname to himself, then in a pair the two sons of Zebedee, sharing the surname of Thunderbolts between them. So likewise in the group of healings Legion comes first in an episode by himself, then the girl and the woman woven into a single narrative.

The similarity of structure is very likely fortuitous, but what is more significant is that Christ takes with him to the third act of healing Peter, James and John as chosen witnesses. Three apostolic witnesses to the third healing (of the second handful), a simple numerical consonance, like the four bearers of the fourth sufferer healed in the first handful. Yet it seems likely that in ch. v the numerical assonance does more than merely underline the numerical scheme. The three miracles of ch. v are chosen from all others to typify the three days' saving work, the passion, entombment and resurrection, to which all the miracles also in their manner bear witness. Similarly three apostles are chosen out of the whole twelve, to bear especial witness to the three days' mystery, to which indeed all the apostles bear witness also. The privilege of the Three, on the three occasions St Mark records it, is always a privilege of closer witness—they enter the chamber of resurrection while the nine are left outside the door, they ascend the mount of transfiguration while the nine remain below, they kneel close to the agony in the Garden while their companions are further removed. The three are chosen witnesses, especially of the three days' work and above all of the third day's, the resurrection.[1]

The three miracles of v are correctly placed with regard to the rest of St Mark's double system of healing and apostolate. Christ calls and heals (i–iii 12), institutes the twelve apostles and their three leaders (iii 13–19), achieves death, entombment and resurrec-

---

[1] A puzzling question is the relation of the 'Peter, James and John' of the gospel tradition to the 'James, Cephas and John, the men who reckon to be pillars' of Galatians ii 9. Are they the Three of St Mark's story, continuing to hold their prestige even though the original James (the Son of Zebedee) has been killed and another James (the Lord's Brother) has taken his place? At least their functions agree: St Paul respects the 'pillars', however grudgingly, as the touchstones of gospel tradition; they are the witnesses *par excellence*. The title 'pillars' may mean the same thing: the function of witnesses is to 'establish', prop, or ground every word; three props form a tripod for the truth, on three pillars it will firmly stand. In I Tim. iii 15 the Church is described as the 'pillar and ground of the truth'.

tion (v), sends the apostolic mission forth, to feed Jews and Gentiles with the bread of life (vi–viii).

The system is consistent enough; consistency is not the issue upon which our difficulties turn, but rather double meaning. The pattern we have just set out is one of prefiguration; it shows the action of God which is released in the ministry of Christ running out into the salvation of the world through the Church, and leaving Christ's ministry behind. Yet the pattern which prefigures these things is represented by the Evangelist as impressed upon the events of Christ's ministry. The same narrative is both a history of the ministry and a prefiguration of its consequences. What is the relation, then, between the two meanings of the story, the historical and the prefigurative?

When our minds ask this question, it is not about the logical or formal relation between the two meanings that we are in doubt. We all know that it is possible to write in a continuous double sense; St Mark was doing so, for example, when he wrote down the story of the sower. It was on the one hand a matter-of-fact account of what happens in a typical Galilean cornfield, but on the other hand it was an allegory of the 'sowing' of God's word, and of the abundant harvest it was destined to bear. Here too was an allegory pointing to the future. Yet prefigurative allegory played its part in present history, by being brought to bear on the minds of the actors. It was a mystery of God's kingdom, hidden from those without, but there and then pressed by Christ on his disciples. It is the same with the extended and enacted parable of things to come which lies in the numerical structure of Mark i–viii. It is not addressed to the Evangelist's readers only, it is a system of signs in the life and experience of the disciples which is significant for themselves. The loose end of the allegorical sense is tied into the historical drama when in the conversation in the boat Jesus presses the riddle of numbers upon his disciples.

It is natural that the allegory should end here. Mark viii 22 ff. does not extend or enrich the pattern of the allegory, for the stream of allegory has flowed back into the main current of Gospel history through the conversation on board the boat (viii 14–21).

What we find in the next section of the narrative is not any extension of the allegory but the continued impact of the mystery it contains on the disciples' minds. Messiah is given to the Nations after having been rejected by Israel, by 'the elders and high priests and scribes' (viii 31). Jesus proclaims the scandal 'openly'[1] and no longer in parables or in unanswered questions (viii 32). The repeated prophecies of the passion and resurrection (viii 31, ix 31, x 33 f.; cf. ix 12 and x 45) take the place occupied by the riddle of numbers in the preceding chapters. There is an enigmatic discussion during the descent from the Mount of Transfiguration which may fairly be said to match the enigmatic discussion in the boat (see p. 4 above), but this time Jesus does not throw the question on his disciples, he gives a formal solution of their perplexity. The 'open' prophecy of the passion is presupposed in this discussion; the matter discussed is the relation of the passion thus prophesied to the figure of Elias just revealed on the Mount, and to the figure of the Baptist as presented in a chain of texts extending through the whole gospel hitherto.

We have made use more than once of the parallel between the spoken parable of multiplying corn with its solution (iv) and the acted parable of multiplying bread with its solution (vi ff.). The parallel is really basic to any interpretation of St Mark as a whole. It is the usual habit of this Evangelist to sketch out a comparatively simple model or theme within a limited compass, and then to work out variations on it with greater subtlety and at greater length. Thus, for example, the whole theme of apostles called and Israelites healed is simply stated in the vocation of the two pairs of brothers and the cure of the two pairs of sufferers. With the vocation of Levi a fresh cycle begins; the theme recurs with complications which take much space to work themselves out. It is the same with the theme of parable and its solution. In iv a series of brief parables (ii 17, 19–22, 25–28, iii 23–30, 34–35) is crowned with a set piece, the parable of the sower, and without further delay the disciples ask for a solution, are reproached with incom-

---

[1] παρρησία. John xvi 25, 29, a text which I take to be not uninfluenced by Mark viii 32, defines the sense of this term by contrast to 'in parables'.

prehension, and given an exposition; a general instruction on the purpose and nature of hidden truth follows (iv 21–34). Here, then, is the model, compact and clear: a parable which is obviously a parable and nothing else, the disciples' incomprehension with regard to it, and Christ's exposition of it. With such a clue in our hands we approach the sequel: a parable which is not so evidently a parable, being a number-pattern expressed in actual events; questioning and incomprehension on the part of the disciples (vi 52, viii 16 ff., viii 32, ix 11, ix 32) long drawn out, and neither so immediately nor so fully relieved; Christ's expositions, reiterated and still not concluded.

The parallel between the multiplication of corn and the multiplication of bread is not merely formal. The one does not indicate to us only how the other is put together, it helps us to understand of what it consists. The corn parable teaches us in general that in spite of the hardness of heart which makes much of the audience of the divine word barren soil, there is still an abundant harvest. The 'parables' of loaves make a more particular application of the principle. There is abundance of supernatural bread and abundance of recipients, even though Messiah is to be rejected by Israel; the gospel is turned towards the Gentiles and the more extended.

In the light of what we have observed let us return to St Mark's parallel twelves and the way in which they are fitted together. We have said that the drama and the movement of the two-sided pattern is provided by the apostolic series rather than by the healing series but that nevertheless the healing series lends itself to the support of the apostolic drama. The eighth healing, being a resurrection, prefigures the Lord's resurrection and provides the appropriate prelude to the sending out of the apostolic mission in vi. The ninth regular healing has the Gentile healing prefixed to it and so provides the appropriate centre for the number-pattern which sets forth the splitting of the mission between Israel and the Nations. And (we may now add) the last four healings being healings of tongue, ears and eyes are the appropriate accompaniment to that phase of the apostolic drama which is the coming home to the disciples of the riddle concerning the loaves.

When we made our original examination of the structure of the healing series, we described it as two handfuls and two over, the second handful going again over the ground of the first handful and the 'two over' repeating the last two items of the second handful. The 'two over', it is plain, are closely attached to the second handful and have the effect of drawing it out from a five into being a seven. And so we may describe the whole twelve, if we like, as a five and a seven, the seven being obtained by repeating the pattern of the five with its last two items reduplicated. And such is the division of the basic twelve which St Mark appears to use in his parallel pattern of the loaves—first five distributed, then seven. The pattern of the loaves takes no interest in the way in which the seven (healings) are built up out of the five, but makes its own new subdivision of the seven on other principles.

The pattern of the loaves is centred upon the middle item of the seven healings, and so the following symmetrical figure results:

Legion, Impure Woman, Jairus's Daughter
5 loaves
(Syrophoenician and) Effatha
7 loaves
Blind Man, Dumb Demoniac, Bartimeus

Of the seven healings one (together with its accompanying extra) is enclosed in the pattern of the loaves, three precede the loaf-pattern and three follow it. The first three of the seven, as we have already seen, form a close group of which two things are noteworthy: (a) they are expressive of the three saving days which culminate in the day of resurrection (b) they are associated with the three apostles who, above the rest, are Christ's chosen witnesses. The last three of the seven do not form a close group, in fact they are not made into a distinct collection by anything else but the fact that, when the pattern of the loaves is finished, there are these three of the healings still to come and these three only. Nevertheless the two things which we have noted with regard to the former triad are both true of these three also: (a) they are made expressive of the three saving days and (b) they are associated with the three witness-apostles.

(a) The last three healings obviously do not express the three days which culminate in resurrection by themselves culminating in resurrection, like the miracles of ch. v. For they are occupied as we have seen with the restoration of the sensitive powers and not with the conquest of death. But St Mark introduces an accompanying shadow of the three last healings, the three prophecies of resurrection after three days (viii 31 closely following viii 22–26, ix 31 closely following ix 14–29, x 33 preceding x 46–52—it could not follow it, since the twelfth and last healing is the full stop to the whole series and must be the last thing before the entry into Jerusalem). The last three healings, then, do not express, except by being the last three, the last three days of Christ's earthly drama. But whatever they fail to express is sufficiently supplied by the threefold shadow which accompanies them, the three prophecies of passion and resurrection after three days.

(b) The three prophecies are followed by interventions of the three chosen apostles. The first prophecy provokes St Peter's famous protest or 'rebuke' to Christ for even speaking so, the second prophecy is followed very closely by St John's description of his unregenerate conduct in silencing the strange exorcist, the third is immediately followed by St James and St John's ambitious request for places of honour on the day of glory. The lesson to be drawn is that the chosen witnesses of a dying and rising Christ are the very men who show their continued incomprehension of the mystery. That they are his chosen witnesses is made clear to us once more by their ascent of the Mount of Transfiguration alone with Christ directly after St Peter's protest and the words of Christ which it provoked.

We said above that the three last healing signs are cut off from their predecessors and made into a group apart by the fact that, when the theme of the loaves ends, there are only three healings out of the twelve left to be performed. If we stand by our solution to the riddle of numbers we can go further—the loaves point forward to the three healings in a more precise way. For the loaf-pattern divides the seven which, added to the five, makes up the twelve, into a four and a three. The loaves offered in the two dis-

tributions are five and seven respectively, but the thousands receiving them are five and four, leaving three thousands still to
come. Thus the loaf-pattern ends with the suggestion 'And three
more still to come',[1] three more thousands, that is. But since the
thousands so far fed have kept pace with sufferers so far healed
the suggestion is strong that as there are still three thousands to be
fed, so there are still three sufferers to be healed.

If the feeding of four thousand contains a pointer to the three
healings which are still outstanding, it points no less to the threefold accompanying shadow of the three healings, the prophecy of
resurrection after three days. For the multitudes wait upon Christ
'three days already' before he feeds them through the hands of his
disciples. Since St Mark's readers presumably kept the Lord's
supper on the day of the Lord's resurrection, and since there is so
much in the narratives of the loaves to evoke the image of eucharistic practice, it was not asking too much of them to expect them
to say, 'Why yes, of course the people of Christ have to wait until
the third day to be fed with the bread of life.' It is easy to set the
suggestion aside with the remark that 'after three days' was the
most trivial of phrases and meant no more than 'Since the day
before yesterday'. But it is fair, in reply, to insist once more on St
Mark's extreme economy of language. There is no clear case of
his using the phrase without reference to the Christian mystery.
This is the first appearance of it in his Gospel and the open prophecy of resurrection after three days follows twenty-eight verses
below. In fact, if this is not to formalise too much, the hint of the
three days follows the ninth healing, just as the succeeding prophecies about the great three days follow the tenth and the eleventh
healings.

We may now perhaps venture to construct a diagram of the
pattern of twelve:

[1] For a mind attentive to simple mathematical relations, an additional force is
given to the expectation of a 3 still to come by the fact that it is the continuation
of a series of which two terms have already been stated. 'Five (thousands), four
(thousands)—why, we are counting backwards, and three (thousands) comes
next: and there we will stop, for we shall have made up our basic twelve: five
and four and three are twelve.'

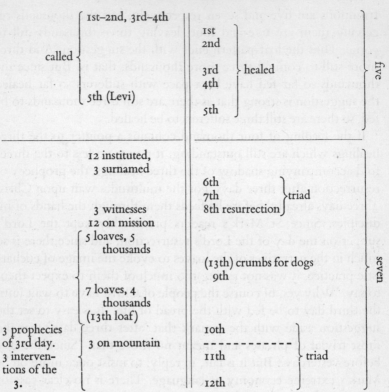

The healing of blind Bartimeus on the road out of Jericho towards Jerusalem brings the system of twelve healings to an end, with all its accompanying complications, and the ministry in Jerusalem can begin. The further it progresses the nearer it brings us to the three days of passion, entombment and resurrection, the days which the pattern we have been studying has so strongly prefigured. When they actually dawn, will not they bring some part of the numerical symbolism back into force? In v the association of the three chosen apostles with the threefold mystery of which they were the special witnesses was emphasised by Christ's taking of them alone with him to the raising of Jairus's child. In ix the same thing was expressed in the carrying of the three to the mountain top to see a threefold mystery, Elias, Moses and Jesus transfigured. The beginning of the passion is marked by a third scene of the same sort.

The three days which contain the heart of the Gospel begin by Jewish reckoning on the eve of Good Friday, or on Maundy Thursday evening by ours. On that evening Jesus eats the Passover with the Twelve and, arrived at Gethsemane, calls the three apostles, Peter, James and John, to a place of privileged witness. They who had seen the raising of the child and the glory on the mountain-top are now called to witness the humiliation of the agony. Three times Jesus visits the three, and three times finds them sleeping.

Since the passage iii 13–v 43 the three apostles have become more and more closely associated with the three days leading to the resurrection. A still earlier passage (i 16–39) familiarised us with the group of four, in which Andrew finds a place beside the other three.[1] Why should not the four, on retrospect, be connected with the four days before the resurrection, as the three with the three days? On Thursday night, as we have seen, Jesus supped in Jerusalem and then went out into the Mount of Olives and admitted the Three into the fellowship of a painful mystery. On Wednesday night he had supped at Bethany,[2] after sitting awhile on the Mount of Olives and admitting the four into the knowledge of a mystery at once terrible and glorious—the sufferings of the Church, the overthrow of Jerusalem, and the advent of the Son of Man. Peter, James, John and Andrew asked him privately when these things should be, and he answered them in his apocalyptic prediction.

The four heard the apocalypse four days (as St Mark would

[1] For the suggestion of a sort of formal bridge joining the four in i to the four in xiii, see below, p. 110.

[2] There is no gap of time between xiii and xiv. The prophecy in xiii ends with the most urgent exhortation to vigilance. xiv continues: 'Now it was passover and unleavened bread two days thence, and the high priests and scribes were plotting . . .'. See *Study in St Mark,* pp. 135–141. 'Two days thence', lit. 'after two days', must be understood by the analogy of St Mark's 'after three days'. 'After two days'='on the second (next) day' will be St Mark's usage when it is not yet evening at the time from which the reckoning is taken. If it is already evening, he says 'On the morrow' (xi 12).

reckon it) before the Resurrection, or, if we are to count the hours, it is three and a half days, half a week, from Wednesday afternoon until dawn on Sunday. The apocalyptic prediction which Christ makes to the four is itself concerned with the second half of a week, the 'days of Antichrist', which, completing the destined seventy weeks of captivity, usher in the kingdom of the Son of Man (Daniel ix 27, xii 7; see p. 88 above). Christ has prophesied the fall of the temple, and being asked when it shall be, says, Not yet; there is a period of waiting first, marked by lesser troubles and persecutions. Then at length the desolating abomination will be placed in the sanctuary, and (this is taken for granted) will involve the desolation of the temple about which Christ had been asked. The abomination would stand, and the most intense persecution would rage, for a number of days specially cut short by divine mercy; the reference is plainly to the most emphatic promise recorded by Daniel, that the great tribulation should not exceed half a week. Then, says Christ, still following Daniel's oracles, the Son of Man will appear on the clouds of heaven.

So, then, four days before the resurrection of the Son of Man Christ recalls to his four disciples the prediction which promises the advent of the Son of Man after four days. We have argued elsewhere, and shall further argue (p. 219f.) that St Mark sees the betrayal and passion of Christ as a type of the Great Tribulation and his resurrection as a type of his advent. It is true, of course, that the four days of Christ's betrayal and passion are literal days, whereas those of the Great Tribulation are, in fact, not days at all, but years: the 'days of Antichrist' are 'half a week of years'. But it is no less plain that 'week of years' is an artificial expression which has no other purpose than that of comparing seven years with seven days and half seven years with half seven days. The comparison which St Mark (on our supposition) draws is implicit in the whole Danielic chronology to which he undoubtedly alludes.

The heart of the Marcan Apocalypse and the clue to its relevance in the Gospel situation lie in the 'shortened days' of the Abomination, and in the advent of the Son of Man which terminates them. The 'shortened days' would be four in St Mark's generous reckoning; he does not count them to us, but there is a flavour of the number four throughout his apocalypse. Four is the only number actually mentioned in it. The Son of Man will gather his elect from the four winds (xiii 27). In Daniel's prophecy the four winds represent the whole extent of the world over which the four bestial empires tyrannise in turn, and it is in the same plane of symbolism to represent the elect as rescued from the four winds when they are delivered. According to Daniel each quarter of the world, each wind, yields its pest; a form of representation followed by the Johannine Apocalypse, when the four horsemen ride out to work havoc at the successive cries of the four cherubic beasts (Rev. vi 1–8). The beasts preside over the four quarters of the sky; the four horsemen themselves derive from the visions of Zechariah where they are manifestly connected with the four winds (i 7, vi 1). No structure of this ambitious sort is attempted in the Marcan apocalypse; but it contains two groups of portents or plagues, a standing feature of apocalyptic and very commonly arranged in numbered sets. Both the Marcan sets are fours in fact. There are the four 'beginning-pains of the travail' which brings forth the world to come, and there are the four direct signs of advent.

'Nation rising against nation, and dynasty against dynasty, earthquakes here and there, famines: these are the beginnings of travail' (xiii 8).

'The sun shall be darkened, and the moon withhold her shining, the stars shall be falling from heaven, and the powers in the heavens shall be shaken. Then shall they see the Son of Man' (xiii 24–25).

The four 'days' of endurance before the Son of Man comes may easily be likened to the night endured by watchmen waiting for the dawn, and when St Mark ends his apocalypse with such a picture, he does in fact divide the watch into four. The watching servants must keep awake, since they do not know whether the householder will return 'late, or at midnight, or at cockcrow, or early' (xiii 35).

None of these fours except the four winds are explicitly counted, but they afford one another some support, and it is reasonable in view of the rest of St Mark's numerology to regard xiii as an apocalypse of fours; the more so because it is explicitly Danielic and the number plays so important a part in the great vision of the Son of Man (Daniel vii).

If the proposed interpretation be allowed even in the main lines of it, we shall at least have something which we can understand. By conventions of symbolism established in the earlier part of his gospel and here put to their final use, St Mark tells us that the resurrection of Jesus is both after three days, in fulfilment of Hosea's oracle (vi 2) 'On the third day he shall raise us (Israel) up (in the person of our Messiah)', and also after four days, as being an enthronisation of Daniel's 'Son of Man'. The two mysteries of the Son of Man's resurrection after three days and the Son of Man's final advent were conjoined in their first open prediction (Mk. viii 31 and 38), and so they are in the realisation.

The three apostles have in the course of the Gospel been consciously associated with the resurrection after three days. It is perhaps only in retrospect that either St Mark or his readers observe that the four apostles, on the only previous occasion of their mention, appeared as the firstfruit of the Kingdom of God, the foretaste of Advent: 'Jesus came into Galilee proclaiming the good tidings of God and saying: The time is fulfilled and the Kingdom of God has come near; repent and believe the good tidings. And walking by the sea of Galilee he saw Simon and Andrew—and going a little further, James and John . . . and straightway he called them.' In the apocalyptic discourse the gathering of the faithful from the four winds is the last consummation. Of this fourfold gathering the call of the four by the lakeside had been the first beginning. They were fishers, themselves fished out of the lake by the Fisher of men, to be the instruments of a fishing which should cover all the corners of the world. Apart from the anomalous call of Levi, who was not an apostle, the Gospel tells of two callings, that of the Four at the beginning of the first 'handful' of healings, and that of the Twelve at the beginning of the second. The call of the Twelve signifies without doubt the call of Israel; it may seem that when he came to write down the apocalyptic prediction the Evangelist saw in the call of the Four the call of the world, and so the apocalypse openly declares for the first time that earthly Jerusalem must fall and that the Gospel must be preached to all the nations.

The call of the Four, coming first in the book, may seem to have expressed the universal aim of that mission which begins in 'the Galilee of the Nations'. But the aim is attained by passing through Israel, and the mission receives definition and immediate direction in the call of the Twelve and the healings which correspond to it. The presence of thirteenth persons and other signs, which we have sufficiently discussed, show that the mission to the twelvefold people is destined to break its bounds; the mystery of the rejection of Messiah becomes more and more clear and, as soon as the twelvefold pattern is completed in the healing of Bartimeus, is virtually actualised in the rejection of Jesus by the High Priests at Jerusalem. It only remains for them to profit by the treason of Judas. But meanwhile Jesus gives to the Four a vision of universal scope which claims the four winds for the Son of Man. The decisive events which follow are an actual crucifixion and resurrection 'after three days', but a virtual endurance of the days of Antichrist and achievement of the Church's final deliverance. For what is suffered and achieved in the Head will be expressed by him through his mystical body.

When we begin work upon the pattern of St Mark's gospel we are likely to feel that the first ten chapters are covered by a net of numbers from which the last four chapters escape; the pattern does not cover the whole book, and the climax is patternless. It does not seem credible that any author should compose in such a way and, when we look back upon the question from the end of our survey, we see that St Mark at least has not done so. There is no puzzle any more about the limited scope of the pattern of twelve healings. It is not and was never meant to be the pattern of the Gospel, it is a pattern within the Gospel. It expresses Christ's ministry to Israel, to which Israel reacts by rejecting Christ. That this will be so is revealed in the narrative framed by the three last healings, and the performance of the last healing is the sign for the rejection to begin. Christ comes into open conflict with the Jewish power in the Temple Courts and, withdrawing, predicts the overthrow of the holy place; he expounds the prediction to the Four on the Mount of Olives. When he ceases to speak we discover that it is now the next day before Passover and that the fulfilment of what has been in store is about to begin. The pattern which spreads over the rest of the Gospel is a pattern of days, the oldest pattern in which the saving events had been set (I Cor. xv 3-4), and a pattern constantly prefigured, as we have seen, in the subdivisions of St Mark's twelvefold design.

The measured days make up the Danielic half-week (xiv 1 ff.) and an emphatic new beginning is made for the great three days (xiv 12 ff.). Friday from dusk to dusk is more elaborately divided. To take the hours of daylight first—early, that is, at the beginning of the morning, Jesus was brought to Pilate for judgment; at the third hour, which is mid-morning, he was nailed to the cross; at noon, the sixth, darkness descended, and continued to the ninth, at mid-afternoon, when Jesus died. Towards dusk he was taken down from the cross and buried.

The divisions of the previous night are not so mathematical. The ancients divided the night into four watches, for such purposes, for example, as sailing by night (Mk. vi 48), but the division St Mark applies to Good Friday eve is less regular. It makes its first appearance in the end of the apocalyptic prediction. The disciples waiting for advent are like a servant told to sit up for his master. He cannot know when he will come, whether 'late' when luckier men are permitted to go to bed, or in deep night (midnight), or when the first streaks of light awaken the cocks, or 'early' when people begin to get about again and the watch is relieved. The Lord's warning, apparently aimed at the future when advent will be impending, drops as it were to point blank range and bears upon the disciples' present state as they expect the Passion: 'Watch, therefore, for you know not when the master of the house cometh, whether late, or in deep night, or at cockcrow, or early, lest coming suddenly he find you sleeping. And what I say to you' (disciples in your present predicament) 'I say to all' (Christians in the days to come): 'Watch.'

The application takes hold of the disciples on the Eve of Good Friday. When it is *late*, they sit at supper with Jesus and learn that a traitor is in their midst. When it is (evidently) *deep night*, they cannot watch, he comes to them again and again in Gethsemane and finds them sleeping. The armed men appear, the eleven run for their lives. When *the cocks are crowing* Jesus, arraigned before the High Priest, confesses, and Peter in the court below denies. When it is *early*, Christ faces Pilate alone. So firmly does the pattern, as well as the substance, of the apocalypse take hold upon the story of the passion.

CHAPTER VI

OTHER MARCAN NUMBERS

Against our expectation, and perhaps somewhat against our wills, we are driven to recognise that the formal skeleton of St Mark's symbolism is arithmetical. Get the counting right, and everything else falls into place; fail to see what St Mark makes of 'five and three', 'five and four', 'five and four and three', and you are left with an invertebrate mass of allusion. His counting is concerned with twelves, whether apostles, healings, loaves, thousands, or basketfuls, and with their subdivisions. But there are other numbers in his Gospel besides these, and it seems only reasonable to give an account of them. For, whether or not they enter into the grand arithmetic, they ought to cast some light on the evangelist's attitude to numbers in general.

The first number we meet is the forty days of Christ's temptation in the wilderness (i 13). The primary interest of this number is plainly typological, not arithmetical; it does not lie (that is to say) in any mathematical relation to other numbers. Christ spent a day in the wilderness for every year that Israel spent there during the great wandering under Moses. Moses himself had made retreats or penances of forty days to save the people from still worse things (Deut. ix 18, 25, x 10; cf. ix 9). Elijah had later made a fast of equal duration in the same region, to obtain the divine words which purified and saved the holy remnant (I Kings xix 8).

So the number 40 is prescribed to St Mark by the subject-matter with which he has to deal. It is an aspect of Christ's fulfilment of the ancient types. Still, there the number is, for whatever reason, with its own arithmetical properties, of which the most obvious is, that it is a multiple or 'power' of four, as its very name expresses (forty, τεσσαράκοντα). And it is a fact, whether accidental or not, that the number 4 continues to run through the next forty-five verses. Returning to Galilee, Jesus calls four disciples in two pairs and proceeds to heal four sufferers in two pairs, the fourthness of the fourth being underlined by the fact that he is brought by four bearers (ii 3).

The next number to be introduced is the vital number, twelve. The first mention it receives is that which is basic to the Christian scheme—the institution of the Twelve Apostles (iii 14, ?16). How the number runs on and subdivides itself and joins up again in the rest of the Gospel has been the subject of our detailed enquiry already; we will not repeat what has been said, but turn to the numbers which measure the increase of the good corn in the parable of the sower (iv 8, 20). 'Thirtyfold, sixtyfold, or a hundredfold'. There are three rates of fertility, just as there are three causes of barrenness—birds, shallow earth, and weeds. 'A hundredfold' is the typical figure for a heavy yield, as we may see from Genesis xxvi 12 and from the Marcan story of the rich man—those who make renunciations for Christ's sake gain a hundredfold (x 30). In the parable of the sower the hundred is roughly divided by thirds. A third should be $33\frac{1}{3}$ and two thirds $66\frac{2}{3}$, but of course the evangelist writes round numbers, thirty, sixty, one hundred. Three numbers, in the rough proportion of thirds, and beginning with a thirty, place a strong emphasis on the number three. Since St Mark likes triadic form in general, it is unnecessary to find any special reason for it here; but it is a fact that the parable of the sower falls in the area of St Mark's first pattern of three. The Three have just been surnamed on the mountain, the group of three great healings is directly to follow, the Three will assist as chosen witnesses at the third. And thirty, the number from which the counting of the yield begins, stands in the same arithmetical relation to the three apostles and three healings (iii 13–v 43), as forty, the number of temptation-days, stands in to the four disciples and four healings (i 14–ii 12).

The first person healed among the three in v is the Gerasene demoniac. 'Legion' is his name and the plurality of demons possessing him is dramatically exhibited when they transfer themselves to 'about two thousand' swine (v 13). 'Two thousand' can scarcely be the complement even of a depleted legion in lax and peaceful days. There is some evidence that biblical speech uses 'two' as an indefinite, where we would say, 'one or two', 'two or three', and the Germans say 'a couple of. . .'. The widow of Zarephath said she was collecting 'two sticks' to bake her last cake (I Kings xvii 12), the poor widow of Mk. xii 42 offers a couple of mites, and in the story of the five thousand there are found to be 'two fishes' for distribution, a number which appears to play no part in the symbolical arithmetic of the loaves, and for which 'a few fishes' is substituted in the corresponding story of the four thousand. Likewise at the first miracle of loaves, the disciples hazard the calculation that 'a couple of hundred dinars' would be required if the crowd was to be catered for. 'The chariots of God' said the Psalmist, 'are twice ten thousand, thousands upon thousands' (lxviii 17). As two tends to signify a mere plural, so, conversely, when we know that a particular number is hinted at, a mere plural signifies two, as in Daniel's famous 'time, times, and half a time'=three years and a half.

It may be, then, that St Mark is telling us no more than that the Gerasene swine 'ran into thousands', but even if this is all, the number is not without its interest. For it suggests to us that flocks and herds may run into thousands; and the only other thousands he mentions at all, the thousands of people fed by Christ, are introduced in the next chapter (vi 33–34) as the objects of Christ's compassion because they were 'as sheep lacking a shepherd'. Here, then, are the people of God seen as sheep panicking or straying and led back to their pasture by their Lord; there by the Gerasene shore were swine driven to panic and destruction because they incarnated the enemies of God and of his people, the demons Christ came to destroy. It was a form of thought close to the old pattern of biblical religion, that the advent of God is for the destruction of the people of his enemies and the salvation of the people of his friends. His enemies are unclean, fitly symbolised by swine, his friends are the sheep of the Good Shepherd. In the New Testament the old texts about God's enemies are freely transferred from men to demons; and so the suggested balance between the thousands of demoniac swine driven to destruction and the thousands of human sheep gathered and pastured becomes perfectly intelligible. But where the number of the swine is (virtually) in-definite—they run into thousands—the number of the sheep is de-fined and elaborated: they are the thousands of the Twelve Tribes.

To turn from the first half of v to the second—we should, per-haps, pay no attention to the statement that the woman who touched Christ had suffered her distress for twelve years, were it not that the girl into whose story she intrudes is found to have enjoyed for the same period the life which Christ's touch restored to her (v 25, 42). It then occurs to us that we are reading the first group of healing stories since the institution of the twelve, and that to find the number twelve thus emphasised in them is parallel to a previous phenomenon. In the group of healings following the call of the four disciples, the number four was found: four bearers brought the fourth sufferer to Christ. There, indeed, the situation was simpler—four called, four healed, four bearers of the fourth. Here it is more complex: twelve called and three surnamed; three healed, the second and third after twelve years, and the third in the presence of the same three who had been surnamed among the twelve. At the scene on the mountain, the Twelve called by that name (according to a strong MS. tradition, twice) and the Three not actually so called, but distinguished by their surnames; at the double scene in v 25–43 the number twelve mentioned twice in description of sufferers, and the Three, not actually so called but listed by their names, assisting at the healing of the last of them. Here is the appearance of a pattern, whatever the 'twelve years' may or may not mean.[1] The two mentions of them are closely followed by the next development in the history of the Twelve—their mission (vi 7).

When Christ sends out his apostles on mission, he sends them two by two. This was the common Jewish usage for the sending of *apostoli* or representatives and, as the Acts of the Apostles shews, the practice was continued in the Church. Later in the gospel Christ sends two disciples to borrow the ass, and again two to engage the supper-room. Nothing could be more natural than

[1] For 'twelvefoldness' as marking the person in need of divine healing, cf. the twelve sorts of evil imaginations which defile a man (vii 21–22).

these missions two by two, and yet once more as we record them we seem to be aware of a piece of pattern sliding into place, as the following table may shew.

1. *Mark i–v*

(a) Disciples called two (i 16) and two (i 19); the four in Simon's house, i 29.

(b) Three disciples surnamed, iii 16; the three in Jairus' house, v 37.

2. *Mark vi–x*

(a) Disciples sent two and two, vi 7.

(b) The three on the Mount of Transfiguration, ix 2.

3. *Mark xi–xvi*

(a) Disciples sent two (xi 1) and two (xiv 13); interposed, the four on the Mount of Olives, xiii 3.

(b) The three on the Mount of Olives, xiv 33.

The first of the three little systems covers the first octave of healings, with the construction of which it is intimately bound up. The second covers the rest of the cures, 2(a) the apostolic mission with the feedings of thousands which hang upon it, 2(b) the three-fold triad of apostles, last healings, and prophecies of resurrection. The third spans the Jerusalem ministry and introduces the passion. No mention of any definite number of apostles less than twelve and more than one has been omitted from the table, except James and John's request (x 35–45). It belongs essentially to 2(b), the extended treatise on the three witness-apostles; but in so far as it is concerned with two of them, it may conceivably be felt to prepare the transition to 3(a).

In vi there are two distributions of numbered groups into small parties. The twelve are distributed in twos when they go on mission, the multitudes are distributed in hundreds and fifties when they sit down to eat the miraculous bread. It is presently discovered that there were five thousand; that is to say a hundred fifties, or fifty hundreds—a symmetrical result.

In the crossing of the sea after the feeding of five thousand, Jesus came to his disciples about the fourth watch of the night, that is, the last, when his disciples' weariness and anxiety would be at the height. In narrating the passion, St Mark divides the day likewise into four periods; in the first half of the morning ('early') Jesus is before Pilate, in the middle of the morning (the third hour) he is put on the cross, at noon darkness descends and continues until the middle of the afternoon (the ninth hour) when Jesus dies. He remains dead on the cross until evening or sundown, when he is taken down. The night before the Passion is not similarly divided into four equal portions or watches, but follows another arrangement, as we have seen (p. 104). We have seen how the three days for which the four thousand waited before they were fed (viii 2) appear to be picked up in the three days for which the world must wait before Christ rises (viii 31, cf. ix 31, x 34, xiv 58).

It is curious how the interval 'after three days' has scarcely been introduced, when it is doubled: after three days Messiah will rise, 'after six days' from the announcement of it his glory is manifested on the Mountain (ix 2). For the progression of numbers 3–6, cf. 'thirtyfold, sixtyfold . . .' (iv 8, 20). The 'after six days' probably has its own symbolical value, like the 'forty days' of i 13. For just as Moses spent three periods of forty days in Sinai without the support of mortal food, so when he heard the divine voice speak out of the cloud (Exod. xxiv 16) it was after the divine glory had dwelt on Sinai and on him for six days. In Mark ix the three disciples both ascend the mountain and hear the voice speak out of the cloud (to themselves and to Moses) after six days. If the analogy is pressed, it will result that the disciples have been under the glory all the six days since the revelation at Caesarea Philippi, but that the glory only becomes visible at the time when the voice speaks from the cloud. It is a further point of connexion between Exodus xxiv and Mark ix that the voice which spoke to Moses from the cloud proceeded to give directions for the making of that one and only authorised tabernacle which was the prototype of the sole temple of God on Mt. Zion. In the Gospel the divine voice implicitly corrects St Peter's proposal that there should be three tabernacles made. Jesus alone is the living oracle and shrine of deity, to whom Law and Prophets testify. By a 'tragic irony', the false witnesses before the High Priest confuse Christ's prophecy of his own death and resurrection after three days with his prophecy of the fall of the Temple (xiv 58). By a divine miracle the veil of the temple rends when Jesus's spirit breaks out of his body on the cross (xv 38).

Such associations of images and ideas would sufficiently account for the 'after six days' in Mark ix 2, unless we wish to press the objection that the actual utterance of the voice from the cloud in Ex. xxiv is what St Mark in his careless idiom would call not 'after six days' but 'after seven'. Nevertheless the number six is there in Exodus, the form 'after n days' is supplied by St Mark's own previously repeated phrase (viii 2, 31), and 'six' fits better than 'seven' into St Mark's simple harmony of numbers.[1] After six days the three go up the mountain, and, by miracle, find themselves involved in a drama for six persons—there are the unearthly three—Moses, Elias and Jesus supernaturalised by the Glory—and there are the earthly three. What remains, but that the latter should prepare three tabernacles for the former?

Apart from numbers we have already discussed elsewhere, few now remain. We need scarcely mention the 'seven husbands' of the Sadducees' riddle; or the two thieves, one to hang at the right hand and one at the left. Perhaps the two thieves are intended to recall James and John's request for the seats at the right and left hand of glory. When Jesus is crucified, the Sons of Zebedee have fled, just as Simon Peter has denied and gone away to weep, when Simon of Cyrene shoulders the cross.

Arithmetically more interesting than these examples is the '300 dinars and more' which, in the opinion of her critics, the woman might have realised for distribution to the poor if she had sold her spikenard instead of pouring it out (xiv 5). The figure outdoes the parallel suggestion of a distribution in vi 37, 'a couple of hundred

---

[1] It also fits another possible line of allusion. The scene on the mountain is perhaps to be viewed as a symbolical 'Feast of Tabernacles' i.e. of booth-making (σκηνοπηγία)—'Let us make three tabernacles' (σκηνάς). And Tabernacles begins on the sixth day from Atonement, of which the themes can plausibly be found at Caesarea Philippi.

dinars' worth of bread'. The act of meritorious charity open to the woman would have been even more splendid. St Mark remains within his characteristic ranges of number—a few hundred dinars for a charitable distribution, anything from two to five thousand in a herd, flock, or crowd of men, decades up to the single hundred for the yield of seed or the reward of enterprise.

One can scarcely put one's finger on an inexplicable number in St Mark. Some have a particular symbolical sense, like the forty days in the wilderness, some are appropriate to particular circumstances, like the 'fourth watch' in which Jesus walked on the water, some are round numbers like the casual use of 'two', and some find their significance in their equality or harmony with other numbers. Sometimes numerical harmonies build up a symbolical system carrying its own riddle, like the system of loaves and thousands, and, indeed, the whole system based upon the number twelve. Sometimes they have no evident effect other than the suggestion of an overruling destiny.

One often hears it said that this or that biblical way of thinking has become utterly strange to us, and then finds the speaker who says so employing it himself quite casually the very next minute. All that has happened in two thousand years is that the form under discussion has changed its sphere; has, for example, been degraded from serious to trivial use, as we see in the case of the play upon words—St Thomas writes, in deadly earnest

> O Salutaris *hostia*
> Caeli quae pandis *ostium,*
> Bella premunt *hostilia*;
> Da robur, fer auxilium.

We have not ceased to play upon words, but we no longer do so at the climax of eucharistic adoration. The play upon numbers has also become a game. If seven bathers went to an unfamiliar riverbank and found seven willows and no more standing in a row, they would laugh, each put his things under one tree, and say that 'it seemed to have been meant'. But when the Israelite writer tells us how the Israelites went down into Egypt a family of twelve increased to seventy (Gen. xlvi 8–27), and coming up out of

Egypt again sat down in an oasis where twelve springs nourished seventy palmtrees (Exod. xv 27), he intends us to understand that it really was meant. Divination was the reading of the book of destiny and numerical coincidence was the stock-in-trade of divination. When Pharaoh dreamed two dreams, one of seven lean kine swallowing seven fat kine and another of seven blasted ears devouring seven good ears, he looked about for an interpreter. The structure of Joseph's double dream was similar. Joseph's dream involved the equation of the twelve tribes with the twelve (zodiacal) constellations, an equation of which the effect was felt from the Blessing of Jacob (Gen. xlix) to the Revelation of St John the Divine (xii 1, xxi 12). Indeed the whole Revelation is one great structure of divination in which numbered sets of things are 'squared' with one another. The Rabbis of the next few centuries developed interpretation by numerical equivalence into what one can only call an arithmetical game of snap, in which licence, triviality and complication held united sway. 'But surely we can keep this sort of thing out of the Gospels'. Can we keep punning out of the *Verbum supernum prodiens*? No, nor will we understand or appreciate the poem any better by turning a blind eye to the puns. We can learn to think and feel like the author, and to discard our prejudices. There is no other way.

It is always useful in matters which touch our hearts to observe our feelings, even when our feelings have to be discounted; for the best way to discount feeling is to uncover it. The interpretation of the Gospels touches our hearts, if we have even a shred of Christian faith; and we know that we have got to discount our feelings, so long as the kind of interpretation we are pursuing is historical. There is only one question, 'How did St Mark think?' And if we find the answer which the facts suggest trivial or dismaying, that is no ground for disputing the conclusion. If the treasure of the Gospel has been given to us in an earthen vessel, we have to accept the fact as one further evidence that the excellence of the glory is of God and not of men.

For it remains that the glory is there. No amount of attention to the mechanics (as it were) of St Mark's arrangement can reduce him to a mere juggler with symbolical arithmetic, or remove one single treasure from his pages. All the divine things he wrote he deeply felt and understood for what they were, and if he chose to string them on a thread of order which was partly numerical we must be patient to follow him.

It is, indeed, an impertinence to invoke patience; it is an author's concern to carry his reader with him. I wish I could have made the preceding chapters easier to assimilate. But defects of exposition may not be the only obstacles. The rules of the science we practise become our standards of what is scientific, and it is difficult for us to take seriously what falls outside them. The science of criticism has recently concentrated on the breaking down of apparent connections in the text with the object of detaching sources underlying it. And it seems unscientific to start doing the opposite and looking for non-apparent connections where apparent disconnection reigns; to desert minute dissection and embrace symbolic synthesis. Yet the authority of a method cannot lie in anything but its appropriateness to a line of enquiry. Did the Jewish writer—did St Mark—supplement logical connection with numerical patterning? If the question is worth asking, the method is worth developing.

CHAPTER VII

MATTHAEAN RECONSTRUCTION, ii

We have counted our way through St Mark, trying to see how the themes of the three pillar-apostles and of the twelve loaves with their thousands of recipients come into the frame provided by the twelve healings. We tried to see how it went, but perhaps we saw it wrong. Who can tell us, unless St Matthew will do so? He has rewritten St Mark, and if his rewriting appears to start from the same interpretation of St Mark as we have been led to adopt, that is the best confirmation we can hope to find.

It is a familiar observation that St Matthew rearranges St Mark freely as far as vi 13 in St Mark's gospel, or as far as the end of xiii in his own. After that he takes what he does take from St Mark much as it comes; he makes additions and omissions, but not rearrangements. It will be seen that the old division between the rearranged and the 'straight' parts of St Matthew corresponds with our division between the ground covered by the theme of the Twelve and the rest of the Gospel. Such a correspondence can scarcely be an accident. What has happened is presumably this. St Matthew has seen that St Mark has a somewhat complicated rhythm, and that the double twelve of healings and of apostles constitute the base of it. St Matthew finds St Mark's pattern too intricate, or anyhow foresees that it will become too intricate when he has loaded it with the additional matter he desires to work into his gospel. He thinks his readers will see their way more clearly if he extracts the base of the Marcan theme and states it first by itself, disencumbered of elaborations. After that he will give them the rest of the Marcan pattern, and they will not lose their way. Now obviously the extraction and separate statement of the basic theme is a work of reconstruction and rearrangement, and so we see that in fact this part of St Matthew's work is freely rearranged. But once this has been done, the rest of the Marcan pattern may be allowed, perhaps, to take its course—it will not require the same degree of active reformation.

When we have extracted the basic theme of the double twelve from St Mark's arithmetical design, how much of the Marcan arithmetic remains? There are the four apostles, Simon, Andrew, James and John, called from their nets in Mk. i and made the recipients of Christ's apocalypse in Mk. xiii. These are the three apostles, Peter, James and John, specially surnamed on the mountain in Mk. iii and privileged to be present at three mysteries—the raising of Jairus's daughter, the Transfiguration, and Christ's prayer before his arrest. And there are the twelve loaves distributed to nine thousands in Mk. vi–viii.

The theme of the four apostles is completely integrated by St Matthew with the pattern of the twelve and swallowed up in it. For him, as we have seen, the four are simply the first four apostles to be called by Christ, and their names reappear as the first line of the apostolic list. They are not heard of again; the Lord's apocalypse is given to his disciples in general, not to the four.

The three receive exactly opposite treatment. So far from being integrated with the pattern of the twelve they are wholly extracted from it. St Matthew suppresses every reference to the Three which falls within the territory occupied by his pattern of the twelve apostles and the twelve healings. Their special surnaming disappears from the apostolic list, their presence at the raising of the ruler's daughter is not mentioned, and the group of three healings in Mk. v which in some way corresponds to the group of three apostles surnamed in iii is broken up by St Matthew's rearrangement. Everything that St Matthew has to say about the three either corporately or individually is to be found in a later part of his Gospel. The only exception is the inescapable mention of Peter's name in the story of his mother-in-law's fever (viii 14). Apart from this exception, the Parabolic discourses of xiii act as an impenetrable barrier dividing the whole theme of the Twelve from the whole theme of the Three.

It is as though St Matthew broke the Marcan system into two parts, the Twelve (corresponding roughly to Mark i–vi 13) and the Three (corresponding to Mark vi 14–x 52). But whereas St Matthew's method of concentrating the whole theme of the Twelve in chs. viii–xii involves considerable rearrangements of Marcan matter, his handling of the Three scarcely involves any. For he does not trouble to transfer the earlier Marcan references to the Three into later contexts, he simply suppresses them, as we have said, and contents himself with the Marcan material contained in viii–x. He adds further material of his own, indeed, but that does not involve him in any rearrangements of St Mark.

The five great discourses of St Matthew's Gospel break the narrative into six parts. Before the first discourse we have the birth of Jesus and his first public appearance (i–iv), after the last discourse we have his passion (xxvi–xxviii). His ministry is contained in the four intervals enclosed by the five discourses (viii–ix, xi–xii, xiv–xvii, xix–xxiii). Of these four intervals the first two are occupied by the theme of the Twelve, as we have already shewn; the last two contain the theme of the Three. Since each theme occupies two intervals between discourses, either can be said to embrace one discourse. In the case of the theme of the Twelve the discourse which the theme thus embraces is actually part of the theme and indeed the very heart of it; it is the Apostolic Charge, and follows direct upon the namelist of the Twelve. The discourse embraced by the theme of the Three is not so obviously central to that theme, but at the very least it is perfectly appropriate to it. It is the discourse on ruling humbly, and deals with the exercise of powers which Christ has specially entrusted to St Peter just before. It springs out of the question, 'Who then is greatest in the Kingdom of Heaven?' and so seems specially to concern the leaders of the Twelve.[1]

The discourse on ruling humbly follows quite closely, though not of course immediately, on Caesarea Philippi and the Trans-

[1] Matt. xvii 25–29 associates Peter with Jesus as a son of the King of Heaven enjoying tax-immunity (in principle). The text continues: 'In that hour his disciples came to Jesus, saying: Who, then, ranks high in the Kingdom of Heaven?' (xviii 1). The answer is, that to qualify as sons we must first become as babes; and, conversely, that babes must be accepted as bearers of the divine Majesty.

figuration. At Caesarea Philippi St Peter received his blessing and his authority; the Transfiguration associated the sons of Zebedee with him. In fact, so far as St Matthew's story is concerned, the Transfiguration is virtually the institution of the Three as a distinct group, for it is the first mention of them his Gospel contains. It is tempting to say that the names of the three Apostles taken into the mountain in xvii bear the same relation to the discourse on ruling humbly as the names of the Twelve, called together in x, bear to the apostolic charge. But that would obviously be to exaggerate.

The Marcan arithmetic of loaves and thousands finds its place in the Matthaean history of the Three. Here indeed is a piece of Marcan work after St Matthew's own heart. Here is a pattern which does not sprawl but is written neatly into a place by itself (Mc. vi 30–viii 21). St Matthew is content to reproduce it virtually as it stands, letting it occupy the beginning of the history of the Three (Matt. xiv 13–xvi 12). All the essential items of the Marcan arithmetic remain and we have every reason to suppose that St Matthew understood the Marcan symbolism and intended to perpetuate it.

Nevertheless, the Marcan pattern, transferred to its Matthaean setting, requires a measure of re-interpretation. There are elements in St Matthew's gospel which would never, one feels, have come to be in the shape in which they are if St Matthew had been composing freely on his own account. He retains them because they still carry their essential meaning in their new context, but they were shaped by the exigencies of St Mark's thought, not of his own. Among these elements we may place the precise arithmetic of the feedings. If St Matthew had been writing for himself, would he have wished to leave the last three thousands still unfed in his story? Would he not have wished to bring seven thousand men to eat the seven loaves? Of the twelve thousands of Israel, five are fed by the Lord in his ministry, and seven through the Church afterwards and concurrently with the Gentile mission. Why trouble to make a further division in the seven between four fed and three still to be fed? St Mark made it for reasons arising out of the place occupied by the feedings in his general pattern of Twelve. St Matthew having loosed the feedings from that pattern, would hardly have made the division for himself, but he can retain it and apply it (as so much in his gospel applies) directly to his own time. Five thousands were fed in Christ's ministry, four thousands have been fed since: there are three thousands more to be fed when St Matthew writes, and then the end will come. The end will come, says St Matthew (xxiv 14) when the gospel has been preached in the whole world for a testimony to all the Gentiles, and it is equally necessary that the predestinate of all Israel should be gathered in before the consummation. The apostles will not finish evangelising the cities of Israel until the Son of Man comes, says the Lord in the apostolic charge (Matt. x 23).

St Matthew has drawn together the whole scope of twelvefold healing in viii–xii, and we expect, perhaps, to see no more healing miracles; but here again the Evangelist is confronted by elements so wrought into the Marcan story that he can scarcely remove them without doing it irreparable damage. The *effatha*-miracle in Mark vii and the corresponding miracle of the blind man near Bethsaida in viii can be dropped from their places without leaving scars—indeed, they leave the Marcan pattern closer-knit. The omission of the *effatha*-story leaves the four thousand directly attached to the Syrophoenician woman, and the omission of the blind man brings the prophecy of resurrection after three days (Mc. viii 31, Matt. xvi 21) nearer to the feeding of the people after three days (Mc. viii 2, Matt. xv 32). So far, so good; but who can narrate the Transfiguration and omit the lunatic boy at the foot of the mountain, when Jesus, like Moses (Exod. xxxii, cf. xxiv 14), redescends the mount of revelation and finds pandemonium broken loose below, and his deputies incompetent to deal with it? Or again, who can bring himself to describe the journey from Jericho to Jerusalem without a blind beggar by the road? Not to speak of the Syrophoenician or Canaanitish woman herself: if she is omitted, the whole system of loaves and thousands is reduced to meaninglessness.

So, in spite of the rounding-off of the twelvefold healing in viii–xii, there remain three healing stories in xiv–xxiii, the Canaanitish woman's daughter, the lunatic boy, and the blind man on the way out of Jericho. The story of the Canaanitish woman belongs to the feedings; the other two stories fall in the section concerned with the three prophecies of resurrection and the three pillar-apostles. It is inconvenient, surely, that there should be two healings only in a section of which the structure is so markedly triadic. St Matthew is easily rid of the incongruity by doubling the person of the blind man (xx 30). Two healing episodes, but three persons healed.

We remember that St Mark's story makes a very exact equivalence between Peter and the two Sons of Thunder on the one hand, and three persons healed on the other, in iii–v. St Peter stands by himself, the other two are a pair, and so with the three healings: the Gerasene stands by himself, the woman and the girl are woven together into a pair. St Matthew effaces the pattern of the Three in that place, but only to employ it later. Peter and the two Sons of Zebedee ascend the mountain in xvii 1, and on their descent one demoniac is exorcised, as though for St Peter. Then presently in xx 30 ff. two blind men are healed, as though for the two Sons of Zebedee. It is, indeed, as though St Peter and the two sons of Zebedee themselves were being healed; for St Peter's folly, the rejection of the Passion, closely precedes the exorcism of the one, and James and John's folly, their request for thrones on the day of glory, immediately precedes the restoration of sight to the two.

There is a third strand in the threefold weft—three apostles, three persons healed, and three predictions of death and resurrection. The third strand conforms to the formality of the rest of the design. The first prediction of the Passion directly calls forth St Peter's folly; and the exorcism of the epileptic presently follows. Two more predictions of the Passion are made, and the second is immediately followed by the folly of the two brothers and the cure of the two blind men.

The formality of the pattern could scarcely be clearer, but the formality of it should not distract us from the meaning of it. The sequence 'prediction of the Passion, apostolic folly, exorcism or opening of eyes' expresses the essence of what is being set before us. The folly of the apostles is a reaction to, or an ignoring of, the prediction of the Passion, and the exorcism exorcises the spirit of perversity which has been thus exemplified; the blindness which is cured expresses in physical form the moral blindness of Christ's disciples.

St Matthew matches one prediction of the Passion with St Peter, and two more with the sons of Zebedee, and allows the two predictions to be given before introducing the two disciples in a double scene where they speak as one. By means of this arrangement, he withholds the theme of the two brothers until after the third prediction in all; and meanwhile the theme of St Peter can continue to run on. That is in accordance with the general balance of this gospel—St Peter is advanced and the sons of Zebedee drawn back into the shade. They appear (outside the general name-list of the Twelve) four times only, at their call by the lakeside, with St Peter on the mountain, in the scene of their request for thrones, and with St Peter in Gethsemane. In St Mark, there are two additional mentions of them: with St Peter at the raising of Jairus's child, and with St Peter and St Andrew at the delivery of Christ's apocalypse. There is also an episode (the strange exorcist) concerning John alone, and there is the special surnaming of the two along with St Peter, in the name-list of the Twelve. What the two lose, St Peter gains: to the Marcan material St Matthew adds the episode of Peter's walking on the water just after the feeding of five thousand (xiv 28–32), the new and impressive account of his surnaming in connexion with his confession of Christ (xvi 17–19), his conversation with Christ at the episode of the stater in the fish's mouth (xvii 24–27), and his question to Christ 'How often shall my brother offend and I forgive him?' (xviii 21). The theme of St Peter runs unbroken from xiv 28 to xx 16, when it is succeeded for a matter of eighteen verses by the theme of the sons of Zebedee (xx 17–34).

St Matthew may have altered the balance of roles as between St Peter and the two brothers, but it remains that the three taken as a group are matched with the three predictions of the three days' mystery, and also with the healing of three persons, the 'lunatic' boy and the two blind men. If we add to them the Canaanitish woman in xv 21–28 we have, in all, four persons healed in addition to the twelve-plus-one of viii–xii. The Canaanitish woman is a sort of double of the Centurion, or rather, the Centurion is a sort of double of her. St Matthew has pulled the theme of the twelve apart from the themes which in St Mark accompany it, and, in particular, from the theme of the loaves and the thousands. Now the Canaanitish or Syrophoenician woman belongs in St Mark equally to both themes; she represents both the one Gentile above the twelve Israelites healed, and the granting of crumbs from the table of the Israelite thousands to the Gentile 'dogs'. St Matthew is in a dilemma: the woman must be assigned either to the one part, or to the other. The choice is not difficult to make. The whole form of the Syrophoenician story ties it to the feedings of the multitudes, whereas another story of Christ's concession to a Gentile's faith will do equally well among the twelve healings. So the Canaanitish woman holds her place among the feedings, and the Centurion deputises for her, as it were, among the twelve healings.

So, then, St Matthew achieves a characteristically balanced result. In viii–xii he gives us the commission of the Twelve, with twelve healings and one Gentile healing in addition, and in xiv–xxiii he gives us the calling of the Three, with three healings and one Gentile healing in addition. It is a balanced result, certainly, but has it not been achieved at too high a price? What has St Matthew done? He has wished to make the basis of the Marcan architecture, the twelvefold calling and healing, plainer for his readers, by setting it apart and dealing with it first within a limited space. But then, in the next part of his book, he confuses us again, by adding three more healings after all. You may tell me that it is perverse of me to make a single sum of the three and the twelve, that this is just what I am not intended to do; and yet I shall inevitably do it. St Matthew who begins by making so much of the twelvefold healing ends by recording for us in detail the healing of fifteen Israelites, not to count the two Gentiles. That is the inescapable fact. How, if at all, does the Evangelist ease the awkwardness of it?

By the very simplest of devices, he supplies us with the means for reducing fifteen to twelve. If we count the persons healed, there are fifteen, but if we count the healing acts, there are twelve; for on three occasions pairs of persons are healed together. St Matthew's pairing is not like the coupling of the twelve-year-old girl and the twelve-years-sick woman in Mark v. There, the two invalids are distinct in their diseases and their cures; they are merely woven into one narrative. St Matthew's pairs are indistinguishable; they suffer as one, act as one, speak as one, and are healed as one. So to talk of 'twelve cures but fifteen people cured' is natural enough. As though we were saying that Christ performed twelve healing acts, nine times laying both his hands on one person's head, and thrice distributing his hands between two sufferers.

viii 2 Leper	ix 20 Issue	
viii 5 (Centurion's servant)		
viii 14 Fevered woman	ix 23 Ruler's child	xv 22 (Canaanitess' daughter)
viii 28 Two demoniacs	ix 27 Two blind	xvii 14 demoniac boy
ix 2 Paralytic	ix 32 Dumb demoniac	xx 30 two blind
xii 10 Withered hand		
xii 22 Blind dumb demoniac		

Let us observe the facts more closely. There are two pairs among the first twelve persons healed, and indeed among the first ten. They count as the third and fourth items in each of the first two handfuls; they are the two violent demoniacs and the two blind men. These are the only simple cases of possession or of blindness among the first twelve; otherwise we have mixed forms, a mute demoniac and a blind-mute demoniac. What we have to observe, then, is that the diseases which are already doubled in the group of the twelve are redoubled by appearing again in the group of the three. The 'lunatic' boy of xvii is, according to St Matthew (though not according to St Mark) a straight case of violent possession like the pair of Gadarenes in viii, while the two blind men in xx are the very double of the two blind men in ix. If we wish to formalise the picture still further, we can say, in a sense, that both the double healings in the first part find their doubles in double healings belonging to the second part, for though the 'lunatic' boy is single, he makes a close pair with the daughter of the Canaanitish woman two chapters before. Both are cases of simple violent possession, both are interceded for by parents, the girl by her mother, the boy by his father. The one reveals the faith of the Gentile, the other the faithlessness of a perverse generation. So, then, we may say that a pair in the second group corresponds to each pair in the first group, but that the pairs in the second group are reduced to unity in different ways: the two blind men by simple coupling in one episode, the two demoniac children through the discounting of one of them as being a Gentile and so as falling out of the reckoning of the Twelve.

We said on a former occasion that St Matthew is revealed by the first paragraph of his gospel to have a highly formal, and indeed a highly arithmetical mind. We have seen abundant reason since to confirm that observation, and we shall see more reason yet. Let us observe some of the results that follow if we adopt the reduced reckoning of the healings, and instead of counting patients count healing episodes. It will follow that the twelve in viii–xii reduce to ten (*plus* one Gentile) and the three in xiv ff. reduce to two (*plus* one Gentile). From these conclusions a point of formal elegance follows—the reckoning by healings gives us a strikingly unequal division of twelve, ten in the first part, and two in the second part. But that is the very same division of twelve as we have within the first part, if we adopt the alternative reckoning and count by persons: ten in the two 'handfuls' running almost straight on through viii–ix, then a break marked by the mission of the twelve apostles in x–xi, followed by the remaining two persons healed in xii. To put it in the barest possible form—10 + 2 in viii–xii: count the 10 + 2 as 10, and add 2 more in xiv–xx.

We may feel impatience at such formality; but St Matthew's formality is never merely formal, it always carries its sense with it.

The cures of the twelve persons in viii–xii constitute ten mighty acts, and what do ten mighty acts suggest to the Jewish mind? What but the ten strokes of Moses' rod, the ten signs given to Pharaoh? Moses smote and healed, Jesus simply heals; that is the difference between the two dispensations. But otherwise the signs of Christ are like the signs of Moses; they are given to confirm a Gospel of salvation, and they are rejected. So a manner of reckoning which enables the twelve new signs given to Israel to be squared with the ten old signs given to Egypt has its value. And no one can complain that St Matthew fails to appreciate it. He exhibits the signs of viii–xii as signs rejected and blasphemed by the new Pharaohs. We saw in a previous chapter how St Matthew draws into the climax of his list the healings which provoked the bitterest hostility. Let us now observe how he follows up the last of them with the highly significant episode of the Scribes and Pharisees asking for a sign. Could moral blindness further go? An evil and apostate generation indeed! (xii 38–45).

The ten signs end at Matt. xii by the one reckoning, and at ix by the other; the first ten to be completed are the two handfuls of persons healed (viii 1–ix 34). The immediate sequel at ix 35 is the sending out of the twelve apostles, an integral part, as we have seen, of St Matthew's architecture. Then there directly follows the episode of John the Baptist's messengers. The point turns on Christ's signs, his mighty works. The Baptist himself needs to receive the report of what men hear or see—the blind obtain their sight, the lame walk, the lepers are cleansed, and the deaf hear, and (through the sending forth of the Twelve) the poor are evangelised. But presently, in reflection upon the consistent hardness of heart shown by Israel to the Baptist formerly and now to himself, Jesus turns his discourse against his nation, and especially against the Galilean cities: if Tyre and Sidon had seen the mighty works Bethsaida and Chorazin have seen, they would long ago have repented in sackcloth and ashes; Sodom would have remained to this day, had it been favoured with the sight of the miracles performed in the streets of Capernaum. Such is the climax of the denunciation, a very close match to the climax of the denunciation in xii which we were studying just now. For when in that chapter Pharisaic perversity asks for a sign, it is reminded of Gentile Nineveh which repented at the preaching of Jonah, and the Gentile queen who came from the ends of the earth to hear the wisdom of Solomon.

The effect of St Matthew's handling of the ten (or twelve) signs in viii–xii is to impress upon us that, whereas God's signs to Egypt were ten plagues, his sign to Israel is twelvefold healing. And so, when the twelve healing works, according to the larger reckoning, are at length completed in xx, we are prepared for a final display of Egyptian blindness by Israel, for the great rejection and the great denunciation it calls forth. Messiah rides into Jerusalem and is rejected by the priests and scribes; he replies with a discourse of unmeasured severity against the teachers of Jewry (xxiii). The apocalyptic discourse follows (xxiv–xxv), just as the apocalyptic parables (xiii) followed the denunciation of those who asked for a sign.

We may now venture to put one thing together with another and guess the grand design of St Matthew's book. We began by attributing to him two forms of structure, one his own and one taken over from St Mark. His own scheme was the scheme of five great discourses arranged at intervals throughout his gospel and dividing it into six parts. The scheme he took over from St Mark was that of the twelve apostles and the twelve healings. We then proceeded to suggest that the Marcan scheme had been cramped by St Matthew into two of the intervals between his set discourses; that is to say, into five chapters among the twenty-eight which compose his gospel—a sad shrinkage when we consider that in St Mark the pattern of the Twelve covers ten and a half chapters out of sixteen. And so it would appear that St Matthew's general plan was not Marcan at all; the Marcan plan has been pinched into one corner of it.

We are now in a position to redress the balance between the Marcan and non-Marcan patterns in St Matthew. Two of the discourses in the non-Marcan sequence of five, the third discourse and the last, are apocalyptic: the apocalyptic parables of xiii and the apocalyptic prophecies of xxiv–xxv. These two apocalyptic discourses are each preluded by denunciations of the Pharisees, and form the respective conclusions to the little twelve of healings contained in viii–xii and to the great twelve of healings contained in viii–xx. The pattern of twelve which St Matthew has taken over from St Mark, though differently handled in St Matthew, runs on as far as it does in St Mark, and ends with the healing of the blind on the way out of Jericho.

Even the Matthaean correspondence between the apocalyptic parables of xiii and the apocalyptic prophecy of xxiv–xxv has its foundation in St Mark's text. I showed in my *Study in St Mark*[1] that the themes of the parable-discourses in iii–iv are rehandled in due order by St Mark in the apocalyptic discourse of xiii. My demonstration was, I hope, conclusive and independent of any errors that my book may otherwise contain. All that St Matthew has done, then, is to strengthen and formalise a relation which the two passages already bear to one another in St Mark. Moreover, in St Mark as in St Matthew, the parables and the prophecies both follow on scenes of conflict and rejection. In Mark iii 1–6 Jesus has outraged the rigidity of the scribes in synagogue itself by healing the withered hand, and in xi 15 we read how he outrages the self-interest of the priests in the temple of God by turning out the market of offerings. In St Mark the second rejection and the second apocalypse[2] follow upon the completion of the twelve healing signs. St Matthew's innovation is to make the first rejection and the first apocalypse also follow upon the completion of twelve healing signs, and this he is able to do by his double method of reckoning the healing signs, first by persons healed, then by healing acts, whether one or two persons at a time are the beneficiaries from such acts.

It will have been observed by the reader that the whole numerical system which we have endeavoured to bring to light in St Matthew depends on double healings, and it may be reckoned as a

[1] Pp. 164–167.
[2] To call the parables in Mark iv a first *apocalypse* is to see them through St Matthew's eyes. See below, p. 213.

128

subsidiary advantage attaching to our thesis, that it explains the presence of so curious a feature in St Matthew's book. Neither his one predecessor nor his two successors in Gospel-writing present anything comparable; and, on narrative grounds, there is little to be said for the double story. When two persons behave simply as one, the interest of the story is, if anything, weakened; and this is particularly notable in the story of the Gadarene exorcism. The Marcan drama contrasts the single person, named Legion and housing an army of demons, with the thousands of swine among whom the army is subsequently distributed. Two men cannot be called 'Legion', and the more persons there are to house the host of devils, the less impressed we are by the hideous concentration of demonic power. But two persons behaving as one have precisely the numerical ambiguity St Matthew's scheme requires: they invite us to call them two persons healed, or the subjects of a single healing, indifferently.

A further incidental advantage to be derived from the thesis of the chapter we are here concluding is that it helps us to see how St Luke came to think of doubling the Marcan number of healings. The suggestions to which he responded stand out fairly clearly, if we are willing to make two assumptions: that he had read St Matthew and that he understood what he read. For here was a gospel with two twelves in it, one twelve ingeniously contained within the other, one reaching a third of the way through the story, and the other reaching out as far beyond it again. The little twelve contained a thirteenth, the Centurion, and the great twelve added a sort of duplicate on its own account, the Canaanitish mother. There were St Luke's facts, and it seems intelligible enough that he should propose to himself two reforms: to set the two twelves out as whole numbers without any overlap of items between them, and to differentiate in a more interesting way between the two thirteenths. They shall not both be Gentiles; one shall be a Gentile, the other a Samaritan. St Matthew's centurion shall remain, his Canaanitish woman shall give place to a Samaritan leper of whom St Luke has heard tell. True, the making up of two whole twelves looks a formidable task. St Matthew has only fifteen Jewish people healed; even if all St Matthew's fifteen are retained, nine more will be required. Yes, but the Samaritan leper had nine leper companions, so there is a solid contribution to the arithmetic.[1]

[1] It is not as simple as this sounds. By dropping Matthaean doubles, St Luke finds room for four more sufferers drawn from his own store of tradition—the widow's son (vii 11-17), the two sabbath healings (xiii 11-17, xiv 1-6) and the high priest's servant (xxii 51).

CHAPTER VIII

THREE MARCAN CRISES

It is impossible to be content with a purely formal analysis of the Gospel. It is an inevitable consequence of the nature of the questions which we have taken up in this book that formal considerations should principally occupy us, but in the present chapter we will turn to some sort of discussion of the light which falls upon the message of St Mark from that simple division of his healing series which we examined first in this book.

We found St Mark's healing narratives to fall into three principal groups, two handfuls of five miracles each, and two more added to make up the twelve. We found the three groups all to end with an identical theme, the restoration of a pair of human powers; first of active powers, to walk and to handle, then of sensitive powers, to hear and to see; the restoration of the sensitive powers being gone through twice over. The three matching terminations are embodied in three narrative settings, and as we compare the terminations we are naturally led to compare the settings in which they stand. Besides the bare formal match between pairs of powers restored to full exercise by the touch of Christ, how much else is there that matches? We will examine the situation of the narrative at the ends of the three groups and see whether any interesting comparison arises.

The first group, that is, the first handful of healings, corresponds with a clearly marked phase in the activity of Christ, his mission in Galilee with Capernaum as his centre, up to the point of his open breach with the scribes in the synagogue at Capernaum (iii 1–6). When Jesus completed the first handful of healings by healing the withered hand in synagogue on the Sabbath day, the Pharisees went out and straightway took counsel with Herod's people how they might destroy him. But Jesus with his disciples withdrew towards the sea, followed by a great multitude from Galilee, and, indeed, from every part of Palestine. He had a boat with him to make him independent of the crowds, and in it he presently set up his teacher's chair, since he was not to use the synagogue. And he gave a formal character to the society of his followers by constituting the body of the Twelve.

Let us leap down from the end of the first group to the end of the second and see what is happening there. We are at a turning-point as serious though not so visibly threatening. After healing the blind man, and so completing the second handful of cures (viii 22–26), Jesus provokes his disciples to confess their faith in order that he may inform them of his destiny. He is to court rejection and death at the hands of the high priests and Sanhedrin (presumably at Jerusalem) and after three days to rise from the dead. Now on the face of it this scene stands midway between two others. It looks forward to the confrontation of priestly authority in the temple at Jerusalem, and it looks back to the confrontation of scribal authority in the synagogue at Capernaum. The scribes would have brought in the Herodian power, if they could, to compass Christ's destruction; the High Priests were going, more effectively, to invoke the power of Pilate. In each case the Jewish authority would be appealing to its regional government. Since St Mark recorded the conspiracy of the Pharisees with Herod's men at Capernaum, he has reminded us of the nature of the threat such a conspiracy held out, by telling us what Herod had done to the Baptist. Moreover, he has told us that Herod viewed Jesus as John Baptist risen from the dead. Decapitating prophets, it seemed, was like lopping the heads of the Hydra—they sprouted again.

The episode which we are considering begins with the statement that Jesus went forth with his disciples into the villages attached to Caesarea Philippi. The very name is ominous. Philip the Tetrarch, Herod's brother, belongs to the story of John's martyrdom at Herod's hands (vi 17), that is the only connexion in which we have heard of him: whereas Caesarea, containing the name of Caesar, reminds us of the Roman power which would crucify Christ. The conversation between Christ and his disciples begins by picking up the echoes of the story of John's martyrdom. The story of John's martyrdom began like this. 'King Herod heard (of Jesus through the mission of the Twelve) for his name had been published abroad. And he said, John Baptist is risen from the dead and for that cause miracles work through him. Others said, It is Elias; and others, A prophet, like one of the prophets: but Herod when he heard, said, John whom I beheaded is arisen. For Herod had sent and seized John . . .' The story of the Baptist's martyrdom follows. At Caesarea Philippi we have the same exordium, but what follows is not the story of John's martyrdom, it is the prophecy of Christ's. 'Jesus asked his disciples, Who do men say that I am? And they answered, John Baptist; others, Elias; others, One of the prophets. But he asked them, Who do ye say that I am?' (The disciples' opinion is insisted on here, as Herod's in the previous passage.) 'And Peter spoke out and said, Thou art the Christ. And he admonished them to tell no one of him, and began to teach them that the Son of Man must suffer many things. . . .'

We know what follows. Peter, protesting against the teaching of the Passion, is admonished as Satan. Now this is very remarkable. Peter, confessing Messiah, is admonished to keep silence; Peter, upholding the glory of Messiah against his suffering destiny, is admonished as Satan. We cannot but remember the texts in which Satan himself, or his demon ministers, had confessed Christ, and been admonished to keep silence. Peter's confession, after all, has something Satanic about it, it is not yet pure. It is unnecessary to run back further than the last text about the silencing of demons, to feel the force of the comparison. 'And the unclean spirits, as often as they saw him, fell before him, crying, Thou art the Son of God. And he laid on them many admonitions not to make him known' (iii 11–12).

The text I have just quoted belongs to the crowd-scene which accompanied Jesus's withdrawal towards the sea, when his life was threatened by the whispering of Pharisees with Herodian officers. The grievance was that he had healed the withered hand on Sabbath, and this was the defence he had given: 'Is it right to help on Sabbath or to hurt? To save life or to kill?' To save life, or to kill; that is the issue for which Christ incurs the threat to his own life. Life is risked, that life may be saved—another's life. But it comes nearer home. For what is it that Christ says in comment on Peter's Satanic error? 'If any will come after me, let him renounce himself and take up his cross and follow me. For he that willeth to save his life shall lose it, and he that loseth his life for my sake and the Gospel's shall save it. For what does it profit a man to gain the whole world and forfeit his life? For what could a man give that would purchase his life? For he that disowns me and my words in this apostate and offending generation, the Son of Man shall disown him when he comes in the glory of his Father with the holy angels.'

It is necessary to insist again and again on the economy of St Mark's writing. His book is not full of sayings about the saving of life and the loss of life; before the scene at Caesarea Philippi the antithesis has only been expressed once, and that is at the healing of the withered hand. The crises which mark the ends of the two handfuls of healings have this in common, that they contain pronouncements of Christ about the saving of life and the destruction of it. Of these two pronouncements, the former is literal, straightforward, and extremely brief; the latter is spiritual, paradoxical, and set out at much greater length. It is as though the saying in iii, were the text, and the saying in viii were a spiritual exposition of it.

It is worth observing the exact order in which the theme is built up. What Christ says in iii 4 lays the foundation with complete simplicity. It is good to save life, bad to kill, whether on Sabbath or at any other time. Complication begins to enter two verses lower down, when, in consequence of Christ's resolution to save life, the Pharisees go out and plot to destroy[1] him. Christ saves life, then, even at the cost of his own, and a new antithesis appears; for 'save life or kill', 'save life or lose[1] life' is substituted. When we come to viii we find Christ calling on his disciples to share his own rejection and penal death, that they may save, not merely the lives of others, but their own in another sense, or in another world.

Most students of the gospel have been puzzled at one time or

[1] In the Greek, to lose (one's own life) and to destroy (another person, or his life) can be expressed by the same verb, and so it is in Mc. iii 6, viii 35.

another over the relation between two things: the emphasis laid on Christ's works of physical healing, and the plain lesson of the Gospel, that we are to live for the spirit, not the flesh, for the other world and not for this. Catholic theology, indeed, has arrived at a balanced doctrine. Man must share the unbounded care of the Creator for the natural life which he has ordained, up to the moment when he is called upon to sacrifice the natural for a supernatural good. When the saint—let us say the Curé d'Ars—heals the sick, and when he mortifies his own flesh to the extreme point that flesh will bear, he is behaving with equal reasonableness. So we may argue, and yet we may wonder whether the evangelists had either felt the force of the antithesis we find in their writings, or arrived at the resolution of it which subsequent reflection has elaborated. We need be in no doubt—St Mark at least is fully aware of the issue. The restoration of physical life (or, as a Jew would say, the life of this world) is good in itself, and a token of the power which preserves man for life everlasting. But occasions may arise when the lower must be sacrificed for the higher.

The evangelist returns to the point a couple of pages further on. We remember that it was in connexion with a disabled hand that Jesus had established the principle, 'It is right to help, not to hurt, to save life, not to kill.' How significant, then, that the lesson of mortification in ix 43 ff. should begin with the example of the hand! 'If thy hand is thy undoing, cut it off; it is better for thee to enter into life maimed, than to go with two hands into the hell of fire.' The withered hand of iii was, we remember, a companion-piece to the paralysed feet of ii, and the discourse of ix follows up the association, and proceeds to the cutting off of the foot. The antitype to the withered hand in the second handful of healings is the sightless eye, and that is the Lord's third example in his parable: 'If thine eye is thine undoing, pluck it out.'

But we have strayed from viii to ix in pursuit of illustration for our theme. Let us return to viii and to the strict parallel between (a) the sequel to the healing of the sightless eyes and (b) the sequel to the previous healing of the withered hand. Peter has been rebuked like the demoniacs of iii 11-12 for a satanic expression of

Messianic belief, and Christ has, in explanation of the rebuke, re-stated the principle of saving life on which the healing of the withered hand was based.

After the rebuking of the demons in iii there follows the ascent of the mountain, and the sequel to the conversation at Caesarea Philippi is also an ascent. In iii Jesus takes all twelve up with him, in ix only the three whose special surnaming is recorded in iii. The rest remain below, but they also have their part to play in the story. In fact, by taking the Three up and leaving the Nine below Jesus shows the significance of the special surnaming of the Three among those twelve whom he took up before. (St Matthew is therefore in perfect sympathy with the rhythms and correspondences of St Mark, when he actually transfers the surnaming of St Peter into a position which makes it the direct prelude to the Transfiguration.) The Three go up, the Nine stay down; the Three show themselves unable to understand the heavenly realities unveiled to them, the Nine, through their immaturity in prayer, are incapable of exorcising the dumb spirit when it is brought before them. 'Who is greatest?' is the woeful topic of discussion, when the Three and the Nine are reunited.

The parallel between iii and viii–ix extends further, but we have carried it far enough to prove our point; we have seen that the match between the ends of St Mark's two groups of healings goes beyond mere formal correspondence; it is charged with a meaning that leads us into the very heart of St Mark's thought. Let us now see whether there is any similar profound correspondence between the third group-ending and the other two.

We found that the middle group-ending coincided with a spiritual crisis, the revelation of rejection, a revelation pointing both backwards and forwards—back to the rejection at Capernaum, forward to the rejection at Jerusalem. We have seen that the rejection at Capernaum coincided with the end of the first group; the rejection at Jerusalem is going to coincide with the end of the third. The end of the third group is the healing of blind Bartimaeus, which opens the road to Jerusalem. Jesus is no sooner arrived in the city, than he throws out the market of offerings, and the high priests and scribes seek how they may destroy him (xi 18).

Of three lines rhyming together in a poem, the first line does not yet rhyme with anything, the second rhymes with the first, and the third rhymes with both the first and the second. It is the same with the sequence of matches in St Mark's narrative which we are considering: the first awakens no echoes, the second awakens echoes of the first, and the third awakens echoes of both the first and second. So in examining the events connected with, and following upon, the healing of blind Bartimaeus, we have to listen for two sets of echoes: echoes of the events similarly related to the healing of the blind Bethsaidan in viii, and echoes of the events related to the restoration of the withered hand in iii. We will begin with the less distant echo and deal with it very briefly.

We take our start, then, from the first and second healings of the blind, in viii and in x respectively. In viii there follows the episode at Caesarea Philippi and the Transfiguration. Jesus moves his disciples to confess his Messianic dignity but enjoins them to silence. He shows his glory on the Mountain and St Peter proposes an ovation of which the ceremony is to be borrowed from the feast of Booth-Making, or Tabernacles as we call it: 'Let us make three booths, one for thee and one for Moses and one for Elias'. Now to take the parallel. The healing of Bartimaeus is followed by Christ's sending disciples to fetch the ass on which he will ride in Messianic triumph, to the accompaniment of shouts which hail the kingdom of David. There is, indeed, a popular ovation, of which the ceremony suggests the feast of Tabernacles. The cutting of branches[1] is as integral to that festival as is the making of booths. The liturgical cries, 'Hosanna! Blessed is he that cometh in the name of the Lord!' are also appropriate to it.

To summarise the parallel: in viii–ix Jesus provokes but sup-

[1] The details of the ovation are progressively brought into line with Tabernacles usage by St Matthew and St John. The conclusion has often been drawn that they read into St Mark's text a suggestion of which he was innocent. In our view, that is to mistake the whole character of St Mark's writing. He is in general not 'simple' but 'enigmatic'. Where slight hints satisfy him his successors insist on unmistakable allusions.

presses the recognition of his Messianic glory. A festal ovation is proposed but not offered. In x–xi Jesus provokes and publishes the recognition of his glory, and receives a festal ovation from the populace. The contrast between the two scenes corresponds exactly to the difference between the two situations. Because what was veiled in viii–ix is unveiled in x–xi, therefore what was merely predicted in viii–ix is effected in x–xi: Jesus brings the High Priests and Sanhedrists down upon him. The rejection at Capernaum will be re-enacted at Jerusalem, but this time there will be no line held open for escape.

Let us now take up the other parallel, the rejection at Capernaum and the rejection at Jerusalem, with the withered hand and blind Bartimaeus as our starting points. It may seem to us that the enquiry promises little; before we undertake it we know all about it. Jesus defied the scribes in the synagogue by infringing the Sabbath, and he defied the priests in the Temple by the apparently opposite action of hallowing the sanctuary and throwing out the market. The scribes at Capernaum tried to contrive his destruction with the aid of Herod's men, and the priests at Jerusalem did contrive his destruction with the aid of Caesar's deputy. Such are the obvious points in the parallel, and it is difficult to suppose there can be any more. For there is so little in the Capernaum incident anyway. The few phrases it does contain scatter over a wide area in the antitype. The rejection at Capernaum is a couple of verses, the rejection at Jerusalem is the history of the passion; and whatever the passion-story is shaped upon, it is not shaped upon the rejection at Capernaum.

Well, clearly the influence exerted by the Capernaum incident must be limited, but that does not prevent it from being powerful at the point where it comes to bear. One pregnant image may have fertile consequences. The pregnant image is not to be found in the episode of the withered hand itself, but in the prelude to it. St Mark devotes two paragraphs to the sabbath-issue in ii 23–iii 6, and the two are inseparable. There is the paragraph of the cornfield and there is the paragraph of the withered hand. Jesus's disciples pluck the ears of corn as they walk through the field on

Sabbath, and Jesus defends them against the charge of desecrating Sabbath by doing harvest work. He makes the corn free to his hungry disciples though it is forbidden by the rule, and quotes the example of David, who, when he and his companions were hungry, went into the temple of God and took the shewbread, though the rule reserved it to the use of the priests. The example is appropriate in so far as it turns on the point of hunger, and in so far as it makes David the authority for the action of his greater Son. But the comparison of the plucking of ears with the taking of the holy shewbread appears somewhat overweighted. The paragraph of the withered hand redresses the balance. For, we now read, Jesus follows the example of David in entering a holy place, the local synagogue, and overriding the authority of those who preside in it.

In so far, then, as David allows hunger to take precedence of ritual law, Jesus imitates him in the cornfield, but in so far as David overrides the presiding power in a holy place, Jesus imitates him in the synagogue. The two incidents are as much united by the example of David as they are by the common topic of sabbath observance.

Let us now turn to the antitype provided in x–xi. Here, it would seem, the example of David can really come into its own, for now the Son of David is not going to enter any mere synagogue, to confront the local scribes, but as David did, the temple itself, and to confront the high priests. The incident will not concern itself with sabbath, for that belongs to synagogue; it will have to do with offerings destined for the temple altar.

Blind Bartimaeus, healed by the roadside, raises the cry 'Son of David'—the first time that we have heard the name of the great king since Jesus himself invoked it in the cornfield. It is as David's son that Jesus enters the city and the holy place, while the populace hail the advent of David's kingdom.

We saw that in ii–iii Jesus imitated David's single action in a double way, by satisfying hunger in the cornfield, by overriding the law of holiness in synagogue. The same thing happens again: Jesus, like David, is hungry, and would have made free with the figs on the wayside tree, if there had been any figs. Jesus, like David, enters the temple and overrides priestly privilege by taking control and expelling the market of offerings. But whereas the two previous antitypes of David's single action were put down side by side and so left, St Mark's story as it progresses reveals a mysterious identity between the cursing of the figtree and the forcible correction of abuses in the temple. David looked for a satisfaction of physical hunger in the temple, but the hunger Jesus desires to satisfy in the temple of his day is God's hunger for the fruits of His vineyard, let out to his treasonable tenants, the Jewish priesthood; of this hunger Christ's physical desire for ripe figs is made the symbol.[1] As the tree is cursed for bearing no fruit, so the priesthood is denounced for refusing fruit to the Landlord's son, and for contriving his death. The tree withers, and the temple will fall. But the tree *withers*. St Mark has a passion for the inversion of his images. In ii–iii the withered hand flourishes and the sanctity of the synagogue is disregarded. In xi the flourishing tree withers and the sanctity of the temple is affirmed. The hand flourishes again, the tree withers; for 'it is right to help and not to hurt, to make alive and not to slay'; and yet 'if thy hand is thy undoing, cut it off and cast it from thee'—the dead wood, the mortified member must be cast out of the Israel of God, lest the whole body should fall into the abyss of fire.[2] The heart shrinks, to record such words. But they are not the pitiless decree of placid power; if

[1] The symbolical value of hunger for ripe figs has a background in the Old Testament. The Lord looking for righteous men is as one longing for the ripening of the new figs after the fresh grapes are finished; there is no cluster for him (in the vineyard), Micah vii 1, cf. Hosea ix 10. The puzzles of St Mark's narrative solve one another. Why are there suggestions of an entry for the feast of Tabernacles about Jesus's arrival in Jerusalem towards Passover? And why does he look for figs before they can be expected? He comes as though to Tabernacles to look for the fruits of the Lord's vineyard, because Tabernacles is the vintage feast, but 'there is no cluster to eat'. 'His soul desires the first ripe fig', but it is not the season of figs. Passover is in the middle of the fruitless season. By arriving at Jerusalem just then Jesus fulfilled Micah vii 1 exactly, in the letter as well as in the spirit.

[2] Cf. Christ's saying about his passion and the coming destruction of the city: 'If they do these things to the green wood, what is to befall the dry?' (Lk. xxiii 31, to be read on the background of xii 49–xiii 9).

Christ killed the tree, it was by dying on it. Whatever died, died in his death, and whatever was vivified sprouted again from his sepulchre.

The rest of the parallel need scarcely detain us. Jesus confronted the scribes in the synagogue at Capernaum for a matter of minutes; he sustained the contest against the temple priests for days or even weeks; they sought how they might destroy him, but they feared the people. When at length he withdrew from the temple, it was to ascend the Mount of Olives, deliver his apocalypse, and prepare for his passion. One detail may be noted. Jesus's withdrawal in iii 7 is consequent upon an abortive combination of Pharisees and Herodians. We said above that the antitype to this in xi ff. is the effective combination of the Sadducean priests and Pilate. And yet in a corresponding position—that is, before the withdrawal of Jesus in xiii 1—St Mark is careful to record a second and equally inefficacious plot of Pharisees and Herodians, to catch Jesus in his speech and put him wrong with Rome.[1] Christ foils his questioners, and other questioners who follow them into the lists. He is left in triumphant mastery of the field of debate. And so the High Priests turn to more sinister methods.

We have now seen what historical significance St Mark's three points of formal division carry, and how he enriches it by symbolical means. The first handful of healings brings him to the rejection at Capernaum, the second handful to the dolorous prediction at Caesarea Philippi, and the two-healings-over to the rejection at Jerusalem.

In relation to the architecture of the Gospel as a whole, what we are likely to find surprising in our conclusions is the emphasis thrown upon the rejection at Capernaum. As to the importance of the other two terminal points, we have never, presumably, been in any doubt. Caesarea Philippi is the dead centre and main turning-point of the gospel, and the entry to Jerusalem is the casting of the die. Let us think a little further, then, about the rejection at Capernaum. What have we discovered about it? This at least, that St Mark saw in it a forcible type or prefiguration of the crisis

[1] C.f. Luke xxiii 2, reflecting xx 20.

which led to Christ's passion. Capernaum prefigures Jerusalem, the synagogue prefigures the temple, and so with the other details of the two events.

Let us attempt to relate our discovery to what we previously observed of St Mark's counting by handfuls. The rejection at Capernaum is occasioned by the healing of the withered hand, that is to say, it marks the end of the first handful of healings. What significance, then, attaches in St Mark's numerical symbolism to his first handful? It plays a part in two different reckonings; it is the first figure in two simple sums, five and three, five and four. It will be sufficient to recall the former of these two sums here.

We have seen reason to think that five and three stand, in St Mark's mind, for an octave, that is, for a week counted inclusively from Sunday to Sunday, the three representing the three days which saw the passion, entombment, and resurrection of Christ, and the five, the five days preceding them. Now when such a scheme is placed before us, our minds immediately turn to Holy Week; if the sixth sign corresponds with the death on the cross, the first sign must square with the entry to Jerusalem on Palm Sunday. But we must remember that St Mark had not read St John's gospel, and St John is the first writer in whose book the outline of Holy Week can be discerned. The student confined to the Synoptic gospels would have no warrant whatever for fixing the scheme of the week on Christ's Jerusalem ministry. St Mark only begins counting the days from Wednesday evening, the fourth eve before the Resurrection, and until he begins to do so (xiv 1), his readers are credited with knowing no other chronology of the end of Christ's life, except that the saving events occupied three days.

St Mark's five-*plus*-three, then, is not a literal week of days; it is not the Holy Week we commemorate from Palm Sunday to Easter Day. It is an octave of mighty acts, in which time is measured by the substance of events, not by the cycles of the sun. Now measured by the bulk of divine action, Christ's life on earth might well divide into five and three, five parts for the ministry, three for the saving passion; a week of heavenly acts, of which the last three occupy literal days, as by a happy chance; but the first five do not. A Gospel narrative which employed such a proportion, assigning, let us say, ten chapters to the ministry and six to the passion, would correspond to the balance St Mark actually exhibits, provided that we are prepared to count in with the passion the events directly provoking it, from the entry into Jerusalem onwards.

By this reckoning, then, the first eight healings are a prefiguration or epitome of the whole Gospel, the first five standing for the whole ministry of which in fact they are no more than a part, and the next three representing the passion, entombment, and resurrection. If this is so, it is only proper that the first five should conclude with a foreshadowing of the crisis which transforms Christ's work from a ministry into a passion; with a foreshadowing, that is to say, of his entry into the temple and his rejection by the priests.

We have been trying to answer the question, why such an emphasis should fall on the rejection at Capernaum, as to place it in parallel with the revelation at Caesarea Philippi and the rejection at Jerusalem. What sort of an answer have we found? A symbolical answer. Historically speaking, the episode had no decisive consequences that we are aware of. The Pharisees whispered to the Herodians and the Herodians did not act. The event is important in what it prefigures, and St Mark makes it the centre of a complete prefigurative symbolism.

CHAPTER IX

THE MARCAN ENDING

Far too much, you might think, has been said and written about the abrupt ending of St Mark's Gospel. And yet the matter has not been settled to the general satisfaction of the learned, and I want to approach it again. I have previously-published statements to revise, and my newly acquired confidence in St Matthew as the expositor of St Mark makes me wish to see what light he has to throw on the ending of the Gospel.

I shall begin by stating two axioms which will fix the limits of the discussion. First, we have no evidence for the authentic text of St Mark beyond the words 'for they were afraid' which conclude the account of the flight of the women from the tomb. St Mark may have written more, but if so it has not come down to us. A second axiom. It is immoral to invoke accident, whether physical accident, such as the damaging of the unique original before even St Matthew saw a copy; or personal accident, such as St Mark's death or arrest in the middle of a sentence, when he had a couple more paragraphs only to write. Such accidents could happen, but they are not at all likely; and history would become a field for uncontrolled fantasy, if historians allowed themselves the free use of such suppositions.

It is only reasonable to try the hypothesis first, that whatever St Mark wrote lay before St Matthew and St Luke. The hypothesis may prove untenable, but it has a right to first consideration. Now there has been a general agreement between scholars that so far as the evidence goes St Matthew and St Luke do not appear to have had a longer story before them in their Mark than we have in the genuine text of ours. For if they had had, we would expect it to have shown its influence by keeping their narratives in step beyond the point where our genuine Mark breaks off. Whereas they keep more or less together with St Mark and with one another up to that point, and then diverge widely.

This is, to say the least, a very superficial and a very inaccurate

144

account of the facts, as we shall hope to shew. But we will accept it for the present, while underlining the limited nature of the conclusion it supports even if it is accepted as it stands. The conclusion is that St Matthew and St Luke had no more *story* in their Mark than we have in our genuine text. But in addition to what we read there may have been a concluding phrase which was not a continuation of the story at all. 'They said nothing to anyone, such was their fear. *But the name of Jesus became manifest in all the world.*' The two later evangelists might both have read a phrase like that, and yet been entirely uninfluenced by it in their several endeavours to carry on the history from the point at which the women fled from the sepulchre. The name of Jesus became manifest in all the world, no doubt, even though the women were too frightened to stop the people they met or to tell them about the angel's message and the Lord's empty tomb. Such a statement is a truism to any Christian and it casts no particular light on the train of events which succeeded the flight of the women and led to the spreading of the Lord's name.

The phrase I have used for illustration is a Marcan phrase (Herod heard of Jesus, for his name had become manifest) but I do not for a moment think that it formed the actual conclusion of the Gospel. All I wish to show is that there are two hypotheses easily compatible with St Matthew and St Luke's having read all that St Mark wrote. Either the original text ended where our genuine text ends or it carried an additional phrase which added nothing of a precise kind to the story.

Each hypothesis has its attractions; the first has the advantage of a blessed simplicity. What St Mark wrote, what St Matthew and St Luke read, and what has come down to us, is one and the same. By the standard of the later gospels St Mark was incomplete, and spurious endings were naturally supplied by ancient industry, as they are still being supplied by modern ingenuity, and for the same reason. The attraction of the rival hypothesis is that it allows us to round off St Mark's conclusion. 'They panicked so' seems an unconventional, a trivial, and a discouraging ending; would St Mark have used it? The hypothesis which adds a rounding-off phrase is not so simple as its rival, for it has to explain the disappearance from all MSS. of St Mark's concluding words. Yet the explanation it is able to offer is easy enough. St Matthew and St Luke established a new standard for what the ending of a gospel should be, and to conform to this standard the spurious conclusions of St Mark were composed. But the spurious conclusions could not be fitted on to the original body of the Gospel without removing the original concluding phrase. One could carry on with the story from the flight of the women, but not from a concluding formula like that which we supplied above. The learned might continue to know that the spurious conclusions were spurious, but the original concluding formula would simply have disappeared from the text. It was so short and probably so unimpressive that it was not worth preserving in a marginal note. The learned scribe might write 'All that follows was composed by a later hand' but he would hardly trouble to add 'The original conclusion was, *But the name of Jesus became manifest in the whole world*'. Most copyists would continue to write out one or other of the spurious continuations, while the scholarly and correct copyists, such as gave us our best Alexandrine manuscripts, would break off austerely at the point at which they were warned that the work of the supplementer began.

Here, then, are two hypotheses neither of which invokes accident or raises intolerable difficulty. Either the text ended at 'they were afraid' or there was a further sentence which was not a direct continuation of the narrative. Which hypothesis is intrinsically more probable? And which is better supported by the evidence?

To take intrinsic probability first. We cannot attempt an answer until we have defined our question more carefully. If we are talking simply about the process of textual transmission, the intrinsic probability of nothing's having been lost is obviously greater than the intrinsic probability of something's having been lost. But we have discussed that point already and will now set it aside. Let us consider something else, the intrinsic probability that a writer such as St Mark was would prefer to end with the words 'For they were afraid' or to add on a round phrase. Here the verdict goes the other way: the chances are that he would prefer to add the round phrase. Dr Lightfoot and others have sufficiently proved that there was nothing out of the way in ending a Greek paragraph with the little word γάρ (ἐφοβοῦντο γάρ—'They panicked so'). What no one has shewn is that it was possible for any narrative writer of St Mark's age to finish a carefully composed book with such a paragraph.

The difficulty is both stylistic and dramatic. Stylistically considered, a light or off-hand ending to a paragraph is one thing, to a book another; dramatically considered, an ending which makes the characters (if I may speak more picturesquely than decently) go to earth with the plot, and sit on it, administers a violent jolt to the readers or listeners. It is useless to invoke St Mark's elementary simplicity of style to explain such a phenomenon. The simpler a story-teller is the more inclined he is to bring his story to a conventional end. Nothing but calculated sophistication could make him want to do otherwise. So long, therefore, as we consider the question in general terms, we must say that a man like St Mark would prefer to add the round phrase.

But perhaps the balance will be reversed when we leave general considerations for particular and argue not from the books which men like St Mark (if there were any) were inclined to write, but from the book St Mark did write. That is the ground I have previously taken, and have concluded from it that St Mark took his pen off the paper at the word γάρ. If I now revise my opinion, it is for two reasons. First, when I defended the abrupt ending, I was arguing against the addition of a whole scene to the Gospel, and that still seems to me as inadmissible as ever. I was not arguing against a mere rounding-off sentence, because I had not it in mind at the time and because I did not see the importance of the suggestion, anyhow. Second, when I defended the abrupt ending I held opinions about the structure of the Gospel which I have since seen reason to modify. I will say no more about my mistakes but discuss the question as I now view it.

There are three sorts of evidence that we might hope to find within the gospel itself. First, structural parallels, second, material parallels, third, indications derivable from the general attitude of the evangelist to his theme. By a structural parallel I mean a text which the structure of the gospel places in parallel with the concluding paragraph, in the way in which, for example, the healing stories in one handful of five are parallel with the corresponding stories in the other handful. By a material parallel I mean a paragraph which tells a story like that which the concluding paragraph tells. And when I look for indications in the general attitude of the evangelist to his theme, I am asking whether the way in which he handles the rest of his book suggests that he is heading for one sort of termination rather than another.

As I now see it, there is only one structural parallel which can fairly claim the title.[1] Although the story of the passion picks up a great number of echoes from all over the gospel there is only one cycle of narrative to which it presents a continuous parallel, and that is the cycle directly preceding it, the Jerusalem ministry. The Jerusalem ministry begins with the mission of the two disciples to find the ass and ends with the anointing at Bethany. The passion story begins with the mission of two disciples to find the supper room and ends with the attempted anointing at the sepulchre. The parallel, therefore, which the very structure of the Gospel recommends to our attention is that between the two anointings.

Jesus received no funeral anointing in the literal sense. The woman in the supper at Bethany anointed Jesus as a mark of honour to the living and perhaps with an extended suggestion that he was the Lord's Anointed. The women who came to anoint him in his sepulchre were disappointed of their purpose, for he had risen. Both stories, then, are stories of surprise; she who would have anointed him for glory learns from the lips of Jesus that she has anointed him for burial; those who would have anointed him for

[1] I shall argue below (p. 221) that there is something to be said for an analysis of the Passion into four episodes, xiv 10–31, xiv 32–72, xv 1–21, xv 22–xvi 8. All the conclusions of episodes previous to the last deal directly or indirectly with the frailty of the disciples and especially of St Peter. The conclusion to the first episode is quoted at the final scene, 'Go, tell his disciples and Peter, He goeth before you into Galilee (there shall ye see him) as he said unto you.' Such an analysis of the Passion supports the view that the flight of the women was intended to be the last event in the continuous story. It does nothing to support the case for a concluding phrase.

burial are made witnesses by the angel of the disappearance of the body they came to anoint. The woman at Bethany is commended. Her generous and affectionate action needs, perhaps, no special defence against the puritanical criticism that her precious perfume would have been better bestowed in sale for the benefit of the poor. But it receives in fact the special defence that it is a burial-anointing only a few days anticipated. No one, then, is to call her zeal misdirected. By contrast, St Magdalene and her companions act inappropriately. Christ has prophesied his resurrection on the third day; it is the third day, and they come to visit his sacred body. Christ has declared the anointing at Bethany to be his burial anointing, and they come to anoint him now. When they find what they should, if anything, have expected to find they turn and run.

The point of the contrast is not, of course, moralistic. It is not that the woman at Bethany was wise and the three at the sepulchre foolish. Both parties acted from devotion and neither knew what they were doing. But the current of divine event cut the paths of their action differently; it struck into the path of the woman at Bethany, and all across the path of the women at the sepulchre. What the woman at Bethany did will be recalled wherever the gospel is preached in all the world; her relation to the gospel mystery is positive, this is she who was providentially moved to anoint for burial the Lord's Anointed who by being buried is enthroned. The relation of the three women to the gospel mystery is negative; they run from it, and are too afraid to publish the great evangel which is destined nevertheless to fill the world.

It is a remarkable fact that the anointing at Bethany ends on the note on which we might expect a gospel to end, the publication of the evangel in all the world. 'Verily I say unto you, wherever the gospel is preached in all the world, what she did shall be spoken of in memorial of her.' It would be surprising if, writing an actual termination to his gospel on the model of this paragraph, St Mark should not bring it round to the same final point. Perhaps, then, that was what he did. 'They went out and ran from the tomb, for trembling and amazement possessed them; and they said nothing to anyone, for they were afraid. But Jesus sent forth his disciples to preach the gospel amongst all nations', ὁ δὲ Ἰησοῦς ἀπέστειλε τοὺς μαθήτας αὐτοῦ κηρύσσειν τὸ εὐαγγέλιον εἰς πάντα τὰ ἔθνη—that, I suppose, is what St Mark might write. The prophecy of world-wide preaching is twice recorded by him, once in the anointing at Bethany to which we have referred, once half a chapter earlier in the apocalyptic prediction (xiii 10). The form differs slightly in the two texts. 'The gospel must be preached among all nations', says the apocalypse; 'The gospel shall be preached in all the world', says the paragraph about the anointing at Bethany. 'All nations' is to be preferred for the last word of the gospel, because it is more appropriate in its place. The women said nothing *to anyone*, but *all nations* were to receive the gospel. The forepart of our proposed sentence, 'Jesus sent his disciples forth to preach', can be collected from iii 14. 'He appointed Twelve . . . to be with him and that he might send them forth to preach.'

So much for the evidence derivable from the structural parallel. We have now to glance at material parallels, that is, at paragraphs anywhere in the gospel which record similar occurrences. Of these we may name two classes, healing miracles and apparitions. The last scene of the gospel records both the apparition of an angel, and the discovery that there has been a resurrection. Jairus's daughter was seen to leave her bed, the angel shows the women the place where Jesus lay but where he no longer lies. Through the resurrection of Jairus's daughter, Christ's resurrection is further related to the whole range of restorations to fulness of life and health of which the girl's resuscitation is the extreme example.

The evidence of the healing miracles is inconclusive. The only relevant feature is the injunction to silence four times imposed by the Healer and notably in the case of Jairus's daughter. 'Say nothing to anyone' said Jesus to the first patient on whom he imposed secrecy (i 44). The women fled from the tomb, and 'they said nothing to anyone'. It may be that the parallel is relevant. If so, it presents a contrast. Jesus enjoined silence on the beneficiaries or witnesses of his cures, and they broke it. The angel gave a message to the witnesses of the resurrection, and they kept silence. Such is the weakness or the perversity of human nature.

Yet the point of the stories about silence vainly enjoined is not, it would seem, to indict human nature but to show that buried theophanies inevitably sprout and manifest themselves. As Christ said in connexion with the parables of the seed and the lamp, 'There is nothing hidden but that it might be revealed'. And so it may not be right to suppose that St Mark would wish to end his gospel with a mere inversion of the oft-repeated story of human perversity: 'As they talked when they were told to hold their tongues, so they held their tongues when they were told to talk.' No, more probably the parallel in the evangelist's mind would be: 'The divine truth will out, whether Heaven itself imposes silence on human garrulity, or human fear suppresses a Heaven-sent message.' And if that is how the evangelist would be likely to think, then the last word of the Gospel would not be the women's failure to speak, but Christ's publication of the truth through his apostles. All the buried seeds of miracle sprout within the story of the ministry except resurrection. The secret of Jairus's daughter was apparently kept and no subsequent miracle of resuscitation opened it up until Jesus himself rose. All the more likely, then, that St Mark should make a point of telling us that the news went abroad in spite of the women's silence.

Twice St Mark actually says that the injunction to silence was followed by publication and so ends a paragraph with a sentence antithetical to its predecessor: 'But he went and began to preach greatly and publish the tale' (i 45); 'But the more he enjoined them (to silence) the more exceedingly they preached . . .' (vii 36). These two cases will have to be our stylistic justification for our proposed final antithesis: 'But Jesus sent his disciples to preach. . . .'

The other material parallels we have to consider are apparitions, and these reduce to two: Jesus seen walking on the water as though he were an apparition, and Elias and Moses appearing in the company of the transfigured Jesus on the mountain top. In the walking on the water, the disciples see a supposed apparition and are distraught; Jesus tells them not to be frightened and comes into the boat. They are still full of ἔκστασις, amazement, for they have not understood about the loaves. The voyage continues and they reach the shore. In the apparition of the angel at the tomb there is the same pattern of initial fear, reassuring words from the person causing fear, and continued amazement (ἔκστασις). But the conclusions of the two stories are necessarily so different as to allow of no useful comparison. Jesus entered the boat and the voyage continued; the disciples still felt ἔκστασις, passionate amazement, but they did not act upon it; whereas the women gave way to trembling and ἔκστασις, and broke off from the cause of it by flight. At the Transfiguration, as at the sepulchre, three witnesses are frightened by a sudden white robed glory and answered by a supernatural voice. Their reactions to the voice are not specified; later, as they are descending the mountain, they are found to be in intellectual perplexity, but that gives us no assistance with the ending to the scene at the sepulchre. The only conceivably relevant trait is the Lord's injunction of silence, which receives the very special form, 'Tell no one what you have seen, until after the Son of Man has risen from the dead.' Then the apostles (not the women) will have to proclaim what they have seen, interpreting the white-robed glory on the mountain and the white-robed glory in the sepulchre by one another. The women, then, may have been so frightened that they told no one anything, but the disciples, sent forth by Jesus, were to publish the gospel among all nations. The story of the Transfiguration does nothing to discredit the supplementary phrase which on other grounds we are inclining to add to the text of Mark xvi.

Last of all, we proposed to look for indications in St Mark's general attitude to his theme, a somewhat ill-defined line of enquiry. It may suffice to recall the parallel which we have shown to play so important a part in his mind, between the three days which bring the resurrection and the mysterious half-week which brings the Advent. Two things are notable; the resurrection of Jesus after his passion is seen as the type of, I would almost say, as the dynamic equivalent for, the advent which puts an end to the passion of the Church and raises the faithful dead. Then, second, the prophecy of the advent carries us no further than the very point at which the Son of Man sends out his angels to harvest his elect from the four winds. The whole mystery of the advent is treated as a single point which puts an end to the Church's terrible half-week. It will not be surprising, then, if the mystery of Christ's resurrection is similarly treated as a single point, one scene, one paragraph, putting an end to Christ's own passion by the assured evidence of his having risen. All in a moment we have the fact that death is dead, the presence of Christ's angel, the promise of the vision of the Son of Man, and the sending of the gospel of the four winds. And if in one aspect the sending out of the gospel is the type of the sending out of the harvesting angels on the last day, in another aspect it is the cause of it. Only when the gospel has been preached to all nations can the end come, says the apocalyptic prediction. But, when the gospel has covered the world, the end will come. And so the apostolic mission, seen as an omnipotent act, seen as the act of the risen Christ, an act divinely complete, is the end of the world. There is no more to be said.

Let us now turn to St Matthew. It is, of course, possible that St Matthew was dissatisfied altogether with St Mark's conclusion, cut it away, and dealt with the end of the narrative entirely in accordance with his own ideas. In that case our suggestion about St Mark's ending will gain neither confirmation nor correction from a study of St Matthew. If, on the other hand, St Mark as we reconstruct him appears to offer to St Matthew the very suggestions on which he acts in shaping his whole conclusion, that will be a positive confirmation of our hypothesis.

There is one point about St Matthew's ending which we may usefully consider first, its brevity. If it were true that St Matthew was entirely dissatisfied with St Mark's stopping-place and wished to do justice to the tradition of Christ's visits to his disciples after his resurrection, he would surely have written more, and on something like the scale adopted by St Luke. St Paul, our earliest authority, gives us a piece of catechism which he had himself been taught and which he handed on to others. Christ died for our sins according to the scriptures, he was buried and rose according to the scriptures, he showed himself to Peter, then to the Twelve (1 Cor. xv 3–5). There were other appearances of the risen Christ recorded, which St Paul adds by way of appendix to the catechetical form. If, then, St Matthew were deserting St Mark for common tradition, it is surprising that he should not even cover the items of the catechism by mentioning first the separate appearance to St Peter which St Luke does, of course, mention (xxiv 34). It is not, after all, as though St Matthew lacked interest in St Peter. On the contrary, we have seen that he was at pains to heighten the high position which St Peter already occupied in St Mark. The simplest explanation for St Matthew's short and formal account of the appearances of the risen Christ is that he is adhering to his role of amplifier and interpreter; that what controls him to the very end is the text he is paraphrasing. The text, that is to say, of St Mark.

Certainly St Matthew amplifies the Marcan conclusion, but he does not begin to do so when the women have fled from the tomb. He begins further back. The point to be marked is the moment of the Lord's death on the cross. From the resumption of narrative after the apocalyptic discourses up to the point of the Lord's death, the scale of St Matthew's account is the same as St Mark's. He makes only one considerable addition, the attempt of Judas to return the blood-money, and if that is counted out, the rest of the Matthaean story uses no appreciably greater number of words than the Marcan. From the moment of the Lord's death the scale changes completely; St Matthew almost doubles the rest of St Mark. He had been content, it would seem, with St Mark's story of the passion; he was discontented with his handling of the supernatural mysteries which furnish the conclusion. But his discontent took the form not of abandoning St Mark but of amplifying him. And the simplest hypothesis about St Matthew's last paragraph of all would be that it is part of the general amplification, not a sheer addition running clean beyond the limit of St Mark's story.

If we compare St Matthew's conclusion with St Mark's, just as they stand, we can say that St Matthew is so far faithful to his original, that the weight remains in the same place, that is, in the balance between two mighty events: Christ's spirit deserts his body, Christ's body deserts his tomb. Both events are perceived through signs only. The flight of the spirit is not literally visible, though there are witnesses standing by; the tokens of it are the rending of the temple veil at the passage of the spirit, and the body left empty of life after its passage. It may be that the flight of the body from its sepulchral prison would have been visible, but no witnesses saw it. The signs of it are the displacement of the stone and the tomb left empty of its occupant. Having given the same sort of account of Christ's resurrection as he had given of his death, St Mark fitly brought his gospel to an end, with a mere adumbration of the appearances of Christ to his disciples which would confirm his resurrection and signify his will. In St Matthew this adumbration takes on the solidity of narrative, and yet the weight remains where it was, in the mighty portents of the cross and the sepulchre.

Not only does St Matthew develop the two portents, he develops them in parallel. 'Jesus let out a loud cry and gave up the ghost; and the veil of the temple was rent in two from the top to the bottom. And when the centurion standing over against him saw that he gave up the ghost with such a cry, he said, Verily this man was the Son of God.' So writes St Mark. The portent was simply an indescribable cry which both rent the temple veil and went to the centurion's heart. Now hear St Matthew. 'Jesus cried again with a loud voice and gave up the ghost. And the veil of the temple was rent in two from the top to the bottom, the earth quaked, the rocks were rent, the tombs opened; and many bodies of sleeping saints arose, and entering the holy city after his resurrection appeared to many. And the centurion and those with him on guard over Jesus, seeing the earthquake and what befell, feared greatly, and said, Verily this was the Son of God.' The parallel with the portents on Easter morning is obvious. There too St Matthew adds to St Mark's story an earthquake, and a guard of armed men overcome with fear.

The extension of the armed guard from the cross to the sepulchre is a Matthaean addition which underlines a Marcan parallel. It also illustrates a Matthaean theme, bribery and corruption. Where St Mark had been content to say that Judas on his undertaking to betray Christ was promised a fee, St Matthew turns the whole episode into the story of a straight bargain on a cash-down basis. 'One of the twelve called Judas Iscariot went to the High Priests and said: What will you give me to betray him to you? And they weighed him out thirty pieces of silver.' St Matthew pursues the luckless history of the money in a paragraph strangely intruded between the delivery of Jesus to Pilate and his trial by Pilate. In a similar way the aftermath of the story of the guard, the bribing of them with the High Priest's money, is intruded between the scene at the sepulchre and the concluding scene at the mountain. The two intrusive narratives have identical conclusions. The money which Judas threw back at the priests was invested in a burial field for strangers, called *field of blood* to this day; the money the priests gave to the guards secured the dissemination of a lie among the Jews, current to this day.

Thus we see St Matthew consistently and characteristically enlarging his Marcan original with the sort of traditions that appealed to him. Another characteristic Matthaean enlargement is the appearance of Christ before the women's eyes to confirm the angel's message by his own word and by physical touch. 'They ran to bring his disciples word. And behold, Jesus met them, saying, All hail. And they came and took hold of his feet, and worshipped him. Then said Jesus unto them, Fear not; go tell my brethren that they depart into Galilee, there shall they see me.' This little scene offers a close parallel to St Matthew's addition to the story of the Transfiguration. The disciples are moved with fear at the voice from heaven, as are the women at the sepulchre by the angel's voice. But 'Jesus came and touched them, and said, Arise, be not afraid'. The general parallel between the Transfiguration and the vision at the sepulchre is, of course, strongly marked in all three synoptic evangelists. St Matthew's account of the walking on the water may also be drawn into the comparison. Peter, moved by the voice of Jesus seen like a ghost over the darkened water, walks to him and encounters him in flesh and blood. 'Jesus stretched forth his hand, and took hold of him, and saith unto him, Littlefaith, wherefore didst thou doubt?'

We see, then, that St Matthew's manner of building upon his Marcan original is much what we might expect up to the point where that original is preserved to us. We can no longer defer our leap into the hypothetical. Let us, then, boldly suppose that St Matthew had the following words before his eyes: 'They went out and fled from the tomb, for trembling and amazement possessed them; and they said nothing to anyone, for they were afraid. But Jesus sent forth his disciples to preach the gospel among all nations.' What is St Matthew to make of this? St Mark is drawing a contrast between the silence of the women and the preaching of the apostles. The witnesses to the empty tomb did not spread abroad the truth of the resurrection; the apostles were sent out by Jesus to do that. But does St Mark also mean that the women never even delivered their message to Peter and his colleagues? It is possible, but by no means clear that he means this; certainly there was no need for St Matthew so to understand him, and it would seem he did not. The women delivered their message, of course.

What appears to have impressed St Matthew is the general point, that the witnesses to the empty tomb did not proclaim what they knew. But he transfers the role of silent witness from the women to the guards. They were silenced, with a vengeance. As to the women, it was not to be expected that they would exceed their commission or turn aside from the carrying to the apostles of the angel's message.

The division of the women's part between the women and the guards can be observed throughout St Matthew's concluding paragraphs. In narrating the portent at the cross, St Mark mentions the centurion for the sake of his awestruck comment, and then goes on to tell us about the women who were watching. St Matthew tells us of the guard of soldiers, overcome with fear, and then of the women also watching. A paragraph further down it falls to him to describe the women sitting over against the sepulchre at the entombment of Christ, and he goes straight on to tell us how a guard was set and the sepulchre sealed. The women and the guard are both present at the apparition of the angel; and most of the fear attributed by St Mark to the women is transferred to the guard by St Matthew. 'For fear of him the watchers did quake, and became as dead men. And the angel said unto the women, Fear not *ye*' (the pronoun is emphatic in the Greek)—nor did they; or at least whatever fear they felt was of a quality which was compatible with 'great joy'. The women in their fear and joy run on their errand to the apostles, the terrified guards pull themselves together and return to their masters, their masters weight their tongues with gold.

So, by means of the two parties of witnesses, the women and the guards, St Matthew has covered the ground which St Mark covered with the party of women alone, and reaches the point, that 'nothing is said to anyone'. On the hypothesis we are considering, there remains of St Mark's text nothing but our reconstructed sentence, 'But Jesus sent forth his disciples to preach the gospel among all nations'. If that is what St Matthew read, we should expect him to do just what he has done, that is, to substitute a short scene for the bare statement. We have already observed such a substitution, when he supplies the dialogue between Judas and the priests at the selling of Jesus's life. There is another example a little earlier in the same chapter. 'When Jesus had finished all these words, he said to his disciples: Ye know that after two days the Passover cometh, and the Son of Man is delivered up to be crucified. Then were gathered together the chief priests and elders of the people into the court of the High Priest, who was called Caiaphas; and they took counsel together that they might take Jesus by subtlety, and kill him.' The Marcan original behind St Matthew's paragraph is the following sentence: 'It was passover and unleavened bread after two days, and the chief priests and scribes sought how they might take him by subtlety and kill him.'

As we might expect, St Matthew's amplification of the conclusion consists in a tissue of his most characteristic ideas and phrases;

none of the detail of it could conceivably be St Mark's as it stands. Just as the women deliver, according to St Matthew, the message which according to St Mark they receive, so those to whom the message is directed are credited by St Matthew with acting upon it. The disciples departed into Galilee; there it was that Jesus gave them his commission to preach the gospel among all nations, or rather, in Matthaean phrase, to *make disciples* of all nations, bidding them observe the prescriptions of the Sermon on the Mount.

We advance the hypothesis we have expounded as a tolerable alternative to the difficult but still attractive supposition that the Gospel ended with the words 'For they were afraid'. If the new hypothesis should be so happy as to seem preferable, then in the matter of endings the dividing line would run between St Matthew and St Luke, rather than between St Matthew and St Mark. St Matthew, we should hold, adheres essentially to the Marcan plan, as we might expect him to do, while St Luke breaks with it, as he could scarcely help doing in view of the fact that he was going on to a second book of divine history; he could not fore-shorten his first conclusion without confusing his second exordium. St John follows St Luke.

In discussing the patterns of the several narratives about the most momentous of all events it is difficult for a believing scholar not to sound more sceptical than he is. 'St Mark wrote thus, St Matthew makes such and such characteristic enlargements.' But where St Matthew so enlarges, there is no reason why he should not be drawing on traditions of fact; a characteristic way of building up narrative, and a certain range of personal interests in the choice of topic, are not irreconcilable with historical truth.

CHAPTER X

THE SERMON ON THE MOUNT

Our concern in this book is primarily with the structure of St Mark's Gospel, and with St Matthew in so far as his reconstructions throw light on what he reconstructs. And yet it seems a pity to make an end without attempting a sketch, however provisional, of St Matthew's architecture viewed in itself. And before we approach the larger question of his Gospel in general it will be well to take a more limited example. How did St Matthew build when he built freely, and not in reconstruction of any Marcan design? The Sermon on the Mount should give him space enough in which to show his hand.

The general shape of the Sermon is not evident at a first glance. What strikes us about it is the rigid formality of its several parts—the eight beatitudes, the six antitheses to the ancient law, the three meritorious works of almsgiving, prayer and fasting. We are naturally inclined to ask whether the formal organisation of the parts is not taken up into some sort of formally organised whole, even though we are as yet unable to see what it is. To read the Sermon on the Mount is to receive the impression that the author is exerting all his skill to present us with a systematic account of Christ's spiritual precepts. And with an author like St Matthew we expect a systematic account to be an account built up round some principle of formal arrangement.

If there is a model St Matthew is likely to have followed it is surely the law from the mountain in Exodus xx–xxiv. The most striking fact about the shape of that passage is that it consists of two parts unequal both in style and extent, the Decalogue, laying down the principles of duty in short precepts, and the Book of the Covenant, applying the principles more at large to the detail of human conduct. It is probable that there is a systematic relation between the Decalogue and the Book of the Covenant, the Covenant Laws being arranged under topics taken in order from the Ten Commandments.[1] But it is unnecessary to suppose that St Matthew had penetrated the principle of the arrangement. He would in any case regard the Covenant Laws as the exposition of the Decalogue, and if he constructed his own great Sermon on the

[1] The sequel to the great Decalogue (Ex. xx 22–xxiii 19) is the old ritual decalogue with a long 'ethical' insertion (xxi 1–xxiii 11) let into the middle of it. (An uninterpolated version appears in xxxiv 17–26). The first two clauses of the ritual decalogue are parallel to those of the great Decalogue (xx 22–23 = xx 1–6). In Exodus xxi the parallel is prolonged by the moving up of the Sabbath command from fifth to third place in the ritual decalogue, so as to keep in step with the second pair of clauses in the great Decalogue (honour the Name, keep the Sabbath). The ethical insertion in the ritual decalogue follows; it is packed into the middle of the Sabbath commandment, Sabbath being the only one of the ritual obligations which involves duty to one's neighbour (That the son of thy handmaid, and the stranger, may be refreshed, xxiii 12). So the ethical insertion works round from sabbath to sabbath, from the sabbath of service (xxi 1–11) to the sabbaths of cultivation and of labour (xxiii 10–12). What lies between the two sabbath paragraphs continues to keep in step with the clauses of the great Decalogue taken in pairs and handled in 'chiastic' order. Here, then, is the whole parallel from the beginning of the ritual decalogue to the end of the ethical insertion.

No gods beside me, no graven image.	xx 23	Ye shall not make with me gods of silver, gods of gold shall ye not make.
Hallow the Name, hallow the Sabbath.	xx 24–xxi 11	An altar for the Name. Sabbath of service, and kindred topics.
Honour thy parents, do no murder.	xxi 12–36	Law of murder and injury, with special mention of parents (15, 17)
No adultery,	xxii 1–15	Theft, property, restoration.
no theft.	xxii 16–20	Corruption of virgins, bestiality, etc.
No false witness, no coveting.	xxii 21–31	Oppression of poor, sharp practice, and withholding dues from God.
	xxiii 1–9	False report and judicial iniquity.

The taking of the Ten Commandments in pairs is the natural division—two commands against heathendom, two in honour of God, two against capital crimes, two against direct violations of property, two against crooked dealing. The parallel supplied by the sequel is not, of course, free from irrelevances; whoever arranged it was handling existing collections which he was not going to alter beyond a certain point.

I owe the substance of this footnote to Miss Aileen Guilding (Mrs Leon Mirsky). See her article in the *Journal of Theological Studies* for April 1948, p. 43.

scriptural model, he would, being himself a formalist in matters of arrangement, be inclined to make his second and longer part comment in some regular order on the contents of his first and shorter part. To speak with more particularity, what we have to expect is that the whole Sermon apart from the Beatitudes will turn out to be an orderly exposition or application of the Beatitudes.[1]

At this point in our argument we encounter an obstacle which makes us feel that fortune has been cruel to us. The Beatitudes are among the few paragraphs in St Matthew's Gospel of which the text is really uncertain. The majority of our MSS. place the blessing upon the meek third, but there is a Western-and-Syriac reading with good early patristic support which places it second. If we are interpreting the order of the Sermon by the order of the Beatitudes, it is vital that we should first make up our minds about the order of the Beatitudes themselves.

I shall argue in favour of the Western-and-Syriac order. If we wish to form an opinion about the probabilities of displacement one way or the other, the first factor to be taken into account is the influence of St Luke on the minds of copyists. The arrangement and development of the Matthaean series is somewhat subtle and elusive, whereas what St Luke has done is strikingly obvious and all the more likely for that reason to impress itself on the memory of the Christian scribe. He has selected four beatitudes which express (or, by a slight rewording, are brought to express) the contrast between present privation and future contentment. Beggars shall be kings, the hungry shall be filled, weepers shall laugh, the despised shall be rewarded. With such a model in his mind, the copyist of Matthew would be inclined to pass direct from the blessing on the poor (in spirit) to the next blessing on apparent misery, the promise of comfort to those who mourn. Finding in the process of revision that

[1] For beatitudes as such we must look to the New Law within the Law (Deut. xxviii, cf. xxiii), not to the Old (Exodus). The Evangelist's point will presumably be that the place occupied by prohibitions in the old law is occupied by blessings in the new. The antitheses of Matt. v 21-48 have a close though not an exact relation to the Decalogue.

he had omitted the blessing on the meek, he would add it in the margin and the next copyist might then replace it incorrectly in the text.

But the principal argument in favour of the Western reading is its intrinsical merit.

(a) It gives us a gradual transition of form from the first beatitude to its successors. All the beatitudes from the third (by this reckoning) to the seventh have the common form: 'Blessed (are) the . . . for they shall be . . .'. The verb always stands last and is always of passive form, even where the sense is active (Blessed are the pure in heart, for God shall they behold, ὄψονται). We are brought up with a jolt, and realise that the series is at an end, when the eighth and last beatitude abandons the form of the previous five and returns to that of the first: 'Blessed (are) the . . . for theirs is the kingdom of heaven.' Now the blessing on the meek has a form midway between the form of the first beatitude and that common to the third and its four successors. It resembles the first in ending with a noun ('kingdom of heaven'—'earth') but it resembles the third in substituting 'they shall' for 'theirs is'; it does not, however, come so close to it as to employ a passive verb or to place the verb at the end. If, then, we accept the Western reading, we can see the form of the beatitude steadily developing until it reaches in the third the shape which it retains:

Blessed (are) the poor in spirit, for theirs is the kingdom of heaven.
Blessed (are) the meek, for they shall inherit the earth.
Blessed (are) the mourners, for they shall be comforted.

(b) The sense of the Western reading is as satisfactory as the sound. The first principle of interpretation is to take the text as it comes. We do not know whether our author foresees how he means to proceed next; we are content to see him build his present sentence on the sentences preceding it. St Matthew writes down one beatitude, and adds another to it. The sense is perfect; we have a self-contained couplet.

Blessed are the poor in spirit for theirs is the kingdom of heaven,
Blessed are the meek for they shall inherit the earth.

The blessed future to which the Gospel looks forward is an empire of heaven exercised upon a regenerated earth. Those in whom the powers and privileges of the heavenly kingdom are vested are those who will inherit or possess the earth. In so far as the kingdom of heaven is anticipated in the Church, St Peter receives the keys of the kingdom of heaven, with the result that what he binds or looses upon earth is bound or loosed in heaven, that is, by divine decree (xvi 19, cf. xviii 18). Or again, we are to pray our Father in heaven that his kingdom and his will may take effect on earth as in heaven (vi 9–11). Such a way of thinking is evidently familiar to St Matthew.

'Poor in spirit' is an expression with a wide range of possible meanings; it receives definition from 'meek'. One characteristic, anyhow, of the spirit or attitude of the poor is that they cannot afford to be impatient or overbearing. And so the whole couplet can be read as a hendiadys, and put together into a single sentiment: 'Blessed are those who share the meekness of the poor, for they shall be clothed with the majesty of heaven and take possession of the earth.'

The beatitudes anyhow contain one undeniable couplet, 'Blessed are the pure in heart, for they shall behold God: Blessed are the peacemakers, for they shall be called sons of God.' If the Western reading is right, they contain three, for according to that reading the initial couplet is followed by another. 'Blessed are the mourners for they shall be comforted: blessed are those that hunger and thirst after righteousness, for they shall be filled.' This couplet expresses the direct relief of distress by the condition opposite to it. The first couplet has no such form. It does not say 'Blessed are the poor in spirit for they shall be enriched', nor 'blessed are the meek for they shall be emboldened'. It is only the third and fourth beatitudes that are phrased in such a way. The fifth deviates again. It does not say 'Blessed are the pitiable, for they shall be pitied' but 'Blessed are the pitiful . . .'. It places the character of the blessed in direct relation to the Divine Nature and so serves as a transition to the following couplet: 'Blessed are the pure in heart, for they shall behold God: blessed are the peacemakers for they shall be called sons of God.'

So according to the Western reading the Beatitudes consist of three couplets, with a transitional line between the second and third and a concluding line harking back to the form of the first. For ease of reference we might say 'Three couplets, the first simple, the second and third each having an additional line attached to them'. But if the Beatitudes fall thus into three divisions, so does the main body of the Sermon. Discounting for the moment certain transitional passages, we readily distinguish two formal units, Christ's interpretation of the commandments (v 17–48) and Christ's interpretation of the three meritorious works (vi 1–18). There remains a third portion of which the structure and the boundaries are less easy to define, culminating in the parable of the houses on rock and on sand (vii 24–27).

The exposition of the three couplets may be looked for in the three parts of the Sermon, but in reverse order, the third couplet in the first part, the second in the second and the first in the third. To put it pictorially, the Sermon crawls backwards up the list of Beatitudes. Such a procedure would surprise us in a modern author, but in an ancient author it should not. For it is only an extension of the familiar arrangement called Chiasmus.[1] Where we say 'A and B; A, that is to say X; B, that is to say Y' the ancients often preferred to say 'A and B; B, that is to say Y; A, that is to say X'. The principle of such an arrangement was that you went on from the place where you were when you began your exposition, instead of jumping back.

A striking and incontestable parallel to the suggested procedure is to be found in the Messages to the Seven Churches. The Messages are an exposition of the Candlestick-Vision on which they hang. In the Vision we read the following texts in order:

(a) One like a son of man . . . his eyes as flaming fire and his feet like burnished brass, Rev. i 13–15.

(b) And out of his mouth a sharp two-edged sword proceeding, i 16.

[1] For *stylistic* chiasmus see N. W. Lund, *Chiasmus in the N.T.* (1942).

(c) I am the first and the last and the living, and I was dead and lo am alive, i 17–18.

(d) The secret of the seven stars thou sawest at my right hand and the seven golden candlesticks, i 20.

The exposition starts where the text of the vision leaves off. To Ephesus St John is directed to write:

(d) Thus saith the holder of the seven stars in his right hand, who walks among the seven golden candlesticks, ii 1.

To Smyrna:

(c) Thus saith the first and the last who was dead and lived, ii 8.

To Pergamus:

(b) Thus saith he who hath the sharp two-edged sword, ii 12.

And to Thyatira:

(a) Thus saith the Son of God who hath his eyes as flaming fire and his feet like burnished brass, ii 18.

The remaining three messages form their titles on the first three and not on the vision, but that is a complication which need not detain us.

A similar but less elaborate example is St Luke's treatment of the temptations in the wilderness and of their direct sequel (iv 1–v 11). Jesus is tempted

(a) to provide himself bread by miracle

(b) to submit to Satan

(c) to throw himself from the temple and force the hand of God.

The sequel shows how

(c) his townsmen attempt to throw Jesus over a cliff and he departs unscathed.

(b) Jesus rebukes and expels Satan in the synagogue at Capernaum and at the door of Simon's house.

(a) Jesus supplies Simon with a miraculous catch of fish.[1]

[1] The hint for antitheses to the temptations is already to be found in St Matthew. Christ refused to demand that stones should be made bread for him, but when the temptations were finished angels came and supplied his needs. St Luke drops the rudimentary antithesis here, to make room for his full three-fold antithesis: he finds a place for the ministering angel on the occasion of Christ's supreme temptation in the Garden (xxii 43), when the tempter who 'left him for a season' in iv 13 must be deemed to have returned (xxii 31, 40,

The reader can study for himself what rearrangements and what introductions of fresh matter it costs St Luke, to obtain this symmetrical result. We will return to St Matthew.

After the eighth beatitude the exposition starts from the point reached. Jesus turns to his disciples and applies the blessing on the persecuted to them. 'Blessed are ye, when men reproach you and persecute you . . . Ye are the salt of the earth . . . Ye are the light of the world.' But the persecuted whose is the kingdom of heaven must be persecuted for righteousness. The demands of the law stand fast and he who looses any least commandment shall be called least in the kingdom of heaven, he who upholds it shall be called great. Except their righteousness exceed that of scribes and Pharisees, the disciples of Jesus shall not enter the kingdom of heaven.

The examples which show how Jesus tightens the law then follow, and in developing them the Sermon expounds the last couplet of the Beatitudes, 'Blessed are the pure in heart for they shall see God, blessed are the peacemakers for they shall be called sons of God.' It is not enough to keep the law against murder in the letter, the whole of our conduct must show a heart free from malice. We should *make peace* with our adversary ourselves and not let his complant against us come into court. It is not enough to abstain from adultery; we must not lust even in *our heart*. Absolute purity of the lips is required in the matter of oaths and asseverations, absolute peaceableness in face of the exactions or the hostility of other men, *that we may be the sons of our Father in heaven*, and perfect as he is perfect.

So much for the interpretation of the law. The Sermon passes on to the three works of merit, and the first of them, almsgiving, or, as it is in the Greek, (work of) *mercy*, brings us to the transitional line between the second couplet and the third, 'Blessed are the merciful, for mercy shall be shewn them.' Only, however, if they set their minds on that divine reward and exclude all others.

46). The angel of Gethsemane, 'putting strength into him,' and the angels of St Mark and St Matthew whose ministry supports a forty days' fast, both equally reflect I Kings xix 8. For St Luke's threefold antithesis to the temptations, compare his fourfold antithesis to the beatitudes.

If they attract attention to their works of mercy and enjoy the reputation of them, they have no reward with their Father in heaven.

The second good work, prayer, belongs to the list of meritorious acts which the Evangelist is following, but falls outside the scope of the Beatitudes. It is all the more remarkable that the end of the paragraph devoted to it should be pulled round into line with 'Blessed are the merciful for they shall be shewn mercy'. 'Forgive us our debts, as we have forgiven our debtors. . . . For if ye forgive men their trespasses, your heavenly Father will forgive you, but if ye forgive not men their trespasses, neither will your heavenly Father forgive your trespasses.' Mercy in the sense of 'alms' has two branches, positive and negative: the positive consists in the uncovenanted relief of distress, the negative in the renunciation of covenants by which the poor are bound to pay us. The lesson which the Sermon here picks out of the Lord's Prayer is exactly illustrated in the parable of the indebted creditor. The servant should have had *mercy* on his fellow servant, as his master had *mercy* on him (xviii 33).

The third good work, fasting, makes an application of the second couplet: 'Blessed are the mourners, for they shall be comforted, blessed are the hungry and thirsty for righteousness, for they shall be filled.' The fasting Jew not only hungered, he also observed the outward signs of mourning. Jesus requires that the mourning should be inward only. 'Be not as the hypocrites of a melancholy countenance . . . Anoint your head and wash your face.'

The first couplet finds its application in a paragraph which generalises the lesson of the three good works and especially of almsgiving. In all our deeds we are to renounce visible present rewards and lay up merit in secret with our Father in heaven; in fact to treasure not treasures of earth, but treasures in heaven (vi 19–21). The Beatitude has promised the meek the mastery of earth, but the meek do not obtain by direct acquisition; they are no other than the poor in spirit, who receive the royalty of heaven by contempt of earthly wealth. These are the heirs of all things on a regenerated earth. To those who seek first the kingdom of their heavenly Father and his righteousness all earthly necessities will be added (vi 19–34).

The exposition of the Beatitudes has covered 72 verses additional to the Beatitudes themselves, and we might be inclined to write off the remaining 27 as appended exhortations rounding the sermon off. Such an account would square well enough with vii 7–27. These verses could fairly be described as a peroration. But vii 1–5 and 6, 'Judge not' and 'Give not that which is holy to the dogs', are new and particular topics and no parts of a general conclusion. Moreover the sequence of thought in this whole region (vi 34–vii 7) is more puzzling than anything else in the Sermon, and we should welcome any light obtainable from a further consideration of the Matthaean method of following set lists.

The list with which we have to do once the Beatitudes are finished is supplied by the clauses of the Lord's Prayer. The Prayer has slipped in unobtrusively in a sort of appendix (vi 7–15) to the paragraph on the second good work. Once established on the page, it exercises on the sequel all that influence which intrinsically belongs to it.

Before we can see how the Lord's Prayer fits into the Sermon we must observe the relation in which it stands to the Beatitudes. It is better not to invoke coincidence too often, so we will suppose one formula to have been arranged on the actual model of the other. The Matthaean arrangement of Christ's Beatitudes is presumably the Evangelist's own, to judge from St Luke's freedom in making a different arrangement; whereas we take the Lord's Prayer to have been already fixed in liturgical use. So we may suppose the Beatitudes to follow the Prayer, and not *vice versa*. We need not exclude from the Beatitudes the influence of all other principles of arrangement, but in so far as they follow the Prayer they do so by promising to appropriate sorts of recipients the boons for which the Prayer asks. It will be convenient to put the correspondences in a table (see next page).

As to the blanks on either side, that in the Prayer contains the sole petition which cannot be construed as invoking a boon on

Our Father which art in heaven, ... thy kingdom come	Blessed are the poor in spirit, for theirs is the kingdom of heaven.
Thy will be done as in heaven, so on earth	Blessed are the meek, for they shall inherit the earth ...
Give us this day tomorrow's bread	Blessed are they that hunger and thirst after righteousness, for they shall be filled.
And forgive us our debts, as we also forgive our debtors	Blessed are the merciful, for they shall obtain mercy; ... blessed are the peacemakers, for they shall be called sons of God.
And lead us not into temptation, but deliver us from the Wicked.	Blessed are the persecuted for righteousness, for theirs is the kingdom of heaven.

mankind. To pray for the advent of God's kingdom and the fulfilment of his will on earth is not a self-regarding request: but the advent of the kingdom will nevertheless enthrone the saints. The hallowing of the Name carries no such implication with it. The two blanks on the other side are less surprising, since on any shewing the Beatitudes enlarge upon the Pater Noster. So the filling of the hungry is built up into a couplet by the prefixing of the comforting of the mournful, and the blessings on those who imitate the divine nature are enriched by the naming of those who by purity of heart merit the vision of God. That only those who are like him can see him as he is, is cited as an axiom by St John (I Joh. iii 2).[1]

If any part of the parallel seems forced it is likely to be the last line. Persecution is not the only trial with which Satan assaults us. But that it is the typical trial is almost a New Testament commonplace, and the first apparent quotation of the end of the Lord's Prayer in surviving literature is St Mark's record of Christ's word to his disciples under the threat of arrest and execution, 'Wake and pray that ye enter not into temptation'. When St Matthew reaches Gethsemane he transcribes what St Mark has written (xxvi 41).

The text of the Prayer makes its appearance in a passage (vi

[1] St John continues: 'And everyone who has this hope in Him purifies himself, as He is pure'.

1–18) where St Matthew is illustrating the Beatitudes with the aid of a conventional list of three pious works. The first and third of the three fit the Beatitudes well enough, but the second, prayer, is unrepresented in any of the eight. St Matthew is all the more fortunate to be able to strengthen the topic with the Lord's Prayer, considered as a prayer, and therefore in its entirety. But he draws out and emphasises that petition to which properly corresponds the Beatitude he is preaching upon in this place. 'Blessed are the merciful for they shall obtain mercy'—'Forgive us our debts as we forgive our debtors'.

Having reunited the Prayer to the Beatitudes at a natural point of contact the Evangelist does not disjoin them again. When in vi 19–34 he moves up into the first couplet of the Beatitudes he moves up at the same time into the first clauses of the Prayer. 'Our Father which art in heaven, hallowed be thy Name, thy kingdom come, thy will be done as in heaven, so on earth'—'Lay not up treasures on earth . . . but in heaven . . . Seek first the kingdom of your heavenly Father and his righteousness, and all these (earthly) things shall be added unto you' (vi 19, 21, 33).

In thus adjusting the earthly to the heavenly the paragraph we are considering draws in the next clause of the Prayer also, 'Give us this day tomorrow's bread'. We are to leave the care of food and raiment to God, God who feeds the ravens and who clothes with glory the grass of the field, flourishing today and tomorrow cast into the oven. 'Care not for the morrow, for the morrow shall be careful of its own; sufficient to the day is its evil.' That is the last word of the paragraph and prefaces a direct transition to the next clause of the Prayer.

We have already read a straightforward exposition of 'Forgive us our debts as we forgive our debtors' (vi 14–15). What meets us in vii 1–5 is a variant form of the same idea—indeed the variation is slight. 'Judge not and you will not be judged' is scarcely to be separated from 'Let off, and you will be let off'. The figure hardly differs, for he who enforces a debt invokes legal sanction. The Sermon has already reminded us that it is by appeal to the judge that the creditor exacts the last farthing (v 25–26). The application scarcely differs either. 'Not judging' merely carries into the provinces of speech and thought what 'letting off' signifies in the province of conduct.

If we are using the Lord's Prayer as a text on which to hang a general catechism, special importance attaches to the words 'As we forgive our debtors'. For it is on these words that our whole duty to our neighbour must be made to depend. To use the Prayer is to make the reception of the blessings for which it prays dependent on two conditions: That we should ask, for otherwise why pray at all? and that we should allow to our fellow men what we demand of God. Pray instantly, and do as you would be done by. Pray—it is a divine principle which we ourselves should follow, not to throw holy things away on dogs; yet the undeterred importunity of the 'dog' showed her to be no dog at all, but worthy of the children's bread. God feeds his children if they ask—why, even men do that. Since God will not deny, be not slack to qualify. Work for others whatever good you desire yourself to receive, that is the Law and the Prophets; otherwise put, that is the signpost to heaven.

That is the Law, and the prophetic comment on the Law, interpreted as the Sermon has interpreted it, following the narrow 'way' (i.e. *halacha,* interpretation) which seeks the particular pleasure of God, not the broad 'way' which leaves open to our own pleasure as much as the letter will allow. The narrow way is the way we seek, our prayers knock at the narrow gate, here runs the high road into the kingdom of heaven; and they are all false prophets who claim to direct us but fail to qualify by well-doing. Only those who do the will of their heavenly Father as Christ's words express it will see the kingdom of heaven or endure the winds and waters of that trial against which the last words of the Pater Noster direct us to pray.

It is, then, the Lord's Prayer which gives shape to the end of the Sermon; the Lord's Prayer and something else besides. In paraphrasing vii 6–11 just above we made an inevitable allusion to the Marcan episode of the children's crumbs given to the dogs; but the whole parallel with the Marcan text is far more extensive, and

stretches from Mk. vi 30 to viii 38. What appears to happen is that
in recording Christ's warning against anxiety over bread and his
exhortation to trust in providential care the Evangelist remembers
how the disciples had worried about the hungry crowd in the
wilderness, and how the prayer of Christ had provided for them
(Mark vi 35–44, 52). On returning from the wilderness Jesus was
met by Pharisees who condemned his disciples for a trifling breach
of pious custom, thereby laying themselves open to the more
serious counter-charge that they were breaking the law itself
(Mark vii 1–13). There is no single episode in the Gospel which
more exactly illustrates the next paragraph of the Sermon on the
Mount—'Judge not, and ye shall not be judged. . . . Why beholdest
thou the mote that is in thy brother's eye, but considerest not the
beam in thine own eye?' (vii 1–5). The parallel continues. The
next episode in St Mark (vii 24–30) shows us Jesus refusing the
'children's bread', that is, the holy things of Israel, to the 'dogs',
but allowing himself to be overcome by the importunity of faith.
Without the aid of the Marcan parallel we might even fail to grasp
the connexion between St Matthew's two themes, 'Give not that
which is holy unto the dogs . . .' and 'Ask and it shall be given
you. . . . What men is there of you who, if his son asks him for
bread will give him stone?' (vii 6–11). The Syrophoenician
woman in Mark vii 24–30 is as one who asks for bread for her
child, but those who, in the next episode (vii 31–37), commend
their friend to Christ ask for the unsealing of his ears: 'Effatha, Be
thou opened' says Jesus. In the Matthaean sermon the request for
opening is coupled with the request for bread. 'Ask and it shall be
given you, seek and ye shall find, knock and it shall be opened
unto you. For every one that asks receives and that seeks finds and
to him that knocks it shall be opened. Or what man of you, if his
son asks bread of him. . . .'

St Mark proceeds to the feeding of the four thousands. The
theme does but repeat the feeding of the five, with which the
parallel we are studying began. But as Jesus and his disciples are
returning by boat after the second feeding, he has occasion to say
to them 'Beware of the leaven of the Pharisees and the leaven of

Herod' (viii 15). 'Beware of false prophets' says the Sermon on the Mount (vii 15). St Mark passes through the episode of the blind man, to which St Matthew has already done justice (the lamp of the body is the eye, vi 22 ff. Why beholdest thou the mote . . . vii 3 ff.) and so arrives at Caesarea Philippi. As they were in the way Jesus asked them the question which led to the revelation of the cross and of the paradox, 'He who will save his life ($\psi\nu\chi\acute{\eta}$) shall lose ($\dot{\alpha}\pi o\lambda\acute{\epsilon}\sigma\epsilon\iota$) it, he who loses his life for my sake . . . shall gain it.' In the Sermon on the Mount we have not yet reached the time for the full revelation of so high a mystery, but we can learn about the narrow way which leads to life ($\zeta\omega\acute{\eta}$) and the broad way which leads to loss or perdition ($\dot{\alpha}\pi\acute{\omega}\lambda\epsilon\iota\alpha$), vii 13–14.

The error of St Peter at Caesarea Philippi shows that it is not enough to confess the Lord, it is necessary to accept his astonishing demands (to take up the cross). 'He that disowns me' (says Christ) 'in this disloyal and offending generation, him shall the Son of Man disown when he comes in the glory of his Father.' Peter has said 'Lord, Lord' (the Sermon seems to reflect) but he must be true to his name and build his house not on the sand of profession but on the rock of performance. 'Many shall say to me in that day, Lord, Lord . . . and I will declare to them, I never knew you' (that is, the Son of Man will disown them). 'Everyone then who hears these words of mine and does them shall be likened unto a wise man that built his house on the rock' ($\pi\acute{\epsilon}\tau\rho\alpha$).

In due course St Matthew comes to give his own version of the events described in Mark vi–viii. When he does so, he very naturally comes under the influence of what he has himself written down in the Sermon on the Mount; he not only reproduces, but strengthens and extends the parallel to the Sermon already present in his Marcan original. He omits (for various reasons) two Marcan paragraphs of which the first, the Effatha healing, supplies the Sermon with (at the most) a word, 'opening', and the second, the blind man, supplies it with nothing at all. He strengthens the parallel between the story of the Pharisees who condemn and are condemned, and the relevant paragraph of the Sermon, in two particulars: by introducing the accusation 'hypocrites' and by describing as blind guides of the blind these men with the beam in their eye (xv 7, 14). The warning against the leaven of the Pharisees is brought into closer similarity with the warning against false prophets, by the explicit statement that the leaven is (false) teaching (xvi 12) and by the coupling of 'Pharisees' not with 'Herod' who was no sort of teacher, but with 'Sadducees', who were a rabbinacal sect. But more striking is the development of the parallel between the episode at Caesarea Philippi and the conclusion of the Sermon through the addition of the blessing upon Peter, the rock on whom the Church of Christ is founded and over whom the abyss shall never close its gates (xvi 18).

We have said above that St Matthew not merely strengthens the parallel, he also extends it. For in his arrangement the parabolic discourses (xiii 1–52) are brought into close neighbourhood with the feeding of the five thousand (xiv 13–21) which begins the Marcan parallel. Now the Marcan material in the parabolic discourses already provides the warning against worldly care or worry (μέριμνα) and the deceiveableness of riches (Mk. iv 18–19, Matt. xiii 22), a warning which the Sermon reflects in the first of the paragraphs we have to consider (vi 19–34). St Matthew adds to his Marcan borrowings a parable of his own, treasure hid in the field. The treasure of this parable stands for that treasure in heaven which is well purchased at the expense of all our worldly wealth and on which the heart should be set (vi 19–21, xiii 44). He follows it with an equivalent parable, the pearl of great price, which reminds us of a later text in the Sermon, and of what not to cast before swine (xiii 45, vii 6). We may say, then, that St Matthew extends the Marcan parallel to the Sermon by adding the parabolic discourses in front of it.

We have digressed somewhat from our original line of enquiry; it is difficult in this type of investigation to know where to stop. Even now we have by no means dealt with all the influences which go to shape the Sermon on the Mount; the allusion, for example, which shows Christ's first discourse to be a continuation of the preaching of the Baptist (iii 8–10, vii 16–20). But we will draw the line here and summarise our conclusions. The Sermon on the Mount is built round four formulae—the eight Beatitudes, the six antitheses, the three works of merit, and the Lord's Prayer. But the four formulae are not all handled in the same way. The antitheses and the works of merit are expounded one by one, as they are stated. The Beatitudes and the Pater Noster are stated as continuous texts and expounded afterwards. If we ask, 'Where is the form of the Sermon? we can see the form of the chapter of antitheses, or of the chapter on good works; but where is the form of the Sermon?' the answer is that the form of the Sermon has been stated in the beginning of it, for the Beatitudes have been stated. That is the answer, or anyhow it is the chief part of the answer. The Evangelist sets out as though to write in exposition of the Beatitudes, ascending from the last to the first. But near the top of the Beatitudes he joins the Pater Noster, and when he has reached the top he descends again, this time taking the parallel stair which the Pater Noster provides.

Whether he is following the Beatitudes or the Pater Noster, the Evangelist is never content with a single form to expound. He has his main form, but he introduces subsidiary forms. He expounds the Beatitudes in terms of the antitheses and the good works; he expounds the Lord's Prayer with the aid of a series of topics from a long passage in St Mark.

Being, as I trust I may call myself, a believing Christian, I take the Sermon on the Mount to be a tissue of Christ's spiritual teaching. But if our analyses are right the tissue was woven in one piece throughout by the Evangelist himself on the frames which they disclose. Leave out from any part of the discourse the framework which is inseparable from the construction of the whole, and see what you have left. Nothing, surely, that has the continuity of a literary source or of a set repetition extending into a catechism. There is no way of disproving that the Evangelist knew or used other men's set pieces, but if he did he handled them with such mastery that the attempt to reconstruct them from his work must be utterly vain. That Q or M or any other shadowy anonymity stands behind his shoulder can be no more than a pious opinion to which neither substance nor detail can ever be given.

CHAPTER XI

ST MATTHEW'S GREAT DISCOURSES

We are now to attempt the general pattern of St Matthew's book. We must take our start from the principal framework into which all subsidiary frames are fitted; and since we have several times already taken it for granted that such a framework is constituted by the series of great discourses, it is high time that we examined our assumption.

In the passages to which we refer we have been content to speak of a fivefold arrangement as imposed by the Evangelist on the material of his Gospel. Such a way of speaking was sufficiently accurate for the purposes we had in hand, but if we wish actually to understand the working of St Matthew's mind it is at least an even chance that we shall find it necessary to count one more term into the series and to speak not of a Matthaean Pentateuch but of a Matthaean Hexateuch. That is to say, that St Matthew did not arrange his Gospel in antitype to 'Moses' (the first five books of the Bible) but in antitype to 'Moses and Jesus' (the first six).

It must be agreed that there is a strong antecedent probability that a writer of Jewish education will use the Pentateuch by itself as his basis and not add any book or books to it. For in Jewish eyes the five books of Moses were a closed canon; Joshua was not the sixth book of the Bible but the first book of a second canon, the Prophets, of which the function was to illuminate the Law. And so for a Jewish author to take the five books of Moses and the book of Joshua as his model might seem to be much what it would be for a Christian author of later date to take the twelve Minor Prophets and the First Gospel as his.

We must concede that the very idea of adding 'Jesus' to 'Moses' is an innovation only possible to a Christian; but then the Matthaean writer was a Christian. In Christian eyes it could never seem an accident that Moses the lawgiver of the old dispensation was forbidden to complete his own work and that 'Jesus' completed it. The 'Jesus' of the Old Covenant is, indeed, a mere shadow compared with Moses, but the Christians know what he foreshadows and so their Pentateuch can become a hexateuch. The most successful argument sprung by Justin on Trypho the Jew is the place of the name of Jesus in the Old Testament.

It is an acknowledged fact about St Matthew that he used and was much influenced by Ecclesiasticus, and the fact is of double interest in the present connexion. For it shows to begin with the attractive power of the name of Jesus in the title of a book. Ecclesiasticus is 'the wisdom of Jesus son of Sirach'. Then, in the second place, Ben Sirach glorifies his name-saint the Son of Nun (xlvi 1–10), making a play on his name (ibid. 1) which St Matthew reproduces (i 21) and emphasising his role as fulfiller of Moses's work. Ben Sirach's catalogue of heroes runs on without a break from Moses and Aaron in the Torah to 'Jesus' in the prophets, which shows that such continuity was possible; and not only that it was possible, but that St Matthew had it in front of his eyes, for he knew Ben Sirach's book.

The Author to the Hebrews was roughly contemporary with St Matthew and he, like Ben Sirach and like the writer of I Maccabees (ii 52–60) compiles a list of heroes (xi). There is a notable division in his list at the beginning of xi 32, between those who receive particular and orderly mention and those who are lumped together for lack of time. The cut is made not at the end of the Torah but at the end of Joshua. And this is the more remarkable because the name of 'Jesus' (Joshua) is kept out, to avoid an anticipation of the climax in xii 2, 'looking unto Jesus the captain and fulfiller of faith' (Joshua had been the captain and fulfiller of the conquest to which the faith of the patriarchs aspired). But even though the name of Jesus cannot appear in the body of the list, it is still apparently necessary for the detailed story to embrace the matter of the 'Book of Jesus' and to cite such curious instances of faith as the fall of the walls of Jericho and the meritorious treason of Rahab the harlot. In mere fact, then, Hebrews xi 2–31 takes a 'Moses-and-Jesus', or hexateuchal, basis, which squares with the 'Moses and Jesus' typology of Hebr. iii–iv.

In spite of the misleading title by which his anonymous epistle has become known, the Author to the Hebrews was admittedly a less Jewish figure than the author of St Matthew. The Matthaean writer has one foot in the Aramaic world, the Author to the Hebrews has both his feet planted on Hellenistic Judaism and the Septuagint. Whether either, both, or neither of these writers were circumcised Jews we shall never know, and to try to bring their work under a simple distinction between what a Jew might say and what a Greek might say is plainly ridiculous. St Matthew felt a pull towards 'Law-and-Prophets' thinking which the Author to the Hebrews did not perhaps equally feel (cf. Matt. v 17, vii 12, xxii 40).[1] But who is to say that no pull in the other direction could be strong enough ever to prevail with the Evangelist? He read the LXX, he used Ecclesiasticus, he was a Christian. It is open to us to enquire without prejudice whether he took a 'Moses' basis or a 'Moses and Jesus' basis for his narrative.

The 'Moses' theory is widely held, but it runs into two principal difficulties. First, it has to allow an epilogue to the five Matthaean books (xxvi–xxviii), itself as long as most of them, so that St Matthew in fact wrote in six roughly equal parts, not in five. A second difficulty is that the five books do not square with Moses's five item by item; the first is not a Genesis nor the second an Exodus, and so with the rest.

The observation on which the whole theory is based is that five of Christ's principal discourses in this Gospel end with a rubric, 'And it came to pass when Jesus had finished these words, parables, or commands to his disciples, that . . .'. In the three middle cases the 'that' clause describes a change of place on Christ's part (xi 1, xiii 53, xix 1) and this appears to be no more than a development of the first case (vii 28–viii 1) where the 'that' clause expresses a com-

---

[1] These phrases belong to St Matthew's reports of Christ's teaching in the days of his earthly ministry. St Matthew had a firm grasp on the truth that the earthly ministry was for the Jews, but that after the Resurrection the mission went to the world. If St Matthew made a full use of his own Aramaic memories in setting forth the Lord's teaching he was only shewing his good sense. It does not at all follow that the balance between Aramaic and Grecian elements in his own mind corresponded to the balance between them in the Gospel discourses, nor that he would see fit to make the whole frame of the Gospel as 'Aramaic' as the discourses it contains.

ment of the people on the words of Jesus, but the next thing that actually happens is a change of place on his part (he descends from the mountain). Of the discourses which thus terminate, the first and last (v–vii, xxiv–xxv) are much the longest continuous speeches which the Gospel contains, while of the remaining three (x, xiii, xviii) each is longer and more systematic than any piece in its own neighbourhood. So we may say that St Matthew has striped his narrative with five notable stripes, and has made the latter edge of each stripe especially sharp by means of the formal rubric terminating it.

From the fact that the latter edges rather than the former edges of the stripes are thus emphasised, the inference has been drawn that in the Evangelist's mind the stripes are felt to terminate whole sections at the ends of which they stand. So, instead of the analysis

i–iv   (unstriped)
v–vii   (first stripe)
viii–ix (unstriped)
x   (second stripe)

is substituted the analysis

i–vii   book 1
viii–x book 2, etc.

Such an analysis represents, perhaps, a fair guess, but by no means a necessary conclusion. For though it is the ends of the 'stripes' which are marked by an identical formula, it is not true that the beginnings of them are any less emphasised; monotony is not the only form of emphasis. Since it is rightly held that St Matthew is a liturgical book designed for lectionary use, let us take an example from the liturgical field. At the end of every lesson in the English daily offices we use an invariable conclusion, 'Here endeth the first (second) lesson', for when we have had it we have had it and that is all that needs to be said. But at the beginning we use a form of particular announcement, specifying book, chapter and verse, because we want to know what it is that we are going to hear. St Matthew would not have given his readers or hearers much assistance if he had introduced the great discourses with an invariable formula like 'Now it came to pass after these things, that Jesus opened his mouth and taught them, saying . . .'.

The introductions of the five speeches are, if we examine them, striking enough. Jesus calls the four disciples from their nets and, in response to the needs of a great multitude drawn from all Palestine, ascends the Mountain and takes his seat; his disciples come about him and he opens his mouth and gives them the truth which the multitudes require, the Sermon on the Mount (iv 18– v 2). Faced with a similar concourse of people, Jesus takes the next step, and sends his disciples as labourers into the harvest, calling together the Twelve, who are named, and addressing to them his missionary precepts (ix 35–x 5). In xiii 1–3 Jesus arranges a vast out-of-door synagogue with a boat for his *cathedra* and addresses his parables to the people, expounding them to his disciples privately in answer to their direct questions (xiii 10–18, 34–36). The two remaining discourses are given in formal answer to questions of the disciples on points of general doctrine: 'Who then is great in the Kingdom of heaven?' and 'How oft shall my brother sin against me and I forgive him?' (xviii 1, 21); 'Tell us, when shall these things be, and what is the sign of thy coming and of the end of the world?' (xxiv 3). We shall hardly find such formal questions asked by the disciples elsewhere in St Matthew.

Since the introductions of the five speeches are no less formal than their conclusions, we have no ground for regarding them as ends to books rather than beginnings, and it seems safest to say that the Gospel is striped with them, and divided by the stripes into six remaining pieces, i–iv, viii–ix, xi–xii, xiv–xvii, xix–xxiii, and xxvi–xxviii.

Such a description can be no more than provisional, for the Evangelist cannot have striped his book for the sake of striping it. The stripes either carry some further meaning in themselves or they are incidental to the execution of some further design. In pursuit of this question it may be useful to ask, At what point in the narrative did the Evangelist expect his readers to become aware of what he was doing? They could scarcely begin to feel the formal discourse as a recurrent feature until it appeared for the third time, i.e. in xiii, and then it seems rather late to be picking up the thread. Does not he, perhaps, put them on the right track from the very beginning?

'Book of Genesis of Jesus Christ' announces the Evangelist with happy ambiguity, and follows it up with a genealogy, like those of which the Book of Genesis is so largely composed, and in which the ancestry of Jesus is traced from the genesis of the people of God in their forefather Abraham, himself the central figure of the Book of Genesis. Free narrative opens out of the genealogy by means of the resumption, 'Now the genesis of Jesus Christ was on this wise . . .'. Abraham's begetting of Isaac had been a miracle, the greatest miracle of birth that the Old Testament contains, yet no miracle compared with the virginal conception of Christ. A second resumption takes the form 'so when Jesus had his genesis', or 'was generated' (γεννηθέντος), and introduces the story of the wise men. When they depart from the scene, the angel directs Joseph to descend into Egypt, in order that there may be an Exodus, 'That it might be fulfilled which was spoken by the prophet, saying, Out of Egypt have I called my son.' Genesis ends, Exodus begins.

Before we plunge into St Matthew's Exodus, let us cast a look back upon his Genesis. It does not contain any discourse of Christ, nor, from the nature of its contents, could it conceivably do so. But it does contain a formal, self-contained piece, the genealogy, and it is to this and not to the birth-narrative that the title 'Book of Genesis' directly attaches. And so, if we are to expect uniformity between one Matthaean 'book' and another, we may enter St Matthew's Exodus with the expectation of finding a set piece in it comparable with the genealogy.

To advance, now, into Exodus (ii 16 ff.): the male children of Israel are slaughtered by a new Pharaoh. God calls his son out of Egypt into the Land of Promise. Jesus passes the waters and undergoes one after another Israel's temptations in the wilderness. It is on such a background that the ascent of the mountain is set, a new Sinai surely, from which Jesus delivers his interpretation of the ancient law. The Sermon on the Mount is a new Law of Exodus, in which the Beatitudes replace the Decalogue. The Sermon is, if not so formally arranged as the genealogy, more formally arranged than any of the subsequent discourses. If the genealogy was 'the book of Genesis of Jesus Christ' who will hesitate to call the Sermon 'Christ's book of Exodus'?

From Exodus onwards the Mosaic writings are largely made up of discourses, divine revelations, and it is natural that the corresponding set-pieces in St Matthew's Gospel should adhere to the discourse-form. What discourse of Christ, then, is to be the Gospel equivalent of Leviticus? There is no single scene in Leviticus which provides the obvious heart of the book, as the scene before Sinai provides the heart of Exodus. Perhaps, then, the Evangelist will take the name for his starting-point, as he did in the case of Genesis. 'Leviticus' is the book about the Levites; it institutes their priesthood, assigns their duties and establishes their revenues. St Paul had already viewed the apostolate as the levitical priesthood of the new dispensation. 'Know ye not,' he says to the Corinthians, 'that they which minister about sacred things eat the things of the temple, and they which wait upon the altar have their portion with the altar? Even so did the Lord ordain that they which proclaim the Gospel should live of the Gospel' (I Cor. ix 13–14). And when had the Lord so ordained? When he sent the Twelve on mission (Mk. vi 8–10, Matt x 9–11). The apostolic charge is the new Leviticus; the apostolic ministry is the priestly sacrifice of the new covenant, as the Apostle of the Gentiles says again: 'Grace was given me of God, that I should be a priestly minister (*liturgus*) of Jesus Christ among the gentiles, performing the rite of God's gospel, that the oblation of the gentiles might be an acceptable sacrifice, sanctified with Holy Spirit' (Rom. xv 16). We may fairly say that St Matthew's Leviticus follows his Genesis in working from the name of the book. It follows it in another particular besides—in beginning with a name-list. The table of the Apostles is the only list the Gospel contains which is at all comparable with the genealogy (x 2–4, i 2–16).

Numbers, like Leviticus, is a shapeless book, and perhaps the name will once more be the best clue to the Evangelist's antitype.

'Numbers' is a fair description of six chapters at the most: the host of God is numbered (Num. i–iv) separated from uncleanness (v) and blessed with the name of God (vi 22–27). The Matthaean parabolic discourse (xiii) is dominated by the parables of husbandry and fishing, which show us the people of God multiplied by the word of God a hundredfold, separated from the wicked and gathered by angels into God's kingdom. The parables stand moreover between two matching paragraphs (xii 46–50, xiii 53–58) of which the lesson is, that the people of Messiah are not to be identified with his physical kindred.

Deuteronomy is a book of far more definite character; it is the old new law, the law of love (I John ii 7–11 *et passim*; John xiii 34). The restatement of the law is occasioned by Moses' death, merely in the sense that his approaching end moves him to urge upon Israel the spirit of all that he had taught during his life. The death of Jesus restates the law more radically, for it gives a new meaning to the love of God and of men which the law enjoins. Christ's revelation of his coming passion was the basis of that cento of his teaching on Deuteronomic topics which St Mark had already collected (Mark ix 33–x 45). St Matthew makes the first piece of the Marcan cento the foundation of his own Deuteronomic discourse (xviii), enriching it with further Deuteronomic material. As we shall have occasion to look into this presently, we will not give the detailed references here.

The last Matthaean piece should stand in antitype to Joshua, and in so far as Joshua is 'the book of Jesus' and records the conquest which fulfilled the promise, it is obviously typical of the gospel within the Gospel, the victorious passion and resurrection of Jesus Christ. Already in St Mark the passion is prefaced by a set piece in almost Matthaean form, the apocalyptic prediction, which condemns Jerusalem to fall as Jericho fell, thus clearing the way to the Kingdom of God. St Matthew's work is already done for him by his predecessor (Mark xiii, Matt. xxiv–xxv).

We began from the position that the Gospel is divided into six parts by five stripes, and we observed that the five stripes are commonly supposed to have something to do with the five books of Moses. We questioned the supposition and have now endeavoured to show that there are in fact six stripes of which the genealogy is the first, and is placed at the very beginning of the first part. This might lead us to expect that each of our stripes or set-pieces would be the beginning of a 'book', composed in antitype to a book of the ancient scripture; and so we should neatly reverse the position which we began by criticising, and which holds that the stripes form the ends of such books. Any such expectation, however, falls at the first fence—the Exodus-theme does not begin with the second set-piece, but two and a half chapters earlier. It seems that the Evangelist was content to 'stripe' his book fairly regularly, to attach the value of scriptural antitypes to his stripes in order, and to allow the rest of the matter belonging to each stripe to accompany it either just ahead or just behind. Any real demarcation between Exodus, Leviticus, and Numbers narratives is as difficult to find in St Matthew as it is in the Pentateuch; the divisions between the middle three Mosaic books are purely artificial. We may reckon St Matthew's Deuteronomy from the first passion-prophecy (xvi 21: Deuteronomy is Moses's farewell discourse) and his Joshua from the passage through Jericho (xx 29).

If we are contrasting St Matthew's hexateuchal scheme with his pattern of twelvefold healing, we shall be inclined to call the latter essentially Marcan and the former St Matthew's own. Yet even in his hexateuchal construction it is not necessary to suppose that St Matthew entirely abandons his role of Marcan expositor. It is probable enough that his own formulation arises from a reflection upon St Mark's work. If St Matthew's opening words, βίβλος γενέσεως, suggest Genesis to the student of the Greek Bible, St Mark's first word, Beginning, makes the same suggestion to a Semitic mind. The imagery of the Baptism of Christ combines the figures of creation and of deliverance from Noachian deluge; the picture of Christ driven out into the wilderness, surrounded by beasts, served by angels, and undergoing temptation, evokes the figure of Adam. There is plenty of Genesis, then, on St Mark's first page.

The beginning is hexateuchally right; the ending is no less so. In

Mk. viii 27–x 45 we have a continuous passage in which we are never allowed for a moment to forget Deuteronomy. Jesus, like Moses, is prophesying his own mysterious departure as the precondition for the achieving of the kingdom. On the Mount of Transfiguration he is marked out as that Prophet like unto Moses to whom Israel is to hearken (Deut. xviii 15). The discourse on ruling humbly evokes a directly preceding Deuteronomic text, the law of the kingdom (Deut. xvii 14–20). The incident of the Strange Exorcist seems to play upon Deut. xviii 20–22, where the success of his word is made the test of the prophet deemed to have spoken presumptuously in the Lord's name. The Marcan sayings about offence tell us that it would be better to lose (physical) life than destroy (spiritual) life; in less grave cases one might be thankful to be let off with the loss of hand, foot, or eye. The text here alluded to seems to be the penalty for wrongful accusation (Deut. xix 16–21). The Marriage Question discusses Deut. xxiv 1–4. The scene with the Rich Man answers to Deut. v 1–vi 13, the securing of 'life' by keeping the decalogue, by honouring the oneness of God, and by putting his will before the claims of wealth. The request of James and John brings back the law of the kingdom again (Deut. xvii).

While these topics are being handled, Jesus takes his journey into Peraea, the region where Moses gave the Deuteronomic discourses, and thence follows the steps of Moses's successor, the Son of Nun, re-entering the Promised Land through Jericho.[1] It would

---

[1] The story of Joshua's conquests is full of apparent prefigurations of Christ's passion; but it is not easy to assess their direct influence on the passion-narratives. St Paul makes it a capital point that Jesus was 'hanged on a tree' and is therefore accursed according to Deut. xxi 23 (Galat. iii 13, echoed by Acts v 30, I Pet. ii 24). The only scriptural examples of Deut. xxi 23 put into practice are Joshua viii 29 and x 26. 'Jesus' hangs the potentates he vanquishes in his great battles. Coloss. ii 14–15 develops the theme of Galat. iii 13: When the law was abrogated by Christ's becoming a curse on the tree, we may say that the flesh nailed there was the law itself, or, again, that it was *the hostile spiritual potentates* whom Christ had thrown off like a garment. In undergoing crucifixion Jesus had gibbeted his enemies, mocked and triumphed over them, as Joshua did (x 23–26). To turn from St Paul to his successors—in the Marcan passion Jesus is mocked as powerless on the cross (Joshua x 24–25), there is a miracle of the sun at the time of his 'battle' (Josh. x 12–14), he is taken down

be absurd to suppose that St Mark wrote these things without seeing what he was doing, but even granting the absurdity, St Matthew can still have had his eyes open where St Mark's were shut and seen the Marcan story run through a Deuteronomic phase to a Joshua conclusion.

Genesis colours the beginning of St Mark because, perhaps, the Evangelist wishes to show the advent of Christ as a new creation. He draws the ending through Deuteronomy into Joshua to show us that, as Moses died and his office was reborn in Jesus the Son of Nun, so Jesus Christ died and was reborn in his own name and person. That may sound to modern ears a difficult comparison, but St Mark makes a comparison of the same sort in vi 14–16. Jesus himself is regarded by Herod as 'John Baptist arisen from the dead', and it is to this fact that Herod attributes the miracle-working power of Jesus' name. The suggestion is plain—if the name of Jesus, continuing the mission of his martyred predecessor, works miracles, how much more will it do so when Jesus arises in person after his own passion! Moses dies and lives again in 'Jesus'. Christ dies and lives again in his own person.

Such thoughts would suffice to turn St Mark's mind upon Deuteronomy and Joshua in his conclusion, just as the thought of a new creation would suffice to make him begin with an echo of Genesis. It is unnecessary to suppose that he saw his Gospel as a continuous hexateuch and, as we shall presently show, anyone who tries to construe it as such runs into serious difficulties. Yet it begins and ends hexateuchally and so the project of reforming it into hexateuchal regularity could easily suggest itself to St Matthew.

He would scarcely find in his predecessor the hint for an expression of the hexateuchal typology by means of set pieces standing out from their contexts. Suggestions for set pieces or formal discourses can be found in St Mark, but there is nothing specially hexateuchal about them. The apocalyptic prediction of Mark xiii is a set piece by Matthaean standards, and as St Matthew glances

and buried at dusk (x 27; Acts xiii 29 appears to make the point) he is walled up in a cave from which he comes forth alive (x 17, 23, cf. 27); St Matthew adds the guard of armed men (x 18).

back through the Marcan story he may find adumbrations of the same form in such passages as the parables (iv), the discourse on clean and unclean (vii 1–23), or the discourses on humility (ix 33–50). Quite apart from any hexateuchal designs St Matthew, with his strong didactic bent, might easily conceive the idea of beginning where St Mark left off and employing throughout the Gospel the valuable didactic instrument which St Mark perfected only in his last pages. When he came to compose his own pieces they served also to carry a hexateuchal pattern, but that was another matter.

As St Matthew advanced with his task he found the pieces he required more and more fully prefabricated by his predecessor. The genealogy and the Sermon on the Mount are not Marcan at all, St Mark's mission charge (vi 8–12) provides the text, but no more than the text, upon which St Matthew's Levitical discourse (x) is preached; the Marcan parables provide the whole form and more than half the matter of the 'Numbers' piece (Matt. xiii), the already strong Deuteronomic antitype in Mark ix 33–50 is merely supplemented in Matt. xviii with further Deuteronomic material[1] and with a parable in illustration of it, the Marcan apocalypse is virtually transcribed in Matt. xxiv–xxv, except that the concluding parables (Mark xiii 28–37) are much supplemented and enlarged (Matt. xxiv 32–xxv 46).

In conclusion to our exposition of St Matthew's hexateuchal pattern we may cast a glance back to the beginning of it. The first of the Evangelist's set pieces, his initial genealogy or 'book of genesis', arranges the generations in three pairs of sevens, six 'weeks' grouped in twos. The mere arithmetic of the arrangement makes several different suggestions to the attentive reader, but among them it is surely proper to reckon a hint of six periods or weeks. Seven such would be a perfect number, a jubilee, a week of weeks. As it is, we have only six, as it were the working 'days' of a

---

[1] As we saw above (p. 186) Mark ix reflects a whole series of neighbouring texts in Deut. xvii–xix. In xvii 1–xviii 14 St Matthew covers the same ground with certain omissions, and proceeds in xviii 15 ff. to add an antitype to another text from the same region, Deut. xvii 2–13.

week of weeks. In six days God made heaven and earth, including (in the sixth) man after his own image; sabbath followed. In six weeks of generations God has made a new creation from the call of Abraham to Jesus his better image. The hope of universal Sabbath follows.

If that is at all how the Evangelist thought, then it would not surprise us if the Gospel story should also strike him as a sixfold work of God, culminating in the enthronement of the new Man through his passion and resurrection; nor would it surprise us if he should see the shadow and prefiguration of it in the first six books of the Bible, 'Moses and Jesus'.

It is unnecessary for our present purpose to estimate the probability of any conjectures about the symbolism of the genealogy. It is enough if we can say that it exhibits a tendency to divide sacred history into six phases, and no tendency at all to divide it into five.

We have now done what we could for the hexateuchal, or 'Moses-and-Jesus' account of St Matthew's structure. But when all has been said, the new hypothesis fails to extricate itself entirely from the difficulties which beset the old. We objected against the pentateuchal theory that it was merely formal—that St Matthew's five dominical discourses matched the five books of Moses in no other particular except in being five. The formality of the new theory may not be so bare as that, but it is still bare enough. The six set pieces it distinguishes can be plausibly told off one for one against their hexateuchal opposites, but with one exception the correspondence is of theme and not of detail. The genealogy derives from Chronicles, not Genesis; Exodus may supply the Mountain but we must go to Deuteronomy (xxviii) for the Beatitudes; the corn which multiplies a hundredfold is not in Numbers but in Genesis (xxvi). The Deuteronomic discourse (Matt. xviii) does make an exposition of texts from the corresponding scriptural book, but even this apparently favourable exception is not so favourable as it seems; it is rather a symptom of a widespread trouble—there is too much Deuteronomy everywhere for the comfort of the hypothesis. The temptations in the wilderness are already written round Deuteronomic citations, and Deuteronomic topics are still being discussed in the courts of the Temple (Matt. xxii 23–40). The scandal is lessened, but the hypothesis scarcely confirmed, by the consideration that Deuteronomy is in its very substance a recapitulation of the other Mosaic writings, so that it is always possible to view them, if one chooses, through Deuteronomic spectacles rather than in their own colour and phrase.

But if we are discouraged by the formality of the relation between the six 'stripes' or set pieces and their scriptural models, we have no less cause for discouragement in the formality of the relation between the stripes and the contexts they stripe. The surrounding cloth is of some other colour; the stripes are neither the beginnings, middles nor endings of complete 'books' homogeneous with them. Sometimes there is appropriate matter in their neighbourhood, that is the most we can say. Since the 'Numbers' discourse of Matt. xiii gathers multitudes into the Kingdom, it is appropriately followed by the arithmetic of the loaves and thousands (xiv 13–xvi 12). The exposition of manifold healing which gives the 'Levitical' discourse (x) its setting derives a levitical flavour from the placing of the leper first among the cured. But such observations will bear little weight. The feeding of the multitudes, considered as such, suggests Exodus more strongly than it suggests Numbers. The Lord's healing works in viii–xii may suggest Leviticus in so far as they are healings, but as a series of mighty works they are apparently used to evoke the memory of the ten Exodus plagues.

An exegetical hypothesis is inevitably psychological. It is plausible if it can plausibly answer the question, 'What did the author intend?' And the plausibility will depend on our being able to see the author intending what is attributed to him. Can we see St Matthew setting out to pattern his book with the curious and, one might almost say, half-hearted formality which the hexateuchal hypothesis seems to imply? Not, perhaps, setting out to do so. But there seems no reason why he should not begin wholeheartedly and continue half-heartedly; for where literary recipes and projects are in question, such a procedure is almost more the rule than the exception. We propose to write on such and such a plan, and begin to do so, but as our work develops it runs on other lines.

An imaginative or historical writer whose work rebels against his project for it expects nowadays to follow one of two courses. Either he gives it its head, lets it find a new shape for itself, and going back over the earlier part effaces the vestiges of the original design. Or else against the grain and by hard constraint he forces the rebellious matter to conform. A novelist might follow the former course, a detective writer more likely the latter: for him the plot is the theme and must be imposed upon the characters. Both courses of action are sophisticated, whether we rewrite or whether we write against the grain. It is not to be supposed that St Matthew did either. He began writing to a scheme and, as he advanced, was captured by other patterns and by fresh interests. What, then, did he do with the original design? He neither abandoned it nor, in any real sense, worked to it; he reduced it to a form within which other matters and, indeed, other patterns could be accommodated.

We have already examined what looks like a small-scale model of such procedure in the Sermon on the Mount. The Evangelist begins arranging the Sermon in orderly comment on the Beatitudes, introduces subsidiary patterns of great intrinsic power, and ends by doing not much more than formal justice to the original design. So with the Gospel as a whole. In i–iv St Matthew concentrates on throwing the traditions about Christ's birth and first public appearance into a continuous and vivid antitype to Genesis and Exodus, and in so doing works his way from the genealogy to the Sermon on the Mount. The Sermon, as we have just been saying, has an elaborate formal development of its own, in the course of which Exodus appears to be forgotten. Descending from the mountain the Evangelist plunges into the arithmetic of the twelve healings and the twelve apostles. Presently there will be the pattern of the loaves and thousands, after that again the pattern of the three apostles and the three redemptive days. As he develops these themes the Evangelist is no longer writing a substantial anti-type to the Books of Moses and of Jesus taken in order. He is content to maintain the hexateuchal frame, a series of set discourses vivid enough in themselves, but often only faintly antitypical to their scriptural models.

It is not only in the Sermon on the Mount that St Matthew seems to reproduce on a smaller scale the grand architecture of his book. We have in previous chapters examined a similar phenomenon in considerable detail. St Matthew so rehandles the Marcan scheme of twelvefold healing as to compress it into a single space (viii–xii) where it is dealt with on its own merits and is the real subject of the narrative. And yet the topic does not end there. By the curious device of a double reckoning based on scenes of double healing, we have seen how the twelvefold scheme extends its arms into later chapters of the Gospel and provides a frame for the theme of the three witness-apostles and the three prophecies of resurrection.

If St Matthew composed at all as we have suggested, he did not stand alone in doing so. The Seer of the Apocalypse made conscious and repeated use of what is essentially the same formula. His dramatic vision of the Son of Man (i) ossifies into a skeleton of titles upon which the impassioned speech of the seven messages is fitted (ii–iii). The vision of celestial glory and the opening of the book in God's right hand (iv–v) runs out into a formal repetition of the breaking of seals (vi), but the visions fitted into the frame so provided are anything but formal—they are the incursions of the four horsemen. It is the same with the management of the trumpets or the vials. Old patterns as they stiffen are not discarded, they remain as frames for fresh designs which stiffen in their turn. The Seer's method is, in a sense, highly artificial, but the effect of it is to allow untrammelled scope to fresh inspirations without sacrificing continuity. We find in St Matthew nothing either so conscious or so elaborate, but then it is no part of our thesis that any two New Testament writers thought or constructed in an identical way.

As in Apoc. iv–v St John is really writing about the great book in the right hand of divine Glory, so in Matt. i–iv the Evangelist's pen is really controlled by hexateuchal typology. There really is a Gospel Genesis (i 1–ii 15) and a Gospel Exodus (ii 16–v 1). And so it is in connexion with this part of St Matthew's scheme that the serious question arises, how far his rehandling of St Mark has been affected by the requirements of detailed and orderly hexateuchal imagery.

If St Matthew is in any case remodelling St Mark, perhaps the first question to be asked is whether St Mark contains anything like a Genesis or an Exodus for St Matthew to remodel. Hardly a Genesis, or even if so, St Matthew can scarcely be said to have re-modelled it. There is, as we saw above, a bare suggestion of Genesis in the first word of St Mark's Gospel, supported by several echoes scattered over the next dozen verses. But it is plain that St Matthew did not build his own Genesis out of these materials, but out of the story of our Saviour's birth, which St Mark had left untouched. The case of St Mark's Exodus imagery is more interesting.

There are, of course, hints of Exodus, as of other scriptural books, scattered throughout St Mark's Gospel; for example, where water is crossed by divine aid or where multitudes are fed in the desert. But there are two moments which stand out with quite a different sort of prominence, involving Jesus himself, his whole existence and action, in a passage of scriptural drama. The moments to which I refer are in the first chapter and the third. In the first Jesus passes through the waters (of baptism), hears the voice of God speak from heaven, endures temptation forty days in the wilderness, is sustained with 'angels' food' and returns to the inhabited land with the message of fulfilment on his lips. This passage is full of echoes, of Adam, for example, as we said above, and of Elijah, but the continuous antitype to the Exodus from Egypt is unmistakable, and would be so, even if we had not St Paul's sermon in I Corinthians x 1–13 to remind us that the passage of the Red Sea finds its antitype in Christian Baptism and the temptations of Israel in the wilderness their antitypes in the trials which test the fidelity of the baptised.

In Mk. iii we have a second spiritual Exodus—the Pharisees are

Pharaoh (even the assonance helps here), their hearts are hardened, they reject Christ's signs and threaten his life, he parts from them in indignation, and withdraws his following towards the sea. Presently he ascends a mountain, and makes a covenant with the Twelve (apostles, as representing the twelve tribes or sons of Israel).

Here is double embarrassment for anyone who, like St Matthew, desires to impose a consistent hexateuchal typology on the Gospel story. What is he to do with two Exoduses, equally complete and equally weighty? And even if he accepts that anomaly, his troubles are not at an end, for the first of the Marcan Exoduses is inextricably tangled with the Marcan Genesis. The baptism of Jesus is a new creation as well as an election of Israel and a passage of the Red Sea waters; his temptation evokes the memory of Adam as well as of the camp in the wilderness.

The easiest way out would be to efface the Exodus symbolism in the first of the two Exodus antitypes, and to preserve the second as it is. Then, in place of one Genesis-Exodus and a second Exodus, we should have one Genesis and one Exodus, which is what we want. But St Matthew cannot do this. He has already provided his own gospel Genesis by the time he reaches the first of the two Marcan scenes under discussion; the first Marcan Exodus becomes his Exodus, he concentrates upon it and develops it, building up the detail of the temptations in the very spirit of I Cor. x. As for the second Marcan Exodus, he breaks it up and disperses it. In fact, he breaks it into three.

(a) The episode of the withered hand and the breach with the Pharisees becomes, as we have seen, part of the climax of rejection which marks the end of the twelve healing signs (Matt. xii 9–16).

(b) The gathering to Jesus of crowds from all the districts of Palestine, his ascent of the mountain and his disciples' coming to him there (Mark iii 8–13) reappear as the introduction to the Sermon on the Mount (Matt. iv 24–v 1). We may say, in fact, that St Matthew has moved Mount Sinai bodily from Mark iii to Mark i, from the second Marcan Exodus to the first.

(c) The 'covenant with the Twelve' disappears—St Matthew

nowhere narrates their institution—but their name-list is transferred from the ascent of the mountain to the mission of the
apostles in Matt. ix 35–x 42 (Mark vi 7–13).

It is worth noting how little inclined St Matthew is formally to
contradict his Marcan original. It would have been easy for him
to combine the institution of the Twelve with their mission, but
he does not do so. In x 1 'Jesus calls to him his twelve apostles' as
an already existing group, and gives them present authority to
preach and heal. We can even suppose that they are the same
group as that which came to Jesus on the mountain, heard the
beatitudes, and were named light and salt of the world; though
indeed the subsequent call of Matthew, one of the Twelve, creates
difficulties for that supposition.

There is the same tenderness towards the Marcan tradition in
the way in which the ascent of the mountain is linked with the
Exodus symbolism of Mark i and Matt. iii–iv. In passing from
Mark i 20 to Mark iii 8 St Matthew does not so much suppress as
summarise the intervening ministry, running together phrases
from the beginning and the end of the Marcan account (Mark i
28–39 and iii 8–13). The comparison of a Marcan catena with St
Matthew's continuous text will show how it has been done.

And he went preaching in their synagogues in all Galilee and
casting out the demons (i 39). And the report of him went forth
straightway everywhere into the whole country surrounding
Galilee (i 28). They brought to him all that were diseased and
demon-possessed (i 32). And he healed many that were diseased
with various sicknesses (i 34). And a great multitude from Galilee
followed, and from Judaea and from Jerusalem and from Idumaea
and beyond Jordan (iii 8). And he goes up into the mountain
(iii 13).

Compare: And Jesus travelled round in all Galilee, teaching in
their synagogues and preaching the gospel of the kingdom, and
healing every sickness and every infirmity among the people. And
the report of him went out into the whole of Syria. And they
brought him all that were diseased, afflicted with various sicknesses, demon-possessed and lunatic and paralytic, and he healed

them. And there followed him great crowds from Galilee and Decapolis and Jerusalem and Judaea and beyond Jordan. And seeing the crowds he went up into the mountain (Matt. iv 23–v 1).

By these means St Matthew hastens from the Red Sea to Sinai, and brings forward his new decalogue-at-the-mountain into the beginning of the Galilean gospel. In a sense, the Sermon on the Mount belongs more properly there than anywhere else, for the Sermon is the systematic account of Christ's *didache*, his scribal, but more than scribal, teaching; and it is in the very beginning of the Galilean ministry that St Mark says (i 22) 'They were astonished at his teaching, for he taught them as with authority and not as their scribes'. The text cries out for illustration. What was this 'teaching' like? The Sermon on the Mount shows Jesus explicitly setting his teaching beside that of current scribalism, and has for its conclusion an actual reproduction of the Marcan text: 'Now it came to pass when Jesus finished these words, the multitudes were amazed at his teaching. For he taught them as with authority, and not as their scribes' (vii 28–29). Through the reproduction of the Marcan verse, St Matthew is carried back from the mountain to the beginning of the Galilean story, and re-advances from there, rearranging his material in that pattern of twelve healings which we have studied elsewhere.

It seems, then, that the requirements of his Exodus typology in ii–v explain to some extent St Matthew's rearrangements of his Marcan original. Further light on the same problem may be derived from a consideration of his 'Leviticus' and 'Numbers' typology. Here, indeed, the facts to be considered are quite simple. The typological influence of the third and fourth Mosaic books is scarcely felt outside the two set discourses which correspond to them. The Mission Charge is St Matthew's Leviticus (x) and the Parables are his Numbers (xiii). Both have Marcan originals, but they are in the opposite order (Parables iv, Mission of the Twelve vi 7–13). And so, for hexateuchal if for no other reasons, St Matthew is committed to the reversing of these two Marcan sections.

Let us now summarise the whole rearrangement of Mark i 1–

vi 13 in Matthew i–xiii from the point of view which, in this chapter, we have ventured to ascribe to St Matthew himself.

(a) For the sake of his Exodus typology he borrows the ascent of the mountain from Mark iii 8–13 and places it after Mk. i 20.

(b) For the sake of Levitical typology he borrows the Mission of the Apostles from Mk. vi 7–13 and joins it to the name-list of the Twelve contained in Mk. iii 14–19.

(c) He embeds this composite Levitical section in his compressed rearrangement of the whole system of twelvefold healing, culled from all over St Mark's Gospel but especially from i–v. The conclusion of the healings brings him to the contested sabbath cure (Mark ii 23–iii 6) and the contested exorcism (Mk. iii 22–30) and so smoothly on through the visit of the Mother and Brethren (Mk. iii 31–35) to its direct sequel, the Parables (Mk. iv 1–34), which supply the model and much of the substance for St Matthew's 'Numbers' discourse (xiii).

Though in the exposition of the foregoing hypothesis we may have fallen into the language of positive statement, we do not wish to claim any higher status for it than that of likely guesswork. All interpretation which is not self-evident is guesswork of a kind, but there is guessing and guessing, and we trust that the first seven chapters of this book, and especially the first three, contain a system of mutually supporting conjecture which inspires more reasonable confidence than the chapter we have just completed.

RETRACTATIONS: THE MARCAN CYCLES

Since I have written about St Mark at such length and so lately, there is nothing for it but that I should pass *A Study in St Mark* in brief review, and say how much of it stands and how much falls, in the face of my latest thoughts. I will restrict my observations to matters of substance. There is much in the book which might have been better expressed otherwise, but I will not be at pains here to alter injudicious adjectives. Nor will I use a style which presumes that my reader has the book in front of him and turns up every reference as he reads. I will hope to make what I say intelligible in itself.

I will divide my retractations into two parts. I will take first by themselves those three chapters (iii, iv and v) which dealt with the cyclic recurrences in St Mark's subject-matter. Then in a further chapter I will deal with all the rest of the book.

In chapters iii, iv, and v I undertook to shew that the recurrence of themes in the successive groups of healing acts did not stand alone but was part of a larger recurrent context. What recurred, I set out to demonstrate, was a whole cycle of themes among which the healing themes found their place. If we could speak of St Mark composing in 'chapters' (not, of course, in the chapters of our printed bibles) we could also say that each chapter embodied the themes of its predecessor in fresh incidents similarly arranged, until the last chapter of all gave those themes definitive expression and revealed them for what they were—the phases of God's redemptive action. Such was the thesis of iii–v, and as a thesis it was sound. And when I look at these chapters again I am happy to find how many genuine cyclic correspondences they describe, in spite of dislocations and artificialities introduced by that misconception of the pattern of healings to which I now plead guilty.[1] And while I am sorry for the mistakes I made, I am encouraged to find how much simplicity and good order are introduced into my

[1] See below p. 224.

old tangles by my new way of construing the pattern of healings. If the new account of the healings sets the narrative cycles straight, that is an important confirmation of its closer approximation to the truth.

My retractation of Chs. iii–v shall take the form of a continuous account of the cyclic movement of St Mark's thought as I now see it. I shall refer to what I wrote in those chapters for the detail of the parallels wherever it is sound, and correct it where it is not.

The beginning of St Mark's gospel, as I rightly said on pp. 53–60, is not written in the standard paragraphs which are characteristic of the rest of it, but in long self-contained sentences of equal length, a sort of prose stanzas: (a) i 1–3, (b) 4–5, (c) 6–8, (d) 9–11, (e) 12–13, (f) 14–15, (g) 16–18, (h) 19–20. They fall into pairs: the prophecies relating to John (a) are fulfilled in his appearance (b); John's prophecies of Christ (c) are fulfilled in his baptism (d). When Christ has, like John, inhabited the wilderness (e) he comes into Galilee proclaiming the kingdom (f). He calls Simon and Andrew from their fishing (g), James and John from their mending of nets (h).

At this point the form changes, and we get the first of St Mark's standard paragraphs, the demoniac in synagogue (i 21–28). I cannot approve the account I gave on pp. 60–67 of the transition from sentence-form to paragraph-form. Without explaining or extenuating my errors I will say what now seems to me to be right.

As far as Christ's entry into Galilee (i 14–15) the pairs of sentences are based upon the same sort of relation, that of anticipation and fulfilment. The pair of sentences concerned with the two callings of fishermen exhibit no such relation, but a simple parallelism: two men are called, and two men are called. So the movement of thought which has carried us through i 1–15 is brought to a stop in a static parallel between two pairs of disciples, Simon and Andrew, James and John.

St Mark takes a fresh start in developing a parallel to this parallel: the two men and two men called are to be matched by two persons and two persons healed, the demoniac and the feverish woman, the leper and the paralytic. It is here that St Mark begins to expand his scale of treatment. The story of Jesus in the synagogue constitutes a paragraph as long as three of the sentences or prose stanzas in i 1–20, while the story of Jesus as guest in Peter's house is actually made up of three such sentences (29–31, 32–34, 35–38). The one story contains the exorcism of the demon, the other contains the healing of the fever.

The units St Mark employs may have trebled in length, but the thought they carry runs on continuously into them from the chain of shorter units preceding them. The relation of preparation to fulfilment exhibited by the first three pairs of sentences and absent from the fourth pair resumes its sway in the first two healing stories. As water to spirit, as wilderness to promised land, as the defeat of Satanic temptation is to the proclamation of the gospel, so is the act of exorcism to the act of 'raising up', and so is Christ's presence in synagogue to his presence in the disciple's house which prefigures the Church; as I explained correctly enough on pp. 67–68. Nor have I anything to revise in my account of the correspondence of the second pair of healings (leper and paralytic) with the first (demoniac and fevered woman).

The account I gave on pp. 69–78 about the sequence of the cycle of Levi and the withered hand (ii 13–iii 12) upon its predecessors was in substance correct, but I am now in a position to express it more naturally because I am free from the dogma which obliged me to treat i 16–ii 12 as a single cycle, four persons called and four persons healed. I prefer now to talk of a pair of little cycles springing out of the pair of callings. After the two callings of Simon and Andrew and of the Sons of Zebedee respectively we have a little cycle perfectly complete in itself, a day's work at Capernaum, first in synagogue, then in Simon's house. The general healing at the house door and the fall of dusk bring it to a fitting conclusion. The early morning episode which follows, and in which Jesus refuses to return to Capernaum, renews the call of the four by summoning them into a wider field, and serves as the transition to a second short cycle. Where the first short cycle had one full healing story occupying a whole paragraph and one very slightly narrated occupying a single sentence or stanza in a group of three, the second short cycle has two full healing stories, the leper and the paralytic, each occupying a complete paragraph. The paralytic corresponds in weight to all the three little episodes connected with Jesus' stay in Simon's house, but in theme it corresponds to the healing of Simon's mother-in-law only. The theme of the renewal of the disciples' call is, as it were, pushed out of the paragraph by the expansion of the healing-story. But it appears as a paragraph on its own, the call of Levi, a further disciple; and so we pass on to a third little cycle written on the model common to the first two and in parallel with both of them. We can see the triple parallel at a glance if we put it in a table:

Call of four disciples, i 16–20	Call of four extended, i 36–39	Call of Levi, ii 13–14
	Contact with leper, i 40–42	Contact with publicans, ii 15–17
New teaching and		New 'wine' of Gospel, ii 18–22
Sabbath exorcism		Sabbath 'harvesting', ii 23–24
contrast Christ and the scribes, i 21–28	Christ and the priests, i 43–44	David and the priests, ii 25–26
	Powers of the Son of Man shewn by	Powers of the Son of Man, ii 27–28
Raising of woman from bed, i 29–31	Raising of paralytic in face of opposition, ii 1–12	Withered man healed in face of opposition, iii 1–6
Many healings and exit, i 32–35		Exit and many healings, iii 7–12

And so the tract of narrative covered by the first 'handful' of healings is found to consist of three successive waves, the first of which throws up two healings, the second likewise two, and the third one. Each wave runs longer than its predecessor and makes more room for controversial exposition. And if we ask why St Mark's thought runs in three waves, the answer is plain. He is building round his healing-pattern, and he builds up his first handful of healings as a couple of pairs healed in correspondence with a couple of pairs of disciples called, *plus* a single person healed in correspondence with a further disciple called. The pattern of apostles and of sufferers provides the skeleton, and the flesh of various narrative simply clothes it.

Apart from the somewhat clumsy representation of these facts, and the unlucky attempt to lump the first two little cycles in one, I see nothing more to retract in my third chapter. It is when we advance to the fourth chapter that the trouble begins. For it is here that my unlucky analysis of the healing-pattern in terms of steadily diminishing 'blocks' each with its 'annexe' begins seriously to force the cycles of St Mark's thought. The mere division of matter in my fourth Chapter is seriously misleading, for it cuts a natural cycle in half. For fear of endless complication I will abandon the attempt to retract in detail, and will substitute a corrected account, largely in diagrammatic form, supporting it by references to such parts of my fourth and fifth chapters as are usable.

The area covered by the handful of healings is the unit that we must take (iii 13–viii 26), and we may naturally expect it to sub-divide into three cycles as the first handful did. Here as there the healings fall into three groups (v, vii 24–37, viii 22–26), but the groups are not as before a two, a two and a one. For, as we have shewn in this present work, the number three exercises a special influence on the first group and attracts into it what in the former handful constituted the forepart of the second group—the purify-ing of the unclean. So the first group is brought up to a strength of three, and the second group would be diminished to one, if it were not compensated by the insertion of the intrusive thirteenth, the gentile healing. And so, in effect, the groups run three, two, one, the first being equal to the other two put together. And what is true of the groups of healings is equally true of the cycles which clothe them: the first (iii 13–vi 6) is roughly equal to the remaining two (vi 7–vii 37 *plus* viii 1–26).

The last two of these three little cycles are closely related in subject-matter; the feeding of the four thousands is central in the latter of them, as the feeding of the five thousands is in the former.

And so the three cycles of the second handful can easily be seen as two, the first simple (iii 13–vi 6) the second subdivided (vi 7–vii 37, viii 1–26). And this appearance of things is confirmed by the way in which the introductory scenes of the three cycles stand to one another. The first two are on a level: one begins with the call of the Twelve (iii 13–19) and the other with their sending on mission (vi 7–12), just as in the previous 'handful' the first cycle began with the call of the Four and the second with their leading forth on a mission. But the third cycle of the second handful has no comparable scene of apostolic vocation to place on a level with the mission and sending of the Twelve, or with the call of Levi in the corresponding cycle of the first handful. What we do get looks, as we have said, more like a subordinate heading. The Mission of the Twelve in vi leads to their being entrusted with twelve loaves for distribution to Israel, of which they handle five almost immediately (vi 30–44) and the remaining seven in the introductory scene of the third cycle (viii 1–9). It seems, then, that we have in iii 13–vi 6 the cycle of the call of the Twelve and in vi 7–viii 26 the cycle of the mission of the Twelve, subdivided into (a) the little cycle of the distribution of five loaves and (b) the little cycle of the distribution of seven loaves.

This inequality in the apparent status of the three cycles in iii–viii does not affect the way in which they are composed, however. They appear quite simply as successive 'waves' of St Mark's thought, each dependent for the elements of its order on the waves preceding it. Every additional wave that runs up in the rising tide of the Gospel climax has one more predecessor than the wave before it and, therefore, a greater number of models on which it might form itself. But the complexity of reference does not in fact accumulate at a mathematical rate, for previous models are constantly being discarded. It might seem theoretically appropriate that each of the three cycles in the second handful should form itself upon the corresponding cycle in the first handful as well as upon its own immediate predecessor, but this does not happen. The second and third cycles of the second handful build themselves upon their immediate predecessors almost entirely. It is only the first cycle which pays any detailed attention to its opposite number in the previous handful, and that seems natural enough. In starting a second handful St Mark is aware of making a fresh beginning and conforms it to a previous beginning. Having made this new beginning he runs on from where he is.

We will now make two tables, showing (a) the conformity of the first cycle in the second handful both to its opposite number in the first handful and to its immediate predecessor (b) the conformity of the three cycles of the second handful to one another.

Call of Four, i 16–20a	Call of Levi, ii 13–17	Call of Twelve, iii 13–19
They left their father, i 20b	Feasting and fasting, ii 18–20	No leisure to eat: Mother and brethren dismissed, iii 20–35
Exorcism with new authority	The power of the New Teaching, ii 21–22	By what power does Christ exorcise, iii 22–30
and new teaching	Cornfield episode, ii 23–27	Teaching from boat: cornfield parables, iv 1–34
in episode of demoniac, i 21–28		Exorcism of storm; exorcism of Legion, iv 35–v 20
Raising of woman in Simon's house, i 29–31	Healing in synagogue, iii 1–5	Raising of girl in ruler of synagogue's house, v 21–43
Many healings, i 32–34	Rejection in synagogue: Many healings, iii 6–12	Rejection in synagogue; *not* many healings, vi 1–6

Most of the detail of these comparisons is correctly described on pp. 80–88 of the chapter I am reviewing.

Having shewn how far the first cycle of the second handful is modelled on its predecessors we will proceed to shew how the second and third cycles follow upon it. We have said above that they borrow nothing from their opposite numbers in the former handful. To be exact, we should say 'Nothing but healing themes'. The healing of the pair of sensitive powers in vii and viii does of course match the healing of the pair of active powers in ii and iii. Otherwise the second and third cycles in the second handful follow upon the first cycle in it, as the following table shows.

Call of Twelve, iii 13–19	Mission of Twelve, vi 7–13	
No leieure to eat, supernatural power behind Christ's mighty acts said to be Satan, iii 20–35	Supernatural power behind Christ's mighty acts said to be John redivivus. No leisure to eat, vi 14–32	
Cornfield parables, iv 1–34	Five loaves for 5,000, vi 33–44	Seven loaves for 4,000, viii 1–9
Stilling the storm, iv 35–41	Walking on the water, vi 45–52	Return by sea, viii 10
Tombs, demons, swine, gentile soil in	Clean and unclean: pharisaic opposition and disciples' incomprehension, vi 53–vii 23	Pharisaic opposition and disciples' incomprehension, viii 11–21
the exorcism of Legion, v 1–20	Gentile exorcism, vii 24–30	
'Talitha cumi', v 21–43	'Effatha' to the deaf, vii 31–37	Cure of the blind, viii 22–26

Nearly all the detail of these parallels, though oddly hashed about, can be found on pp. 88–104. It will be seen that the new arrangement delivers the author from the special cause of embarrassment which he was forced to acknowledge on p. 100.

We must now take up the 'two over' which are added to the two handfuls of healings to make up the twelve, and we must see in what cycles of narrative they are embedded and how these cycles are shaped upon their predecessors. I handled the matter on pp. 104–122. I made nonsense of the relation of the 'two-over' passage (viii 27–x 52) to the preceding movements of St Mark's thought, through failure to pick out the model it principally follows; and I introduced an unnecessary new feature called first 'the Truth' or 'the Teaching' from its content, and later 'the Para-cycle' from its form. Unable to evolve this section of the gospel from the preceding sections, I evolved it from itself and concentrated my attention upon its interior development. In so doing I made a number of observations which were perfectly sensible in themselves, but I failed to do what I set out to do, and that was to reveal the cyclic structure of the gospel.

The 'two healings over' are closely modelled on their two direct predecessors, and so we naturally look for the model of viii 27–x 52 in the last two cycles of the second handful, i.e. in vi 7–viii 26. We saw that those two cycles were somewhat weakly divided and inclined to take on the form of a single piece; and the passage which follows them and with which we are now concerned appears to lose the middle bisection entirely. At the same time it develops a subdivision of its own into three parts, each beginning with a prophecy of resurrection after three days, followed by words of the disciples flouting the principle of the gospel and meriting rebuke (viii 27–ix 1, ix 30–50, x 32–45). If we are to regard each of these texts as the beginning of a little cycle, we shall have one such cycle (ix 30–x 31) without a single healing in it, an anomaly in the structure of the gospel as we have known it hitherto. Whatever terms we like to use, we must agree in any case that the interior movement within viii 27–x 52 proceeds in three waves; much of the detail of the correspondences between them can be found on pp. 119–120 of *A Study in St Mark*.

I said that my analysis failed through failure to detect the principal model of viii 27–x 52. What that model is, I have partially explained in Chapter viii above (pp. 131–136). What I was concerned to shew in that chapter was that the terminations to my three principal groups of healings, the first handful, the second handful, and the two over, correspond with critical points in the development of the gospel narrative, and that these critical points echo or rhyme with one another. That is to say that, for one thing, the situation after the first healing of the blind powerfully evokes the situation after the healing of the withered hand. As I put it in Chapter viii, 'the parallel runs on'. To use the language of our present discussion, the 'two over' cycle finds a continuous model in the first cycle of the second handful. I will now make a table of the correspondences of the 'two over' cycle with its two models, and for this purpose I shall neglect the threefold development within the cycle itself.

Jesus comes near to lose his life for saving life. He admonishes the demons who confess him to be silent, iii 4–12	Opinion of Herod and others concerning what Jesus is. The Baptist's passion prefigures Christ's, vi 14–29	Opinion of Herod and others quoted. Peter confessing, is admonished as Satan. Jesus prophesies his passion. Saving and losing life, viii 27–ix 1
Jesus ascends mountain with three surnamed apostles and nine more, iii 13–19	Jesus ascends mountain to pray and descending amazes his disciples, vi 47–52	Jesus ascends mountain with the three apostles and descending amazes the nine and the crowd, ix, 2–15
Jesus's exorcism discredited as demonic. He warns his critics of everlasting sin, iii 22–30	Dispute with Pharisees about disciples. Exorcism of child for parent. Healing of deaf stammerer, vii 1–37	Dispute of Pharisees with disciples. Exorcism of deaf-mute child for parent. John discredits strange exorcist as schismatic; the rebuke of Jesus warns of everlasting death, ix 16–50
Jesus turns from mother and brethren and declares that his faithful hearers are his kindred, iii 31–35	Pharisees tempt Jesus with request for a sign, viii 11–13	Pharisees tempt Jesus with marriage question. He says, 'Leave father and mother and cleave to wife.' Says the kingdom of heaven is the children's, x 1–16
Parable: cares and riches choke the word. But good ground bears a hundredfold, iv 1–20	The disciples may rely for bread on the power that fills 5,000 with 5 loaves, etc., viii 14–21	Rich man turns back. The disciples who have made sacrifices are promised a hundredfold, x 17–31
(Jesus's sailing companions terrified and amazed, iv 35–41.)		Jesus's travelling companions terrified and amazed. Request of James and John, x 32–45
	Healing of the blind, viii 22–26	Healing of the blind, x 46–52

It will be seen at a glance that the second column of the table contributes little to the formation of the third; it is the first that provides the substantial model. We will comment a little more fully on the use made of that model, resuming from the point at which we left off in Chapter viii. We came as far as to show how the Transfiguration in Mark ix echoes the ascent of the mountain in Mark iii. The next scene in iii is the so-called Beelzebul-controversy. The power of Christ's exorcism provokes the blasphemy, 'He casts out demons by the prince of demons'. Christ's reply is, that the Spirit of God must be recognised in his works. Satan does not cast out Satan; exorcism is by the name, power or spirit of God. The story in ix works round to a fresh application of the same point. On descending from the mountain Jesus and the Three find the Nine wrestling vainly with an exorcism which their prayerlessness, says Jesus, prevents them from achieving. The high privileges which the Three have just enjoyed, and the impotence which the Nine have meanwhile exhibited, naturally prompt the question 'who is greatest?' The Twelve discuss it as they walk, and draw upon them Christ's rebuke when they next pause for rest. While the rebuke is in their ears, John tells his Master about the strange exorcist whom they had silenced, because, not being one of their company, he had presumed to exorcise in the name of Jesus. Jesus' answer is in principle the same which he gave to those who had accused him of exorcising by Beelzebul. The power of the Spirit is its own evidence. If the Name of Jesus works through the exorcist's lips, it is not likely that the man is in bad faith. Jesus proceeds to warn his disciples of the danger of thus resisting the spirit or otherwise giving offence to believers. As he had spoken to his Pharisaic critics of a sin unforgiven in the world to come, and attaching to the blasphemy of the Spirit, so he reminds his disciples now of an offence which may bring a man to the punishment of everlasting fire.

Let us continue the parallel, taking the next paragraphs in iii and in ix–x respectively. In iii the mother and brethren of Jesus ask for him and are at that juncture of events refused, in consideration of a better claim. 'See, my mother and my brethren,' says Jesus, directing his eyes upon his hearers. The next paragraph in x shows Jesus asserting that the claim of marriage is above all other natural ties: 'For this cause' he says, quoting Genesis, 'will a man leave father and mother and cleave to his wife, and the twain shall be one flesh.' The parallel here appears to support the mystical doctrine of St Paul. Our Saviour's union with his Church (represented in ch. iii by those who hang on his lips and do the will of God which he expounds) is to be compared to a man's union with his wife: both unions override the ties of blood.

And this aspect of the lesson of the visit of the brethren and Mary, the universality of Christ's love (Behold my mother and my brethren!) is illustrated in the reception of the little children in x 13–16. It would be superfluous, therefore, to seek a separate archetype in iii–iv. We pass to the next piece of it, the parable of the Sower. Some of the seed that takes root is choked by the cares of the world and the deceitfulness of riches—the only reference to wealth which the first nine chapters of St Mark contain. In the parallel we read of the man in whom the seed so took root that Jesus invited him to follow him, but he refused because his possessions were great, and Jesus went on to comment on the snare of gold. But we, said Peter, have forsaken all and followed. Then, said Christ, you, and all who have made such renunciations, shall gain a hundredfold in this life, and everlasting life besides. The good seed in the field, unchoked by the worldly weeds, was, we remember, to bear thirty, sixty, or a hundredfold. Such is the growth which, in the symbolism of the parable, defies not only the weeds of wealth, but the scorching noon of persecution; and in the parallel it is remarkable that those who renounce possession are promised a hundredfold, *with persecutions thrown in,* an unexpected point, unless we have the type text iv 14–20 in mind.

So much for the cycle, or triple cycle, contained in viii 27–x 52. There remain two pieces more of comparable extent, the Jerusalem ministry (xi 1–xiv 11) and the Passion (xiv 12–xvi 8). The whole Jerusalem ministry offers a continuous parallel to the preceding piece (viii 27–x 52) as well as to the much-used model iii–iv. As in iii 1–6 Jesus had broken with the scribes in Synagogue, so now he breaks with the priests in the Temple; and the parallel runs on.

	Disciples confess Messiah, viii 27 ff.	Disciples prepare Messianic Entry, xi 1 ff.
Christ as a new David, ii 25	Christ in Glory: 'Let us make three tabernacles', ix 2 ff.	Ovation as at Tabernacles: hailing of David's Kingdom, xi 7 ff.
who, hungry, overrides the priesthood, ii 26	Jesus expels demon from boy's body, ix 14–27	Jesus comes hungry to Jerusalem and overrides the priesthood in expelling traders from God's house, xi 12 ff.
Healing of withered hand, iii 1–5	Power of prayer, ix 28–29	Withering of fig reveals the power of prayer, xi 20 ff.
	Discussion on greatness and authority: only Christ's name authenticates. Failure to receive in the Name is damnation, ix 33–50	Christ's authority questioned. He acts in God's name. Rejection of God's representatives brings final overthrow, xi 27–xii 11
Pharisees and Herodians, iii 6		Pharisees and Herodians, xii 13 ff.
	Marriage Question, x 1 ff.	Marriage Question, xii 18 ff.
	The Commandments of the One Lawgiver, x 17 ff.	The Commandments of the One Lawgiver, xii 28 ff.
	God to be served in Jesus, x 21 ff.	Messiah shares God's throne, xii 35 ff.
	Snare of riches, x 22 ff.	Abuse of riches and power, xii 38 ff.
	Those who give all receive a hundredfold, x 28 ff.	Poor widow gives all, xx 42 ff.

Withdrawal of Jesus: Peter, James, John, Andrew etc. on the mountain: parabolic discourses, iii 7–iv 34	Question of James and John, x 35 ff.	Withdrawal of Jesus from Temple to mountain and question of Peter, James, John, and Andrew answered by apocalypse, xiii
	Christ hailed as Son of David, x 46 ff.	Christ anointed, xiv 3 ff.

To begin with the first column: we have done much of the work here already (ch. viii above). We have seen how the withered hand is connected with David's taking of the shrewbread from the temple priests, and how in x–xi Jesus, hailed as Son of David, withers the barren fig and overrides the priests in the temple. And we have seen how the two themes of withering and conflict with the priests are worked out and worked together in the parable of the wicked husbandmen who withhold the fruits and kill the landlord's son. The parable carries us as far as xii 12. So much for the defiance of the priests, in antitype to the defiance of the scribes at the healing of the withered hand. The defiance in iii is followed by (a) the withdrawal of the Pharisees, who plot with the Herodians, (b) the withdrawal of Jesus and his following. The model is followed, with much expansion, in xii 12–xiii 2. (a) In xii 12–13 the priests withdraw, baffled, and send a party of Pharisees and Herodians to ensnare Jesus; and (b) in xiii 1–2 Jesus withdraws from the temple, prophesying its overthrow as he goes. The expansion of which we speak consists in the succession to the Pharisees and Herodians of other learned questioners, the Sadducees first, then the Good Scribe; after dealing with whom Jesus passes to the attack and confutes first the doctrine, then the morals of the rabbis. Only then, when he has been proved the master of debate, does he make his own withdrawal from the temple.

We might suppose that the long expansion in xii filled out by the questions of the learned would have caused St Mark to lose touch with his model in iii, but it proves to be otherwise. When Jesus finally and dramatically departs from the temple, St Mark recalls how he had left the synagogue before in a way no less dramatic—it has been, indeed, a veritable exodus from Egypt, with a great multitude following, and directed towards the sea, like the march led by Moses. Like Moses, Jesus arrives at a mountain and there institutes a new covenant by the appointment of the Twelve. Virtually none of the detail of this withdrawal applies to the withdrawal from the temple; the point I am making is that both are solemn withdrawals, marked by the symbolism of finality. When Jesus withdraws from the synagogue, he turns his back on Egypt; when Jesus withdraws from the temple, he prophesies that not a stone of it will remain upon another.[1]

Withdrawing from the synagogue, Jesus ascends a mountain, and calls the Twelve to him; withdrawing from the temple, he sits on the Mount of Olives. In iii the name-list of the Twelve is given, beginning with Peter, James, John and Andrew in that order. On the Mount of Olives in xiii the four names recur in that order, which is nowhere else used by St Mark. The four now ask for enlightenment about the fall of the temple and the accompanying apocalypse, and Jesus replies in the longest continuous discourse which St Mark has recorded for us. The only unbroken discourse which approaches it in length is Christ's reply to his disciples' question about the meaning of his parables. He answered them in a string of further parables (iv 11–32). In iii–iv Christ's long answer to his apostles' enquiry is not, admittedly, given on the mountain to which he summoned the Twelve, but only after he had descended from the mountain and uttered a number of parabolic sayings in public (iii 30–iv 8). But in the antitype which he writes in xiii St Mark broadens and simplifies his effect: all the parabolic discourses of iii 30–iv 32, whether privately or publicly uttered, are treated as one and made the models for Christ's apocalyptic discourse, and Christ remains on the mountain to deliver it.

The parallel between the parabolic discourses and the apocalyptic prophecy is verbal, close, orderly and detailed, and I am surprised if anyone, having examined the evidence, will contest

[1] Cf. Apoc. xi 8: the city where the Lord was crucified is 'allegorically Sodom and Egypt'.

its force. I have said all I need to say about it in my previous book, pp. 155–166.

I will not here repeat what I there said, but invoke external support, the authority of St Matthew. He arranges the middle part of his gospel—that is to say, the story of the ministry—in two balanced sections leading up, the one to the parable-discourses, the other to the apocalyptic prophecy. He grasps the parallel between the two and strengthens it. St Mark, for his part, did not write the parables as an apocalypse, but in the course of following out his parallel he found himself nine chapters later writing an apocalypse on the topics provided by the parables. St Matthew, on the other hand, having studied St Mark through to the end and (I should suppose) learnt him by heart, reads the apocalypse back into the parables. So St Matthew's parables contain explicitly eschatological passages, and we observe, in particular, that he grasped the force of the equation between the landlord sending forth the sickle (Mk. iv 29) and the Son of Man sending forth his angels (Mk. xiii 27). 'The harvesting' he writes 'is the consummation of the world and the reapers are angels. . . . The Son of Man shall send forth his angels, and they shall gather out of his kingdom all offences and workers of iniquity. . . . Then shall the righteous shine forth as the sun . . .' (xiii 39–43).

To turn now from the first column of our parallel to the second. In the eighth chapter of this book we traced this parallel also for a certain distance. In Mark viii we saw Jesus provoking his disciples to confess his glory and then veiling it. In xi we saw him sending his disciples for the ass and provoking a public recognition of his glory. In ix Jesus ascends the mount of Transfiguration and is offered, but does not receive, an ovation with Tabernacles' ceremonial. In xi he ascends Mount Zion and receives an ovation with 'Tabernacles' ceremonial. We left the parallel there, but it continues.

After the descent from the Transfiguration, Jesus cast a demon out of a boy and explained his disciples' inability to do what he had done by their lack of the power to pray. After the entry to Jerusalem, Jesus cast the traders out of the temple and (an act

mysteriously equivalent to the other) withered a barren fig. Peter
expressing astonishment at the withering of the fig, Jesus said that
had his disciples faith to pray, they might remove mountains. St
Matthew supports the parallel between the two sayings about
prayer, for he borrows the epigram about the removal of the
mountain to adorn Christ's answer to his disciples about their inability to exorcise. As to the parallel we have suggested between
casting out a demon from the human person and casting out pro-
fane traders from the temple, St Mark himself supports it by his
suggested equation between the raising up of Christ's human body
after three days and the raising up of the fallen temple after three
days (xiv 58). And St Matthew supports it by the parable of the
house swept and garnished, where the house from which demons
are cast forth is the human person (xii 43–45).

To take the next point of comparison. After the exorcism in ix
we have Christ's disciples disputing on greatness. Christ turns
their thoughts another way. Men are not to be accepted because
they are great, but because they represent God. Christ is to be
accepted in a child, and he who sent Christ is to be accepted in
Christ. Now to turn to xi–xii. The Priests question Jesus about his
authority or power. He gives them no direct reply, but utters a
parable. The landlord keeps sending his accredited messengers to
collect the fruits of his vineyard, but they are not accepted. All of
them are handled roughly, and the master's own son is murdered.
The question about tribute money follows, and continues the
theme. The landlord requires his rents, that is to say, the Heavenly
King demands his tribute. Can it be right, then, for his subjects to
pay tribute to an earthly, an idolatrous king? Is it lawful to give
tribute to Caesar, or not? There is no separate model for the story
of the tribute money in Mark ix, a fact which discontented St
Matthew, who set about to supply the lack (xvii 24–27). In his
version the whole discussion about true greatness and the receiving
of little ones is given a new introduction. Those who collect the
tribute of the God of Israel, that is to say, the temple-tax, approach
St Peter and ask him whether his Master pays it or not? The
tribute-money is provided by the miraculous catch of a fish with

money in its mouth, but the point of the story is that Christ pays to avoid giving offence, while maintaining his freedom as a matter of right. The King's children do not pay tribute, he says. The saying claims for Jesus, and it would seem for his disciple too, the status of a king's son and leads on to the disciples' question, 'Who then is great in the kingdom of Heaven?' And so the rest follows much as in St Mark.

To return to the Marcan parallel itself. On the one side we have the Pharisees' question about marriage and divorce, on the other side the Saduccees' question about marriage and resurrection. The two questions have the same form. Pharisees and Sadducees both take their stand on texts from Deuteronomy, Jesus answers both by first reinterpreting Deuteronomy and then citing earlier parts of the Mosaic writings in support of his interpretation. To proceed: in x we have Jesus and the rich man discussing salvation by the keeping of the commandments of the only One who is good, and in xii we have Jesus and the scribe discussing the question which commandment is greatest and laying emphasis on the Oneness of God. In x Jesus recommends the rich man to add to his formal observance of the commandments of the only God a complete self-devotion to the following of Jesus; and in xii Jesus turns from his discussion with the scribe to complain that the scribes fail to associate Messiah with the throne of the all-ruling God. In x there follows the rich man's refusal and Christ's warning against the dangers of wealth; in xii this is matched by Christ's denunciation of scribal pomp and avarice. In x he promises reward to his disciples who have left all and followed him; in xii he extolls the poor widow's offering above the easy contribution of the rich, because she had given all she had, her whole living.

So much for the parallel between Mark xii 18–44 and x 1–31. It is notable that, just where the parallel with St Mark's other model—the model provided by his third chapter—is weakest, the parallel with x is most strong and clear; one model makes up the deficiencies of the other, or, to speak more realistically, St Mark does not attend equally to both models at once, since it is hard to serve two masters. In the next passage he reverses the balance of his attention. We have seen above that the apocalyptic prophecy in xiii runs carefully and in order over topics provided by the parables in iii–iv. By way of compensation, the prophecy draws little on the request of James and John in x 35–52. In both texts, indeed, Christ is answering a question of James and John, though on the second occasion Peter and Andrew join the sons of Zebedee. Both questions have to do with future glory and (this perhaps is the most striking thing) in answer to both Christ promises his disciples, in the first place, martyrdom, and evades an exact answer to their question. May James and John have the seats to the right and the left? They are not Christ's to give, except to those for whom God has prepared them. May Peter, James, John and Andrew know when the last things will be? Of that day or hour none knows, not the angels in heaven, not the Son, but the Father alone.

To continue the parallel we are exploring: in x we have blind Bartimaeus, and whatever corresponds to him in xiv it will not be another healing; for Bartimaeus is the twelfth and last, there are no more. Nevertheless here is a person as bold as Bartimaeus, discouraged like him by the onlookers but like him owned by Christ. Bartimaeus comes with an acclamation of the Lord's Anointed, 'Son of David, Son of David'; the woman in the supper room at Bethany comes with his anointing, an alabaster box of flowing nard, and pours it on his head.

That completes our account of the Jerusalem Ministry (xi 1– xiv 9). There remains only the Passion. The Passion is simply modelled on the Jerusalem ministry, so far as it is modelled on anything. It is perhaps surprising at first sight that the parallel between ii 23 ff. and xi 1 ff. should not continue through the Passion, for if the breach with Jewry in the first octave of healings matches the breach with Jewry after the twelve healings are complete, how much more should the three great miracles with which the octave ends (ch. v) foreshadow the Passion, Entombment and Resurrection. And so they do, but only in general and symbolically. It is obvious, on reflection, that they can provide no detailed model for the course of events in the last section of the Gospel.

Mission of two disciples to prepare festal entry, xi 1–6	Mission of two disciples to prepare festal supper, xiv 12–16
Entry to the festival. The hunger of 'David'. Old rites reformed, xi 7–18	Entry to the feast. 'David', plotted against, gives 'shewbread to his companions'; new rite instituted, xiv 17–25
The power of prayer, xi 20–25	The power of prayer, xiv 26–42
High Priests march upon Jesus, xi 27 ff.	High Priests' servant and men march upon Jesus, xiv 43–52
Debate of Jesus against high priests and scribes. He maintains against them the session of Messiah at God's right hand, and predicts the fall of the Temple, xi 29–xiii 2	Trial of Jesus by High Priest and scribes. His prophecy of the fall of the Temple is twisted against him. He maintains the session of Messiah at God's right hand, and is condemned, xiv 53–65
Warning to Peter and his companions that they stand fast before Sanhedrins and Governors, xiii 3–13	Peter denies in the court of the Sanhedrin. Jesus stands before the Governor, xiv 66–xv 5
The Abomination of Desolation and the agony of the Saints, xiii 14–23	Crucifixion and agony of Jesus, xv 6–47
The Son of Man appears and sends his angels to gather the elect. Jesus receives 'burial anointing' from woman, xiii 24–xiv 9.	Message, summoning disciples to see the Son of Man, given by angel to women who come to anoint Jesus after burial, xvi 1–8

In xi Jesus sends his disciples to fetch the ass which shall carry him into Jerusalem for the feast; in xiv he sends two disciples to prepare the supper room where he may eat the festal meal. The form of the two stories is the same—Jesus, by supernatural insight, tells his disciples what they will find and how they will be answered.

In xi Jesus as a new David comes hungry to the Temple and, in a spiritual sense, finds nothing to eat; the fig tree disappoints him. That cannot be the end, divine purposes are not frustrated, and

David, we remember, when he came hungry to the temple, ended by giving holy bread to his companions. The priests in xi disappoint Jesus, but the householder in xiv welcomes him and supplies what is needed for the feast. Jesus breaks a loaf into twelve pieces for the twelve: here at length is the shewbread of the New Covenant, of which we have seen so many prefigurations. David gave his companions the shewbread, and went on his way, hunted by his persecutor. It would be superfluous to point out how large a place the type of the persecuted psalmist-king plays in St Mark's passion-history. It begins to affect the narrative where the new David, at table with his companions, says to them: One of you shall betray me, 'He that eateth with me' (cf. Psalm xli 9, 'He that eateth my bread hath lifted his heel against me').

After his disappointment over the fig tree and the temple in xi we hear Jesus speaking to his disciples and especially to Peter on faith and prayer, by means of which the acts of men become the instruments of omnipotence. The impression left on a careless reader may be that if we pray hard enough we can get anything. Gethsemane is the corrective; not all prayers prove prayable, not, for example, 'Take this cup away from me'. While giving the pattern of true prayer in his own person, Jesus is exhorting his disciples, and especially Peter, to pray, after warning them of their need; they reject the warning ('Though all break down, yet will not I') and they fail to pray ('Simon, sleepest thou? Couldst thou not watch for an hour?'). The texts on prayer in xi and xiv belong together. Between them they supply much of the Lord's prayer. 'Abba, Father, thy will be done; forgive us our trespasses as we forgive them that trespass against us; lead us not into temptation.'

Two theories are possible about the relation of this pair of texts to the Lord's prayer, and both support the parallel between the texts. Either St Mark was acquainted with the Lord's prayer in something like the Matthaean form, or he was not. If he was acquainted with it, then he has incorporated part of it in the text about prayer in xi and more of it in the text in xiv, and he can hardly have done so without noticing what he was doing. If, on the other hand, St Mark had not the Lord's Prayer, the most natural supposition (which you and I, no doubt, will think outrageous) is that St Matthew composed the Prayer. But if he composed it, he at least recognised the Marcan parallel we are demonstrating, for he drew phrases from either side of it into the Lord's Prayer.

To continue with the parallel. After the text about prayer in xi we saw high priests, scribes and elders march upon Christ to demand from him an account of his acts. The upshot of it was, that they feared to lay hold on him; they left him, and went their way (xii 12). It was otherwise when men with swords and staves from the high priests, scribes and elders marched upon Jesus in Gethsemane. They laid hold of him, and his disciples it was who left him, and fled.

In the remainder of xii the debate between the scribes and Jesus is renewed. He declares that Messiah's destiny is to sit at God's right hand, a doctrine reprobated by the scribes; and, leaving the temple, prophesies that no stone of it shall stand upon another. After Christ's arrest in xiv, his debate with Jewish authority is renewed in the High Priest's house. Hostile witnesses misrepresent his prediction of the fall of the temple, and in answer to the High Priest Jesus reaffirms with reference to himself his doctrine of Messiah's session at God's right hand. The priests and scribes condemn it as blasphemy.

After leaving the temple in xiii Jesus gives Peter and his three companions his apocalypse; and first warns them not to be dismayed by rumours but to stand fast before sanhedrins and synagogues, governors and kings, and to give their testimony in the power of the Holy Ghost; and this is what St Peter most signally fails to do as he hovers on the verges of the sanhedrin which condemns Jesus (xiv 66-72). The apocalypse goes on to reveal heathendom triumphant, and the desolating abomination set up; that will be the crisis of the Church's martyrdom. All that the Church undergoes hereafter is prefigured in the present sufferings of Christ; he is traded to the heathen, and the desolating abomination is indeed set up when the Roman gallows lifts the King of

the Jews into the air. The desolating abomination is so called because it desolates the temple, and already when Christ dies
the veil of the temple is rent from top to bottom; when
the spirit departs from his torn body, the presence departs from
the Temple.

But, says the apocalypse, in the days of the Church's last
martyrdom deliverance is at hand; they shall see the Son of
Man, and he will send forth his angels to gather his elect. The
women who come to the sepulchre on the third day after
Christ's own passion encounter an angel, whose commission is
to gather the Son of Man's elect, that they may see him. 'Tell
his disciples and Peter, he goes before you into Galilee, there shall
ye see him.'

But what are the women doing at the sepulchre? They have
come there to anoint the Lord, like the woman at the supper which
follows the apocalypse in xiii–xiv. It was in her mind to anoint
him for glory, but, said he, she is beforehand to anoint my body
for the burial. He had his burial-anointing by anticipation in the
supper room at Bethany. When the two Marys and Salome came
to the sepulchre on the third day, there was no body to anoint.
The sun had risen, and Christ has departed.

It only remains to consider whether the interior development
in three waves or little cycles which we have hitherto found in the
main divisions of the Gospel plays any part in the Jerusalem ministry or in the Passion. In the Jerusalem ministry it is about as marked
as in viii 27–x 52. There are three sections of very unequal length,
xi 1–19, xi 20–xiii 2, and xiii 3–xiv 11. All begin with dialogues
between Jesus and his disciples. He sends two to fetch the ass, he
answers Peter's astonishment about the withering of the fig, he
answers the question of four disciples about the last things. The
endings match—the first and second end with Christ's exit from
the temple and the city, the second and third with his commenda-
tion of a woman's generosity—the poor widow's mites, the
woman's alabaster box of ointment. In general, we may say that
the first little cycle provides a text which the second expounds.
The demand for fruit and the challenge to the priestly authority

in the temple (xi 13–18) are set forth in relation to one another in xi 20–xii 12. The brief words of xi 18 'The chief priests and the scribes . . . sought how they might destroy him; for they feared him, because all the multitude admired his teaching' receive abundant illustration in xii 12–44. The public teaching given in the second little cycle touches not only upon the fall of the priesthood and temple (xii 9–11, xiii 1–2) but also on the glory of the Son of Man at the right hand of God (xii 35–37). In the third cycle a full instruction is given to the disciples about these two great predictions.

It is difficult to feel much confidence in a triple division of the last section of the Gospel (xiv 12–xvi 8). There are so many subdivisions and minor correspondences between the several parts of the passion-narrative. If we wished to prove the thesis that St Mark never varied from the use of triple form, we should be forced to adopt the division, Last Supper (xiv 12–31) arrest and trial (xiv 32–xv 21) Passion and Resurrection (xv 22–xvi 8). The first contains the institution of the cup, the second Christ's acceptance of it, the third his drinking it. But we should be obliged to admit that the middle cycle is further doubled upon itself: betrayal to the priests, condemnation, mockery, denial by Simon Peter, xiv 43–72; betrayal to Pilate, condemnation, mockery, Simon of Cyrene carrying the cross, xv 1–21. There are, therefore, virtually four sections, not three. All end with the theme of the failure of disciples—(a) Peter's denial prophesied, xiv 29–31, (b 1) Peter's denial, xiv 66–72, (b 2) another Simon carries the cross, xv 21, (c) the women run from the sepulchre, xvi 8. But it may well be that a different division of the Passion would be just as reasonable, and I should prefer to say that in any case the triple sub-division of the main sections of which St Mark is composed fades gradually out with the healing-pattern. For it was, as we have seen, the healing-pattern which provided the firm skeleton round which it took shape.

Before we take leave of the topic it will be as well, perhaps, to tabulate the division of the Gospel as we have reformed it:

Exordium, i 1–15

First triple cycle, containing first handful of healings, i 16–34, i 35–ii 12, ii 13–iii 12.

Second triple cycle, containing second handful of healings, iii 13–vi 6, vi 7–vii 37, viii 1–26.

Third triple cycle, containing the 'two healings over', viii 27–ix 29, ix 30–x 31, x 32–x 52.

Fourth triple cycle, containing the Jerusalem ministry, xi 1–19, xi 20–xiii 2, xiii 3–xiv 11.

Fifth (triple) cycle, containing the Passion, xiv 12–(xiv 31, xiv 32–xv 21, xv 22–) xvi 8.

The last thing that I desire to do is to insist on the regularity of St Mark's cyclic structure. The table is neater than the facts, if only because it fails to show in what a variety of places the several short cycles find their models. That St Mark's thought runs cyclically is a thesis which needs no advocate. All I am concerned to show is that the cyclic formation corresponds to the pattern of healings, and that, conversely, the pattern of healings explains some things which would otherwise be obscure about the cyclic formation, and especially the choice of models for new cycles from among those already composed.

RETRACTATIONS: MISCELLANEOUS

In the first chapter of *A Study in St Mark* I discussed the state of the question in Marcan scholarship, and I do not wish to qualify what I wrote about that. Incidentally I made a defence against the argument that if St Mark's construction were as important to his meaning as I contend, it is surprising that St Matthew and St Luke should have treated it with such little respect (pp. 26–27). My defence conceded too much, anyhow with regard to St Matthew. What I should now say about St Matthew's handling of St Mark's order may be gathered from Chs. iii and vii in the present work, pp. 38–53, 116–128.

In the same chapter I introduced a discussion on Papias's notices of 'the Elder's' opinion about St Mark and St Matthew (pp. 10–21). My object was to remove an obstacle. Papias's Elder seems to tell us that St Mark is to be valued for his Petrine matter, but that his order is haphazard. This being our earliest tradition about the composition of St Mark's gospel appears to discourage any enquiry which interprets St Mark's meaning from his arrangement. I argued that the Elder's opinion ought to be nevertheless discounted because it could be shown to be part and parcel of a view about the composition of St Matthew which we all of us now hold to be erroneous and indeed refutable. I stand by my argument but I find it necessary to point a moral which it implies. It is still being widely taught that when St Matthew is credited by Papias with putting together or systematising the *logia* or oracles, what is meant is that he made a collection of Old Testament oracles or prophecies concerning Christ. This is an impossible interpretation, because 'the *logia*' in the sentence about St Matthew is no more than a shorthand expression for 'the dominical *logia*' in the preceding sentences about St Mark.[1] St Peter, St Mark's apostolic authority, did not make an 'arrangement' of the dominical logia, but St Matthew the apostle made his own arrangement of the

[1] And, indeed, in the title of Papias's whole work.

logia. Now it may be that 'the logia' by itself and in no particular context would be more likely to mean the Old Testament 'oracles' than any others. But 'the *dominical* logia' cannot mean this. We must compare 'dominical logia' with 'dominical day' and 'dominical prayer'. The adjective in its Greek and Latin forms is a Christian appropriation from secular use, where it means 'Imperial', 'belonging to our Lord Caesar'. 'Dominical logion' can no more mean 'oracle about the Lord Jesus' than 'dominical rescript' can mean 'Rescript about our Lord the Emperor'. It simply means 'the divine teaching of the Lord Jesus'.

In Ch. ii I made an attempt on the pattern of twelve healings and got it wrong (pp. 36–44, 52). This was the grand calamity of the book and the parent of many errors. I was not the victim of mere phantasy for I was attempting to give an account of real facts. I appreciated the rhythmical repetition of healing themes in the successive groups of healing narratives, and I tried to determine the formal character of the matching groups in which these recurrent themes are successively found. It is here that I went wrong. I observed quite correctly that the healing stories are split into smaller and smaller groups by the intervention of other material as the Gospel proceeds. I should now say that this fact is a by-product of the development of the other material, particularly the teaching (see pp. 8–10 above). But at that time I took it to be the effect of a formal principle in the arrangement of the healing narratives themselves. The groups of healings get smaller and smaller and yet continue to support the whole healing theme, so that the theme becomes more and more condensed. There may be some truth in this—as the healing act is repeated in one example after another it becomes more and more charged with echoes and overtones from preceding examples, and so more fit to point the way to the supreme act of healing, Christ's death and resurrection. But my attempt at a numerical formalisation of this progressive concentration of healing ought not to have satisfied me. The principle I used was that of a regular declining series, 4, 3, 2, 1. But I was obliged to make the following admissions. (a) There are single loose units following each of the serial numbers (4, 1; 3, 1;

2, 1; 1, 1), and why should there be? (b) Even so the system is not regular, for the second loose unit is lacking. (c) The first group is not a perfectly continuous succession of healing stories; it is so divided in the middle that it is just as reasonable to call it two 2s as one 4. What I now think about the sections which carry the correspondences of healing sequence I have sufficiently explained in this present work.

In the rest of the chapter (pp. 45–51) I have little to retract. On pp. 49–50 I showed how the exorcism of the Syrophoenician girl picks up the themes of all the three great healing miracles which stand next before it, the Legion, the Impure Woman, and Jairus's Child. The facts are correctly stated, but I should now judge the significance of them differently. The three great miracles express the salvation of Israel through the work of the three great days from Good Friday to Easter Day. The 'intrusive' Gentile healing which Christ accorded to the Syrophoenician mother's faith shows as well as it is possible for a single episode to do how Christ will do everything for the Gentiles which his triple work has accomplished for the Jews.

On p. 51 I pointed out the systematic variations on the theme of the son or daughter healed at the prayer of the father or mother. I no longer think it reasonable to treat the healing of Simon's wife's mother as an irregular representation of the theme of the mother and the son. According to my present opinion that theme is not represented in the gospel at all. The way I should now interpret the facts is this. The Evangelist is showing us how the Gospel fulfils the prophets. Elijah and Elisha raised the son at the mother's prayer; Jesus fulfils or completes the work, granting first the prayer of the father on behalf of his daughter, then of the mother on behalf of her daughter and last of the father on behalf of his son.

With Ch. vi of *A Study in St Mark* we reach one of the chief stumblingblocks of the book, as the reader will find virtually admitted on pp. 154–155. For I found myself driven to claim that St Mark wrote his gospel on two principles simultaneously throughout. First, there was the wave-like movement, cycle after cycle exemplifying with constant variety and increasing force that plan of divine action which obtained its ultimate expression in passion and resurrection. Second, there was a correspondence of the whole of the last half of the Gospel (ix–xvi) to the first three eighths of it (i–vi). And it seemed impossible that St Mark should have seen his book both in the form of a wave-like repetition, each wave striving to outrun its predecessors, and in the form of a single long model (i–vi) with a single antitype or fulfilment of even greater length (ix–xvi).

My difficulties arose from my cardinal error about the pattern of healing. Since I had neglected the division by what I now call 'handfuls' and based my analysis on small continuous groups of healing-stories, I was led to give a corresponding importance to little cycles of narrative each containing one such group of healings, and to neglect the longer complex cycles embracing each a whole 'handful' of cures. The Gospel took on the appearance of a continuous wave-like progress made up of some dozen little waves, and I was at a loss how to deal with certain more extended parallels, or how to explain the harking-back of certain later symbolisms to early models. And so I was glad to catch at a supplementary hypothesis capable of supporting observations which the analysis into short cycles failed to accommodate. The elements of sound observation and of speculative error continued in Ch. vi of *A Study in St Mark* may be conveniently listed under two heads.

I. (a) The beginning of the 'two over' line or movement (viii 27–x 52) matches the beginning of the line preceding it in a continuous and highly important parallel, as we have just seen (p. 206 f. above), but it does also match the very beginning of the line before that, which is the first line of all; the themes of i 1–28 reappear at Caesarea Philippi and at the Transfiguration, as is shewn in detail on pp. 155–157 of the Chapter we are criticising. And it is quite right to draw the inference, that so vigorous an evocation of the beginning of the whole Gospel at a point roughly half way through its course marks this point as an important new beginning comparable with the original exordium.

(b) The line which contains the Jerusalem ministry (xi 1–xiv 11) reflects the place from which the second line takes its beginning (iii–iv), as we have said in Ch. viii (pp. 138 ff. above) and with greater detail on pp. 158–167 of our former work. This parallel is also of great importance.

It was, however, a mistake to treat the parallel of viii–ix with i (a) and the parallel of xi–xiii with iii–iv (b) as parts of a continuous parallel, placing the whole of viii 27–xvi 8 in antitype to the whole of i–vi. To make out so ambitious a scheme we were obliged to fill the gap between (a) and (b) and the gap from (b) to the end with weak and formal correspondences, of which we were candid enough to admit the flimsy character.

II. Because St Mark counts his healings as he goes along, we have shewn in Ch. v of this present book, pp. 86 ff., that he is led to see 'five plus three' healings as an octave, as it were a week of divine acts, the first five being common days, the last three the saving days from the Friday of the Passion to the Sunday of the Resurrection. Because he thinks in this way, the first octave of healings and the narrative embracing them (i–v) do specially prefigure the whole gospel work in St Mark's eyes. He wakes up, it would seem, to the significance of the octave as he finishes the first handful and begins to work towards the triad succeeding it, i.e. at the beginning of iii, the crisis in Capernaum. So, when he comes to the crisis at Jerusalem which the Capernaum crisis prefigures, he feels the force of the model he had himself constructed at that point. But (again) it was an error to argue from the symbolical value of the octave or 'little gospel' in i–vi to a systematic antitype in viii–xvi.

What I wrote in general about the prefigurative way of thinking in Ch. vi was well judged and I uphold it. I quite rightly pointed out that the prefigurative force of the octave or little gospel runs on after the end of it, so that as the resurrection of Jairus's daughter prefigures Christ's resurrection, so the sending forth of the disciples on mission to Galilee prefigures their sending forth into all the world; and so the feedings of multitudes with the attached incidents prefigure the sacramental church extended to embrace the Gentiles. It may be that I have forced certain points, but in general I think favourably of pp. 148–152 of *A Study in St Mark*.

Chapter vii deals with the ending of the gospel, of which I have already written my retractation in Ch. ix of this book. I have nothing to retract in Ch. viii, where I discuss the historical sense of the Gospel. The material is, indeed, set out in the 'double cycles' of my old analysis. I should now set it out in the 'triple cycles' which make up my five great divisions, and should endeavour to show in what relation the articulations of cyclic structure as I now see them stand to the articulations of historical sequence. But the question is of secondary importance and I will not attempt it here. I will also allow Ch. ix to stand, in which I maintain that there is no reason to suppose that any of our New Testament writers believed the general shape of the gospel events to have been other than St Mark describes.

Chapter x deals with 'the Messianic Secret', or, more properly, with the allied themes of Christ's discouraging the publication of certain healing miracles, and Christ's preservation of the secret about his person and office. The chapter contains, I hope, only one new error, the underrating of the enigmatic quality of the parable of the Sower (pp. 241–243). A juster estimate appears on p. 245, and in Ch. i (p. 9) of the present work. But if my tenth Chapter propounded no new errors but this, it perpetuated old ones; for it arranged the development of the themes of secrecy and disclosure round the imperfect structural machinery which we have been criticising here. What the facts about secrecy and disclosure really show is simply that these themes are consistently and steadily unfolded throughout the Gospel. Such a gradual unfolding is in natural harmony with any analysis of the narrative which acknowledges a forward movement stage by stage as the general shape of the story. I do not think it necessary actually to reconstruct my Chapter here before my reader's eyes, or to prove to him in detail that the account I now give of the cyclic structure of the Gospel can be happily reconciled with what I formerly wrote about secrecy and disclosure.

What I wrote about the Son of Man in Chs. xi and xii still satisfies me, except that I (a) misdated *XII Testaments* and (b) failed to define with sufficient care what I was attempting to do. I was not attempting to make any contribution to the historical exegesis of Genesis, Daniel or Enoch. I was concerned with the books as they exist for us, and as they existed for Israel and for the Church, not with the meaning of their presumed authors on the day when they wrote. It was irrelevant to my purpose to determine (for example) whether 'Son of Man' was anything like a set phrase or title for the author either of Daniel or of Enoch. It was enough to show that St Mark uses the set phrase in allusion to Daniel, and that 'Enoch' develops the same Danielic figure under a similar description and in a way which offers an interesting parallel to what St Mark does. But I did make some historical statements about the older authors—for example, that 'Daniel' was writing out of Genesis in one place and out of Hosea in another—and I did not keep a sufficiently clear distinction between paragraphs in which 'Daniel' means the actual author of the Old Testament book and paragraphs in which 'Daniel' means a literary person existing for St Mark and his contemporaries.

Chapter xiii deals with Loaves and Thousands. My error about the Syrophoenician exorcism, which was part of my error about the healing-pattern, involved an error about the feeding of the four thousand. I have explained both how I erred and what I think in a long article in *The Journal of Theological Studies* for April 1953. Most of the points I made in the article and some others can be found in Ch. iv of this present book.

I wish to withdraw Ch. xiv entirely. It gives a very unsuccessful account of the series of occasions on which groups of apostles are mentioned by St Mark. The reader is asked to accept in place of it what I have said in Ch. v above, pp. 90–103.

Chapter xv was put forward as the most tentative of speculations. My thesis was that the thirteen persons whose cures St Mark describes might perhaps correspond not in general only but to some extent in particular with the tribes or patriarchs of Israel. My revised position about the Gospel as a whole allows the working out of such a suggestion with greater simplicity and force than my original position permitted. For example, it is no longer necessary to modify the traditional order of the tribal names. But on the other hand the *a priori* probability of St Mark's having thought in such a way has been weakened by Dr M. de Jonge's new study of the Testaments of the Twelve Patriarchs. He has made it seem overwhelmingly probable that this apocryphal work was compiled from Jewish sources by a Christian writer of about A.D. 200. We can no longer say, as I did say, that anyhow St Mark was acquainted with a popular and edifying book in Greek setting forth a detailed tribal typology under the persons of twelve patriarchal figures. All we can say is that the Twelve Testaments and other documents prove that from the first century B.C. onwards the legends of the Twelve Patriarchs were being elaborated in the Synagogue, and that St Mark or his teachers may have heard or read such material. It seems hardly worth reconstructing what I wrote in Chapter xv until a more thorough study can be made of the whole position of the patriarchal legend in the first century.

Chapter xvi treated of the date at which St Mark was composed; I have no fault to find with what I wrote.

INDEX OF SCRIPTURAL REFERENCES

INDEX OF NAMES

235